HIS IMPERIAL MAJESTY

HIS IMPERIAL MAJESTY

A Natural History of the Purple Emperor

Matthew Oates

BLOOMSBURY WILDLIFE
LONDON · OXFORD · NEW YORK · NEW DELHI · SYDNEY

BLOOMSBURY WILDLIFE
Bloomsbury Publishing Plc
50 Bedford Square, London, WC1B 3DP, UK

BLOOMSBURY, BLOOMSBURY WILDLIFE and the Diana logo are
trademarks of Bloomsbury Publishing Plc

First published in Great Britain 2020

A catalogue record for this book is available from the British Library

Library of Congress Cataloguing-in-Publication data has been applied for

ISBN: HB: 978-1-4729-5012-3; ePub: 978-1-4729-5013-0;
ePDF: 978-1-4729-5014-7

2 4 6 8 10 9 7 5 3 1

Typeset in Bembo Std by Deanta Global Publishing Services, Chennai, India
Printed and bound in Great Britain by CPI Group (UK) Ltd, Croydon CR0 4YY

To find out more about our authors and books visit www.bloomsbury.com
and sign up for our newsletters

*To CH, where I fell under the spell of this,
the best of all possible enchantments.*

Contents

Foreword

If you've ever heard softly spoken but impassioned words about British butterflies on the radio, the chances are you were listening to Matthew Oates. You may also have seen him, in a purple-ribboned hat, on television programmes such as *The Great British Summer, Butterflies: A Very British Obsession* and *Wild Britain*. Matthew talks about butterflies, for butterflies and even to butterflies.

He is also an accomplished writer and poet, citing influences such as Edward Thomas, Richard Jefferies and W H Hudson. Matthew writes for *The Times* Nature Notebook column and has written a number of well-received books, including *Beyond Spring* (2017) and *In Pursuit of Butterflies* (2015). His latest book, a celebration of the 'jewel in the crown' of Britain's butterflies, the Purple Emperor, is, in many ways, the culmination of his life's work and a singular, ruling passion.

Matthew worked for the National Trust for almost 30 years, as Advisor on Nature Conservation and latterly as National Specialist on Nature, before retiring to a life in which he can fly freely among the butterflies he loves. He is a life member of the charity Butterfly Conservation and one of the earliest members of the Knepp Wildland Advisory Board – the panel of expert ecologists overseeing our rewilding project in West Sussex, the context in which I first got to know him, nearly 20 years ago.

Over his long career Matthew has studied the life cycles and habitats of some of the UK's rarest butterfly species, such as the Duke of Burgundy, High Brown

Fritillary and Marsh Fritillary. But it is the Purple
Emperor he loves – with a devotion bordering on
insanity. The Emperor, of all butterflies, defies standard
study methods and the kind of controlled laboratory
experiments usually relied upon to identify cause and
effect. Elusive, unpredictable, fast- and high-flying,
aggressive, a hooligan among butterflies, the Purple
Emperor simply does not play ball. This is clearly a
purple flag to Matthew's scientific curiosity, and his sense
of fun. Who else could have conceived The Emperor's
Breakfast experiment, laid out on a linen tablecloth deep
in Fermyn Woods to tempt the Emperor's decadent taste
buds (it has a penchant for fox scat and intoxicating oak
sap) with pickled mudfish, rotten bananas, Stinking
Bishop cheese, fresh horse manure, crushed grapes, a wet
bar of soap and Pimm's Number 1? The results of the
experiment – a clear win for Big Cock shrimp paste
from Thailand and 'belachan', a putrid fermented-krill
relish from Malaysia – have provided Purple Emperor
aficionados ever since with the secret ingredients to
spread on gateposts, and even themselves, for a close
encounter.

Matthew has followed the Purple Emperor in the
wild since it first erupted into his life in July 1970, in
woods near Southwater, when he was a schoolboy at
Christ's Hospital in West Sussex. His subsequent pursuit –
a pilgrimage, no less – has taken him to all the legendary
'sacred groves' of the Emperor in the UK: Alice Holt
Forest on the Hampshire–Surrey border, Bookham
Commons in Surrey, Bernwood Forest near Oxford,
Savernake Forest in Wiltshire, and the Purple Emperor

mecca, Fermyn Woods in Northamptonshire. For years, like fellow Emperor addicts and his own growing band of groupies – the 'People of Purple Persuasion' – Matthew took the bulk of his annual leave during the Purple Emperor flight season, in high summer. His quest covered 18 UK counties, and now takes him to Europe.

But he has also, over painstaking days and weeks, studied the highly challenging immature stages of the butterfly through the rest of the year, and has found over a thousand eggs and larvae. Anyone who has ever tried to search for a Purple Empress's egg will know what an achievement this is. It is hard enough seeing the camouflaged larva hibernating in the fork of a sallow branch when Matthew is pointing right at it. His years of peering into mottled shade and rattling branches seem to have given him psychic antennae. In all, Matthew has seen the adult butterfly for 50 consecutive years and either the egg, caterpillar, chrysalis or butterfly in every month of the last 10 years.

But it is his study of Purple Emperors in the nascent habitats of the rewilding project at Knepp, barely a mile from his first sighting in Southwater Woods as a boy, that has provided some of the most exciting new information about the species. The development, over the last 15 years or so, of by far the largest Emperor population in the UK, has revealed the true characteristics and preferences of this evasive species. Matthew's observations here are exploding myths that have surrounded the Purple Emperor for decades. Contrary to previous belief, the Emperor – Matthew asserts – is not a 'woodland species', confined to oak-rich woods; it thrives in extensive sallow scrub, where it can be seen flying low and rigorously chasing females. This discovery is ripping up and rewriting the textbooks, and will be hugely significant for the future conservation of this scarce and stunningly beautiful species.

Purple Emperor-watching with Matthew, and his distinguished and equally ebullient butterfly colleague Neil Hulme, on their annual safaris at Knepp is far from the genteel pursuit most would imagine butterflying to be. With Matthew dressed to challenge in head-to-toe purple, shepherd's crook in hand and a lucky Jay's feather tucked into his purple bandana hat band, it swiftly devolves into a raucous, adrenaline-fuelled spectator sport akin to the old football matches between Millwall and West Ham United. The Emperors themselves seem to play to the crowd, attacking each other, or birds, or dragonflies, and sometimes the onlookers.

This is Matthew's genius: to make the study of butterflies fantastic entertainment; to bring the sometimes rather dry and, to many, indecipherable work of the scientist alive to the layperson; to inspire new audiences with the majesty of butterflies and the thrill of the chase. He teaches us *how* to look for Purple Emperors, to cherish his beloved 'spirit of place', the arc of the seasons, the myriad miracles of the butterfly life cycle. One of the greatest naturalists of our time, Matthew is also one of science's most articulate and generous communicators, the kind of champion nature now needs, more than ever.

Isabella Tree, author of *Wilding*
Knepp Castle, West Sussex
September 2019

Adrift on the wind

The remarkable world into which you are venturing begins at spring's zenith, deep in the southern counties, when the thistledown-like seed of the trees which children know as pussy willow drifts downwind. This seed may settle, fortuitously, where clay has been slopped out along a woodland ride, following ditching work; for pussy willows, or sallow trees to give them their proper name, are pioneer coloniser plants of bare clay. Some seed may also come to rest in a nearby clearing, where mature trees have recently been felled, to be sold as timber and replaced by another generation. Outside the forest edge, seed may also land on the embankments of a new road cutting, created to feed a developing industrial estate, and on brownfield land awaiting redevelopment close by. If most fortunate, seed will settle on clayey fields abandoned by arable farming.

Some of this seed will germinate, perhaps among violets and primroses, to set in progress a remarkable sequence of colonisation, exploitation and relationship within an ever-changing matrix of winners and losers, in a continuum that runs towards woodland senescence, beyond, and back again.

Sallow seedlings become whips, which soon develop into young trees, growing at least a metre a year. Within four years some will commence flowering. Chiffchaffs feed on the flies that visit the pollen-laden yellow flowers of the male sallow and the soft green flowers of the female. Blackcaps nest within the tangled brambles below. From mid-May onwards, the sallow foliage becomes pockmarked by the feeding blemishes of moth larvae, leaf beetles and weevils. The lower leaves are avidly browsed by cattle and deer and, higher up, young bark is stripped in midsummer by squirrels.

Later, when summer is at its highest, and the sallow foliage develops a blueish tinge, a giant butterfly, bold, brown and brazen, flies powerfully in to deposit her eggs on the uppersides of the leaves, favouring shady foliage growing below the canopy. She is wary, yet determined, and large enough to see off flocks of young tits out a-hunting in the sallow thickets, should she wish it – and

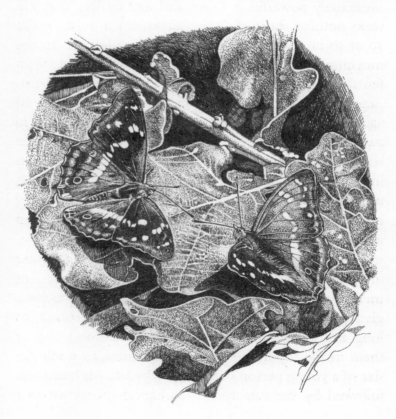

she often does. She is particular as to where she places most of her eggs, seeking out the situation where the resultant tiny caterpillars, or larvae, will fare best – leaves with certain characteristics, which are determined in part by microclimate conditions. Should the weather be clement, she will traverse tracts of landscape, rural and suburban, to seek out new habitat patches. She and her kind are inclined towards pushing limits.

Somewhere upslope, along the crowns of tall oaks out of the wind, her mate awaits her, should she require his services. He is stunningly beautiful, with shimmering wings of iridescent blues, purples and violets, and is immensely powerful in flight, and well he knows it. He seeks nothing short of divine supremacy, at least for the 10 or so heady days that constitute his adult life. In the mornings he may search the sallow thickets for virgin females. In the afternoons he will establish territories in canopy gaps up in the treetops, which he will defend against all-comers, even birds. This he will do while awaiting the arrival of a female still in need of male services. Sometimes, he may descend to feed on indelicacies on the woodland floor, for this butterfly is tropical in both appearance and habit, and like many of his far-flung cousins he seldom visits flowers but instead imbibes minerals in solution.

Yet he, like the female, is almost a year old, having undertaken a slow but remarkable journey of metamorphosis that began with an egg half the size of a glass pinhead the previous high summer; involved 10 long and loathsome months of caterpillarhood, five of them in the soporific state of hibernation, to reach the size of a young person's little finger by late May; and was followed by the cataclysmic biological meltdown that we call pupation (only the nervous system stays intact), and three weeks of hanging upside down from the underside of a sallow leaf, waiting, brewing, scheming.

People, too, arrive here, sun-hatted, bearing cameras and binoculars, and the odd notebook. They have come to seek, adulate, and take away memories of encounters with an aloof insect that is prone to bizarre and extreme behaviour – and which at times stimulates bizarre and extreme conduct in us. Few of them may think about what they are truly seeking, but it is far more than cheap-thrill outdoor goggle-box entertainment, or mere escapism, for our relationship with beauty and wonder runs deep, and with nature, deeper still. Many of their experiences will be highly humorous, for the path they are treading reaches the nether regions of British eccentricity. Above all, they are seeking adventures with this, the most storied of butterflies, and one which is capable of doing almost anything.

Welcome to the world of the Purple Emperor, the one the Victorian butterfly collectors saluted as His Imperial Majesty (or *HIM*), the Emperor of the Woods and the Lord of the Forest, to name but three of many salubrious epithets. This is the one butterfly they most wanted to possess, to form the centrepiece of their precious collections. This is the one today's butterfly enthusiasts most want to experience and understand. It is mysterious, elusive, ebullient, enthralling and highly amusing, and it transports us into a world that is very different from the one we know – yet is a reality in which we feel wondrously at home.

This book explores the mysteries and complexities that surround one of the most alluring, if confusing and deceptive, elements of British wildlife. Its roots reach back into the early Victorian era when English naturalists fell heavily under the Purple Emperor's spell. I am not the first to devote an inordinate amount of time to this insect, and will not be the last. Eventually, we may even comprehend why, and understand the butterfly, and what it means to us. This book is part of that continuum. I hold the torch now; others have held it in the past; more will come, and eclipse me, with my full blessing. The book's aims are, simply, to inspire and enable people to go out and study, record and fully appreciate this, the most magical and enthralling of butterflies.

This book is, however, not a definitive ecological account of the Purple Emperor. It is, as the subtitle indicates, simply *a natural history*. Neither is it a vigorous scientific thesis, but an account written by an impassioned naturalist for fellow nature lovers. There is some science in it, or at least scientific endeavour. As a seldomly seen, canopy-dwelling winged insect, the Purple Emperor does not lend itself easily to scientific study. Sample size is a big problem, as one sees so little of this species: tracking individual Purple Emperors in the wild is nigh on impossible (with today's technology), and following the egg-laying females is unusually difficult. These problems seriously disadvantage scientific research into this recalcitrant insect. Better techniques and technology are required.

The butterfly does, however, stimulate rampant hypothesising. This is what fascinates me, and others before me. We need to be careful here about what is actual and what is hypothesis: I have probably blurred the two in places in these pages, though not deliberately, and the book may even read the better for it.

Because the Purple Emperor is a fantastically strong and entertaining character, I have anthropomorphised in many places, contrary to modern fashion. If at times this seems somewhat over the top, it is because the butterfly's enthusiasm and behaviour know no bounds, and it regularly goes over the top. Don't blame the author, the messenger – blame the butterfly. Likewise, if you find that this book rampages all over the place, it is because that is precisely what the Purple Emperor does, and that is how people have interacted with it over time. I have tried to provide some structure and coherence, but my subject is essentially a free spirit.

If we ever start to understand it adequately, the Purple Emperor will doubtless reinvent itself and throw us back into perplexity, and reassert itself as a wondrous enigma. It is that sort of beast – mythical, fabulous, chimerical and utterly captivating, stimulating interest which generates a new hypothesis with each venture into its world.

CHAPTER ONE

A glorious history

The hunting gene – The meaning in a name – The pursuit of
iris in Victorian and Edwardian times – W H Hudson, a voice
against collecting – The Emperor's legacy in literature and art

Incredibly, only one person has died in pursuit of the
Purple Emperor in Britain. This is not for want of
overexuberant endeavour. The lone victim was an
eminent, if oversized, Victorian gentleman who met his
maker after falling out of a sallow tree while searching
for Purple Emperor eggs. It is probable, though, that the
butterfly has stimulated a number of heart attacks,
seizures, apoplexies, terminal winebibbings and the like,
not to mention divorces and separations, only these have
not been recorded in entomological history.

Make no mistake, this is the one butterfly the collectors
of old sought with an ardency which will alarm some of
today's readers. This was the cherished prize above all
others, even the Large Blue, the ultimate rarity, and the
giant Swallowtail drifting unattainably over impenetrable
reed beds.

The truth is that this insect stimulates the hunting
gene within us more than any other British insect,
generating an adrenalin rush rivalling that produced
by close encounters with our rarest birds and mammals.
It is, inter alia, the country sportsman's butterfly. It
pushes people prone to eccentric behaviour to exceed
themselves, and the British are by all accounts prone to

eccentricity, including naturalists. Be warned: it can set off obsessive behaviour that in the sphere of natural history is associated mainly with the activities of bird egg collectors. Tread warily with this butterfly; it can ensnare minds, and the only way to avoid this is to be thoroughly open facing, and to share one's experiences.

The literature canon of what should be the peaceful pastime of Emperoring does not help, for it too stimulates behaviour that is eccentric, if not downright extreme. It winds readers up, for the sound reason that the insect itself is a monumental wind-up merchant. C G Barret, writing in his 10-volume *Lepidoptera of the British Isles* (Vol. 1 Butterflies, 1893), highlights the problem: 'The male is an exceedingly bold, swift and powerful insect; not destitute of curiosity, as it will sometimes fly across a field to look at an intruder; and then when struck at with a net, will more frequently fly at – and past – its assailant than from him …'. W S Coleman, in another classic Victorian butterfly book, *British Butterflies* (1860), is more succinct: 'Cowardice is not one of his attributes.' This butterfly gets under our skin, and our relationship with it goes back a long way.

The Purple Emperor is not included in the descriptions of 20 British butterflies offered by Thomas Moffett in the first attempt at a book on British insects, his *Insectorum sive Minimorum Animalium Theatrum*, of 1634, written in Latin. A bland description of the butterfly appears in the second book published on British insects, John Ray's *Historia Insectorum*, which appeared posthumously in

1710: '*Papilio major nigra seu pulla, alis supina parte maculis albis notatis*' (a basic translation reads: 'large butterfly black or blackish, wings showing white spots and bands'). This was based on a specimen, almost certainly of the Emperor, caught by the Reverend Mansell Courtman of Castle Hedingham, Essex, in 1695, and presented to Ray, a friend and near neighbour. The absence of reference to purple suggests that the specimen was a female. The insect is also included in Petiver's *Papilionum Britanniae Icones*, published in 1717, with the description: '*Papilio oculatus e fusco aureo mixtus, umbra purpurascente*' ('eyed butterfly of shining dusty mix, gaining a purple shade').

When English or vernacular (common) names started to come into being, the Purple Emperor was first called Mr Dale's Purple Eye, in 1704, by James Petiver, a London apothecary regarded as the forefather of butterflying. The Mr Dale referred to here is Samuel Dale, a naturalist-physician from Braintree, Essex, and an associate of Ray. By 1741 it had become the Purple Emperour or Purple Emperor. All subsequent authors refer to it as the Purple Emperor, though some also use other names, as synonyms: viz. the Purple Highflyer (in use 1747–1832), the Emperor of the Woods (1747–1832), the Purple Shades (1795), the Emperor (1832) and the Emperor of Morocco (1853). Effectively, by 1800 the butterfly's name had been firmly established as the Purple Emperor.

The name 'Emperor' refers to the *toga picta*, or purple cloak, which only Roman emperors (of the later era) and victorious generals celebrating official state triumphs were entitled to wear. The Tyrian purple dye used to colour it had been discovered by the ancient Phoenicians. It was incredibly expensive, as it had to be laboriously

extracted from a group of medium-sized sea snails native
to the eastern Mediterranean.

Carl Linnaeus (1707–1778), the founder of the modern
system of naming organisms, placed the butterfly in the
family Nymphalidae, which includes the fritillaries and
aristocrats (such as our familiar Peacock, Red Admiral and
Small Tortoiseshell) and now also the browns (formerly
the Satyridae). Linnaeus gave the butterfly the scientific
name *iris* in his *Systema Naturae*, published in 1758, after
studying specimens in a Leipzig museum. In Greek
mythology, Iris was the winged messenger of the gods,
who appeared in the guise of a rainbow, or with
shimmering golden wings. Iris appears spectacularly at the
end of Book IV of *The Aeneid*. Virgil describes her descent:

Ergo Iris croceis per caelum roscida pennis
Mille trahens varios adverso sole colores
Devolat

A modest translation of this stupendous piece of Latin
verse reads: 'Then dewy-winged Iris flew down through
the golden sky, (and) drew countless shimmering colours
from the sun's rays.'

The origin and meaning of *Apatura*, the name of
the genus of emperor butterflies globally, has been a
source of considerable, if somewhat academic, debate.
The genus was erected (devised) by Johan Christian
Fabricius (1745–1808), a Danish zoologist who specialised
in insects, and was a student of Linnaeus. H N Humphreys,
writing in his classic Victorian work, *The Genera and
Species of British Butterflies* (1859), states, 'The name of the
genus, Apatura which was given to it by Fabricius in

1807, and which should more properly have been Apaturia, is generally said to have been taken from one of the names of Aphrodite or Venus, in reference to the beauty of the insect. But I have a fancy that Fabricius had in view rather one of the names of Athena, indicating deceitfulness, in reference to the deceptive effect of the purple gloss.'

I R P Heslop, who dedicated much of his life to pursuing and understanding the Purple Emperor after reading Classics at Cambridge, believed that the genus name is derived from the ancient Greek verb to deceive or trick, *apatao*, again referring to the changing nature of the male's wings. E M Emmet, an Oxford Classicist, examines all these theories in his *The Scientific Names of the British Lepidoptera* (1991) and concludes that the dominant theme is that of deception.

Whatever the truth is, the genus name is wholly appropriate, and not simply because of the deceptive colours on the male's wings. As I will argue throughout this book, this butterfly consistently fools and misleads us, and not merely visually, for it tricks the human mind – and there is to many of us a mysterious element of near-deity about this species, a *mysterium*.

The names Purple Emperor and *Apatura iris* are partly responsible for the aura that surrounds the butterfly, and for the insect's mystery that has intrigued and captivated so many. *Apatura iris* has metaphysical cadence and resonance, and is part of the deep magic that surrounds this insect. Uproar will ensue should taxonomists dare to alter these names, which are held sacrosanct.

By 1800 the Purple Emperor had attained the rank of being first and foremost among our butterflies. A H Haworth writes in his *Lepidoptera Britannica* of 1803: 'In the month of July he makes his appearance in the winged state, and invariably fixes his throne upon the summit of a lofty oak.' The term 'lofty', a de rigueur adjective of the then-fashionable Picturesque movement, was repeated in accounts of this species in most books about British butterflies for well over a century. For example, Richard South, writing in *The Butterflies of the British Isles*, the main butterfly textbook from the time of its publication in 1906 through to the 1970s, begins:

'As befits his rank, the Emperor has lofty habits ...'. Haworth's account continues: 'He performs his aerial excursions; and in these, ascends to a much greater elevation than any other insect I have ever seen, sometimes mounting higher than the eye can follow; especially if he happens to quarrel with *another Emperor*, the monarch of some neighbouring oak: they never meet without a battle, flying upwards all the while, and combating with each other as much as possible; after which they will frequently return again to the identical sprigs from whence they ascended.'

In *British Butterflies* (1860), the popular beginner's book of the late Victorian and early Edwardian eras, until superseded by South, W S Coleman writes: 'By universal suffrage, the place of highest rank among the butterflies of Britain has been accorded to this splendid insect, who merits his imperial title by reason of his robe of royal purple, the lofty throne he assumes, and the boldness and elevation of his flight ...'. Note, again, the use of the (now wretched) adjective, 'lofty'.

By the mid-1800s, the blood was well and truly up. One William Sturgess of Kettering writes in deeply Purple prose in *The Entomologist's Weekly Intelligencer* journal of 1857: 'It was a pledge that in due time his majesty would pay us a visit, though as a novice, I could entertain but a very faint hope of ever becoming more than a distant acquaintance of so high a personage. You may, therefore, judge how agreeably surprised I was to learn, one scorching day in July, that his majesty had been caught regaling himself on the imperial delicacies of dead stoats, weasel, etc. [a gamekeeper's gibbet]. I did not neglect the first opportunity of visiting the spot, and had the satisfaction of seeing, within the space of an hour, three Emperors descend from their thrones to breakfast upon the delicious viands'. All told, he took 80 specimens that season, suggesting that the butterfly was both numerous and hungry.

Edward Newman, in *An Illustrated History of British Butterflies* (1871), writes of the Emperor's depraved feeding habits: 'I would gladly have depicted the Emperor of our insect world as banqueting on ambrosia ... or quaffing the nectar of flowers, but this would not be truthful: in this and other cases of depraved appetite, we can only lament a fact as incontrovertible as it is unsatisfactory.' Of course, the Victorian butterfly collectors duly exploited these tastes, as illustrated in the paragraph by Sturgess, above.

The Entomologist's Weekly Intelligencer for 1857 also includes the following wondrous account of pursuit and capture, by the Reverend W G Wilkinson, Rector of Hyde, near Fordingbridge, Hampshire: 'There I saw, for the first time in my life, the Purple Emperor on the wing in great abundance, but could not obtain a single specimen. The sight of it, however, inflamed my desire of obtaining it ...'. Suitably inflamed, the account continues, breathtakingly: 'The creature made a lordly swoop in my direction, which had the singular effect of taking the breath out of my body; a furious but futile dash of my net sent him careering off amongst the trees.' The reverend gentleman was clearly most wound up.

The saga continued: 'On returning home from bathing ... I again encountered the Emperor ... He flew *bang* at me. I aimed a blow with my towel, and sent him sprawling on the ground, but before I could hit him again he was up and away. I pursued him in a most excited chase, but to no avail – he gained every step, and left me exhausted.' The titanic battle between the Emperor and the vicar ended emphatically: 'The royal city is taken! I went down and looked for it every day, saw it twice, knocked it down again with my towel, but all in vain. So I took the net, went and waited two hours without seeing him: at last he came. I saw him on the other side of the field – raced across, and took him easily. Strange to say, as soon as I had caught him, I felt a pang of sorrow that I hadn't got *two*.' And that's exactly the point: this insect always leaves you wanting more. It creates insatiable desire.

H N Humphreys, writing in *The Genera and Species of British Butterflies* (1859), states: 'The capture of the perfect insect, which appears towards the end of June, or in July, is difficult, on account of its elevated flight, which it delights to take in the neighbourhood of lofty oaks, over the top of which it skims with a power and rapidity, that seem at first to place it quite out of reach of the Lepidopterist, even when armed with his very best appliances, such as a small light net at the extremity of a long, pliable rod ...'. This contraption became known as the 'high net'.

Extreme measures were often necessary to capture this butterfly. The most remarkable account was published in *The Entomologist* magazine in 1888, concerning an adventure in south-west Hampshire: 'In August 1877, whilst driving in a dog-cart from Christchurch, I saw *Apatura iris* flying along the hedge of a bare roadside. I immediately gave the reins to a friend ... and pursued it with the dog-cart whip, and through a piece of luck I managed to hit the under wing above the upper, and so disable it enough to capture it. It was a fine male and not in the least damaged.' Perhaps the butterfly is, after all, to blame – for deliberating winding people up, or even driving them insane?

That episode can perhaps be bettered in eccentricity only by Dr Henry Guard Knaggs's suggestion, in his best-selling *The Lepidopterist's Guide* (1869): 'to shoot, with dust shot or with a charge of water (as they do Humming Birds in S. America), the Emperor as he sits in state.' The good doctor also recommends 'pelting with stones', and 'fumigating and vapourising'. The worrying truth is that all these have been tried, some quite recently. One would-be collector bemoaned in *The Entomologist* (1881): 'I saw about a dozen *Apatura iris* flying round high oaks and scotch firs, but sticks, stones, and clods of earth availed not at all to bring their imperial majesties within the reach of the long net I had provided for them.'

Gentlemen of the cloth were especially susceptible to such bizarre practices. The Reverend F O Morris recalls, in 1853, how a renowned collector, the Reverend William Bree, Rector of Polebrook near Oundle, Northamptonshire, trapped a feeding male under his tall hat.

Some collectors were more measured in their approach. One young collector, writing in *The Entomologist's Record* in 1892, states: 'Of *Apatura iris*, one was captured, two more were seen. My brother and I had a long chase after one – including a climb up two trees; but to no purpose. The one we caught we disturbed as it was drinking at a stream, it flew up and pitched in a tall ash nearby, so we sat down and enjoyed a smoke, and in about ten minutes were gratified to see "His Majesty" come down and, after several circles, alight on a stone, just in shallow water. We allowed him to get comfortable, and my brother managed to get the net over'.

Sometimes luck sufficed. An account in *The Entomologist's Record* for 1904 runs: 'One day I saw three *Apatura iris*, one of which sat on the ground within three yards of me, but when I tried to reach it, it successfully pleaded a previous engagement ... but on another day I got a nice male which an old woman had caught in her hands sitting on a flower in her garden.' That, incidentally, provides a rare record for a Purple Emperor visiting flowers. Doubtless the old lady knew that the butterfly was valuable and was rewarded for her diligence – indeed, servicing butterfly collecting was a major local industry in the New Forest for almost a hundred years.

So, there were two main techniques for capturing *Apatura iris*: exploiting the insect's tastes for imbibing unsavoury juices, notably by baiting for it; and netting it with a 'high net' on the end of a long, cumbersome pole. These techniques were not met with unrestrained approval. The Reverend G M A Hewett writes in *The Entomologist's Record* for 1895: 'I would go a long way to make sure of netting *Iris*. But, though I would go a long way, yet I cannot screw up my courage to carry about high meat or a 30-foot net. The former makes one so very unpopular in a railway carriage, and the latter so very ridiculous.' Rest assured that the reverend gentleman found other ways of making himself look very ridiculous, involving the pursuit of the Purple Emperor caterpillars, a pond, a soaking, and subsequent cold-shouldering in a railway carriage.

J W Tutt describes collectors using the high net at the popular collecting locality of Great Chattenden Wood, near Rochester in Kent, in his *British Butterflies* (1896): 'These (both males and females) had a custom of flying for a few hours (11 a.m. to 3 p.m.) to the highest point of the wood, and soaring around a few oaks that topped the hill. Here they settled and became easy prey. With a large ring net fixed on the end of a long hop-pole about twelve or fourteen feet in length … we have seen as many as nine amateur collectors standing in a line at three or four yards distance, and netting every specimen as it came up. … in one year (1881) alone, some two or three hundred specimens were captured.'

F W Frohawk provides accounts of both techniques in his *Natural History of British Butterflies* (1924), adding: 'In Chattenden Woods, Kent, where these butterflies formerly occurred abundantly, the females were in the habit of resorting to the highest ground, the brow of a large hill. On the summit of which there were a few oak trees; these were the favourite resort of this species, and large numbers were captured yearly.' He continues: 'From the height at which this butterfly usually flies, a large net fixed to a pole about fourteen feet or fifteen feet long is usually required for its capture; this is, however, a rather unwieldy implement when a strong wind blows.'

These descriptions, by Tutt and Frohawk, are the first in the entomological literature of Purple Emperors assembling on hilltops within woods, where the males establish territories and to which females in need of mating may fly. Those oaks stand on that wooded hilltop today, and are still used by the Purple Emperor.

Frohawk also describes baiting at Chattenden: 'Owing to this butterfly's great appreciation for decaying animal matter to feast upon, this habit has been taken advantage of by collectors; large numbers have been caught by hanging up a savoury bait ... no fewer than ninety-seven of these butterflies were captured in a few days by two men – a dealer and his friend – as they swooped down to feed on the provided banquet hung upon the lower branches of a neighbouring oak.' Yes, butterfly collecting had become such big business that professional dealers, in dead specimens and live stock (caterpillars, etc.), came into being during the 1850s. They still exist today, trading on eBay and at entomological trade fairs.

Some collectors also sought the larvae, in order to breed pristine Purple Emperor specimens for the cabinet. Mostly, they 'beat' for larvae, by thrashing sallow branches with a stout stick, catching some of the dislodged invertebrate biodiversity in an upturned umbrella or, better, an entomological beating tray or a sheet spread out on the ground. This, however, is an incredibly inefficient way of obtaining this insect, as the larvae adhere strongly to the silk pads on which they rest (Heslop describes obtaining a single larva from a marathon 55 hours of beating, during 1953 and 1954). We are informed by Humphreys that the caterpillar of the Purple Emperor was first discovered on 26 May 1758, by pioneer entomologist Dru Drury near Brentwood, in Essex.

The pursuit of *iris* ignited intense passions. Perhaps the grandest collection of British butterflies ever amassed was that of Sir Vauncey Harpur Crewe (1846–1924) of Calke

Abbey, Derbyshire. Sir Vauncey deployed his gamekeepers as assistant collectors, under his trusty head keeper Agathus Pegg. He was also a chequebook collector, purchasing valuable specimens at great cost. Unfortunately, he was a recluse and may well have suffered from obsessive-compulsive disorder. He had the habit of descending on the New Forest with his entourage and taking over an inclosure (as the New Forest's planted woods are known) for a weekend or more, stationing flunkies at the entrances to deter other collectors. This generated a series of rumpuses, as he was denying access to open access land. *Iris* was, predictably, an obsession. On a sunny morning in late June 1893, Sir Vauncey arrived, net in hand, in the grounds of the Gothic mansion his cousin John was renting from him on the Calke estate. They were both avid collectors. A cataclysmic row ensued, and Sir Vauncey immediately ordered his staff to evict his cousin and pull the mansion down. This was quickly done. Only the Purple Emperor could possibly have evoked such passion. We should accept this episode as the first record of *Apatura iris* in Derbyshire.

Butterfly collecting was not quite universally approved. The nature writer and champion of the embryo RSPB, W H Hudson (1841–1922), detested it with a hatred that almost defies words, and wrote disparagingly about it on several occasions. He avoided the Purple Emperor because it was so heavily targeted and treasured. Strangely, it seems that he saw his first Purple Emperor in the very woods where I saw mine, near Newbuildings Place in West Sussex, as he was a close friend of the owner – the poet, Islamist, anti-imperialist, radical thinker and rampant womaniser Wilfrid Scawen Blunt (1840–1922). Here's Hudson on butterfly collecting, from *Hampshire Days*: 'Lyndhurst is objectionable ... because it is the spot on which London vomits out its annual crowd of collectors, who fill its numerous and ever-increasing brand-new red-brick lodging-houses, and who swarm through all the adjacent woods and heaths, men, women, and children (hateful little prigs!) with their vasculums [for plant collecting], beer and treacle pots [for moth collecting], green and blue butterfly nets, killing bottles, and all the detestable paraphernalia of what they would probably call "Nature Study".'

Hudson was a man way ahead of his time, who sought a deeper relationship with nature than butterfly collecting could enable. Of one collector, a parson, he wrote, again in *Hampshire Days*: 'I cannot imagine him in white raiment, with a golden harp in his hand ... he could see nothing ... but an object to be collected.' Hudson's first book, a novel, was titled *The Purple Land That England Lost* (1885). It was later republished as *The Purple Land*. Those titles might be highly appropriate for a book, a novel perhaps, on the exploits of late Victorian butterfly collectors.

Butterfly collecting waned during the First World War, and further during the Second. It continued to decline as our butterflies themselves dwindled in number due to large-scale habitat loss, especially after it ceased to be run as an official school hobby at boys' boarding schools during the 1960s. Finally, butterfly collecting was driven underground by the Wildlife and Countryside Act of 1981, which afforded protection to many of the most

wildlife-rich places in the UK, 'Sites of Special Scientific
Interest' (SSSIs), and to some of our rarest butterflies.

Something wonderful arose from out of all this
eccentricity, lunacy and sheer bloodlust: somehow, this
butterfly, this insect, this mere animal inveigled its way
into our national psyche. It has been there for some time
and is flourishing there today. It is celebrated in our
visual art, rampantly, and increasingly so. It is prominent
in designs and advertising – on postage stamps, greetings
cards and tea towels – as a powerful symbol of the
importance of the mysterious, precious and elusive, as a
holy grail, to be sought out and attained.

The wonder all started when the Purple Emperor and
Iris the goddess became intertwined, in English literature
and verse. Alexander Pope set it all up in *The Rape of the
Lock* (1712):

> *Some to the sun their insect-wings unfold,*
> *Waft on the breeze, or sink in clouds of gold.*
> *Transparent forms, too fine for mortal sight,*
> *Their fluid bodies half dissolv'd in light,*
> *Loose to the wind their airy garments flew,*
> *Thin glitt'ring textures of the filmy dew;*
> *Dipp'd in the richest tincture of the skies,*
> *Where light disports in ever-mingling dyes,*
> *While ev'ry beam new transient colours flings,*
> *Colours that change whene'er they wave their wings*

The Purple Emperor appears in full glory, alongside
other sylvan butterflies, in *The Borough, Letter 8*, a lengthy

poem by George Crabbe, published in 1810, part of which reads:

Above the sovereign oak, a sovereign skims,
The Purple Emp'ror, strong in wing and limbs

To John Masefield, Poet Laureate from 1930 to his death in 1967, the Purple Emperor is a dark prince that haunts the oak woods, in *King Cole* (1921); to W B Yeats the butterfly is a dark stain upon his hand, in *Another Song of a Fool* (1919).

There are four allusions to the Purple Emperor in George MacDonald's *Phantastes* (1858), the pioneer adult fantasy novel written by a profound Christian mystic. This perhaps inspired the butterfly's spectacular appearance in J R R Tolkien's *The Hobbit* (1937), when Bilbo Baggins climbs to a treetop to find a way out of the dark forest of Mirkwood. The butterfly also appears in John Fowles's *The Collector* (1963), as an elusive rarity, something to be desired, pursued and captured. Most recently, *The Purple Emperor* is the title of a volume in Herbie Brennan's children's fantasy series *The Faerie Wars*. It seems that the very name of the Purple Emperor inspires magic and mystery.

CHAPTER TWO

The modern era

*I R P Heslop and Notes & Views of the Purple Emperor – The
two Fs: forestry and farming – Denys Watkins-Pitchford ('BB'),
and breeding and releasing – Ecological studies at Bookham
Common, and a method for surveying for Purple Emperors –
Media interest, The Emperor's Breakfast and modern
communications – Fermyn Woods: BB's dream fulfilled –
Knepp Wildland: paradise regained – Introduced populations –
Butterflies and the law*

Ian Robert Penicuik Heslop (1904–1970) lit what can
loosely be termed the 'Purple torch'. He was the lead
author of a fantastical monograph entitled *Notes & Views
of the Purple Emperor*, published in 1964. Heslop's writings
encapsulate the state of mind which this insect forces on
to people. A crack shot and a trophy hunter, he defines
'big game' early on in the book as a beast of the chase
about which one can recall the detail of every capture,
and concludes that the Purple Emperor is the big game
of our butterfly fauna. Heslop made such an impression
at Cambridge University shooting club that the Heslop
Cup was established in his memory, and is still disputed
each February between Cambridge and Oxford.

Notes & Views of the Purple Emperor is an eclectic
collection of papers, most of which had already been
published as articles in entomological periodicals.
Strangely, several published articles offering new
information are not included. The book leads more into
Heslop's world of rampant theorisation than into

ecological truth, but is perhaps the richer for it. *Notes &
Views of the Purple Emperor* captivated and inspired me
when I read it aged 16, though it sent me down many a
cul-de-sac. It is a mindset, but so is the Purple Emperor.

Heslop was a colonial administrator in Nigeria from
1929 to 1952, governing a province the size of Wales.
Whilst in Africa, he specialised in collecting the huge,
wary and elusive pasha butterflies of the genus *Charaxes*.
But his heart was Purple, and it was the Emperor that
called him home. He returned to England, choosing to
teach Latin at private boarding schools within the Purple
Empire, in Wiltshire, Hampshire and West Sussex. There
he studied the Purple Emperor, while amassing the 202
meticulously set specimens in his collection, which
resides in Bristol Museum along with his diaries and
papers. His pursuit of the Purple Emperor almost rivals
Captain Ahab's obsessive quest of the great white whale
in Herman Melville's *Moby-Dick* (1851); both whale and
Purple Emperor are mighty leviathans. I published a
short biography of Heslop in *British Wildlife* in 2005.
Further biographic details are provided in a fascinating
account by Robinson *et al.* (2017) of Heslop's discovery
of a now-extinct Nigerian subspecies of the Pygmy
Hippopotamus (*Choeropsis liberiensis heslopi*).

Heslop was one of the last great collectors of British
butterflies, and certainly the greatest of the Purple
Emperor. He became captivated by this elusive species
through reading the entomological literature. He saw his
first specimen at Brockley Warren, Somerset, in 1918, at a
distance, and had another unexpected and tantalising
glimpse while attending officer training camp near
Mytchett, Surrey, in 1923. His first real day in pursuit of

the Emperor was in July 1933, during his second colonial leave from Africa. Accompanied by his Cambridge friend Baron de Worms and a Colonel Labouchere at Bignor, West Sussex, 'I missed one *iris* up an oak tree by the skin of my teeth and had a certain shot at another in flight accidentally balked by Col L.' Ten days later, he missed another specimen at Bignor; it was 'the bitterest disappointment of my entomological career'. Twenty-one years later he found a larva at Bignor, which developed into an adult that July. His diary entry reads 'BIGNOR REPAYS ITS DEBT' in red capitals. He had taken his first specimen nearby, at Petworth, West Sussex, in mid-July 1935. It was swept off a diseased oak with a net fixed to a long pole. His unpublished memoir states: 'This was my first capture of His Imperial Majesty, the Purple Emperor, monarch of all the butterflies.' I drive past that spot, Fox Hill, regularly, and think of that moment each time. It is somehow stained there, within the memory of the place.

Heslop's pursuit of the Purple Emperor knew few bounds. He redeveloped the Victorian technique of taking specimens of this arboreal species with a 'high net', a series of ferrule-linked bamboo poles extending to a staggering 10 metres. This instrument necessitated great strength, mathematical calculations and precision timing. It was used only to capture specimens perched on trees bordering broad rides and roads, owing to the difficulty of bringing it to the ground without losing or damaging a specimen. His daughter Jane tells that the pole was so heavy that its end had to be kept on the ground, and the net aligned to drop over a perched Emperor as the pole was pushed into rapid descent.

Heslop caught nearly a hundred specimens with this weapon.

At Whiteparish Common, south Wiltshire, the Purple Emperor was attracted to the weeping bough of a diseased oak. Heslop exploited this by fixing a killing jar to the end of a pole 7 metres long. Several specimens were secured by this 'lethal cup', including a unique aberration. He also tried a variety of baits, in an attempt to exploit the insect's unsavoury predilection for seeking sustenance from damp, decaying matter. Thus, in 1953, a trailer load of manure was tipped into part of Bentley Wood, south-east of Salisbury in Wiltshire, from 'Brigadier Fanshawe's pig farm'. Cow manure, deer skins, treacle, something wacky called amyl acetate (a flavouring agent which smells of apples and pears), rotting bananas, and combinations of sugar, strawberries and beer were tried. Most worked to some extent, at least in hot weather. However, no panacea was found. Eventually Heslop discovered sap runs and bleeds (small or large flows of sap) on oak trunks and boughs, to which the butterfly is naturally attracted. His diary recalls that one day at Bentley Wood, 'on a weeping limb, very low down, I had the good fortune to pluck off, between finger and thumb, two male Purple Emperors which were already there; and two more as they came in and settled within the next 15 minutes.' Conventional netmanship was occasionally deployed: in July 1968, 'there was a brawl among *iris* along the road as a result of which I caught all three participants.'

Heslop reached his personal Elysium on 21 July 1969 when, after staying up all night watching the Apollo moon landing on TV, he visited his beloved Bentley Wood and caught a pristine male Purple Emperor lacking almost all vestiges of the normal white markings, an acute aberration or variation. His diary reads: 'Never have I taken an insect more easily! It was just flying peacefully along the track at knee height.' This was close to where the main Bentley Wood car park is now situated, a place where people gather each summer to view this butterfly. A week later, close by, Heslop was to see his last Emperor. The following spring he fell heavily on cobbles, and never recovered from a badly broken hip. He died just before I saw my first Purple Emperor.

I never met Heslop, but I did meet his close friend, the renowned and much-respected Baron Charles de Worms; notably on one incredibly hot day when he clambered out of his huge old silver Bentley, clad in a string vest, Boy Scout shorts of considerable antiquity, and hobnail boots, and proceeded to rub rancid Danish Blue cheese into a Forestry Commission gatepost as a bait for *iris*. This occurred at the height of the long hot summer of 1976, the last summer of widespread butterfly collecting, the last summer when men patrolled the southern forests armed with nets, intent on capturing the demigod *iris*.

After that summer, nets were forsaken in favour of more benign cameras, and the hobby of butterfly photography was born. Strangely, although I could not kill a butterfly to save my own life, least of all a Purple Emperor, I feel deeply connected to the old collectors and regard them as my spiritual ancestors. Heslop felt the same, stating in *Notes & Views of the Purple Emperor* that he felt the collectors of yesteryear almost come to life in their writings about the Purple Emperor.

A postscript is provided in full *laudator temporis acti* vein by Clive Simson in his book *The Butterflies' Fly-past* (1994). He describes, gloriously, but somewhat too wordily to be quoted in full here, his first capture of *Apatura iris*, in what was clearly Bentley Wood, in front of 'two accomplished' entomologists – Heslop and de Worms, in all probability. The butterfly, a naive and overambitious male, landed on his car. 'Your bird', said one of the distinguished gentlemen; a cow-shot to deep midwicket followed, culminating in successful capture and a wild celebratory war dance by the bald-headed Simson, with Heslop and de Worms walking off down the July rides, their shoulders shaking. Such were the highs of butterfly collecting.

Heslop was also a pioneer conservationist, and the Purple Emperor's first champion. In 1956 he raised funds to purchase 46 hectares of Blackmoor Copse, part of the Bentley Wood woodland complex, as a nature reserve specifically for this butterfly. Having saved the wood from coniferisation, he went on to oversee the reserve's management. Today, Blackmoor Copse is a Wiltshire Wildlife Trust reserve, where the Purple Emperor still flies.

Above all, Heslop's writings, alongside those of his co-authors Roy Stockley and the pioneer butterfly photographer George Hyde, inspired many collectors, young and old, to think more fully about the butterfly, and of its needs, and to view it as being more than just a piece of elusive beauty to be hunted down, captured and possessed. *Notes & Views of the Purple Emperor* is by no means a definitive account of the ecology of the Purple Emperor, but a gateway towards the development of such understanding. The frustrating thing about it is that it was published prematurely: if Heslop had sat down to write the book in the early autumn of 1969, just after he had retired, he would have written a near-definitive account.

While minds were turning from collecting to conservation, the Purple Emperor began to experience new threats. The activities and values of the Forestry Commission from the 1920s into the 1970s, and occasionally beyond, posed a very real threat to the Purple Emperor and other butterflies — and helped to fire conservation-minded naturalists into action. For many years the Commission was geared towards replacing native broad-leaved woodland with non-native conifers, and regarded sallows as noxious weeds of which forests had to be purged. Forestry Commission policies were undoubtedly the main factor behind the severe decline of the Purple Emperor during the twentieth century.

In 1970 a major rumpus blew up in the New Forest, the most famous and treasured of all butterfly and moth collecting grounds, when it became apparent that the Commission intended to replace the Forest's inclosures with conifers, leaving only cosmetic fringes of broad-leaved trees. They were stopped only by government intervention. The Commission's influence on butterfly habitats in privately owned woodland was equally severe, though it was merely following government policy.

Another sad example is provided by the tale of Bernwood Forest, another renowned butterfly locality, north-east of Oxford. The Forestry Commission purchased the larger blocks of this forest during the 1950s. Most of the indigenous broad-leaved trees were then felled, and replaced with conifer crops. Broad-leaved regrowth was sprayed off, by air, using the now long-banned herbicide 2,4,5-T. The even more infamous pesticide DDT was also deployed, again by air, to kill off infestations of the Large Pine Weevil, well into the 1960s. But forests have amazing powers of recovery, and so do insects, and populations recovered to the extent that Bernwood Forest was made into a Forest Nature Reserve in the 1980s, not least for its butterfly populations. That dark history can now be forgotten. Somehow the Purple Emperor survived, though with some human assistance, in the form of breeding the butterflies and releasing them into the wild (known as 'breeding and releasing'). Another massive problem for Purple Emperors was the wholescale clearance of woodland for agriculture, kick-started by the Second World War food shortages. Removal of woodland continued after the war, and increased considerably after 1973 when Britain joined what was then the European Economic Community or Common Market. The Common Agricultural Policy, which came into being in 1962, was strongly focused on increasing agricultural productivity. Woodland was being grubbed out (the term in use) in the Purple Empire right the way through into the 1980s to make way for more farmland. Doing nothing was no longer an option for butterfly enthusiasts, or for naturalists in general.

Heslop and Stockley's writings, augmented by those of Hyde, paved the way for conservation efforts for the Purple Emperor, primarily in the face of forestry policies. *Notes & Views of the Purple Emperor* inspired the practice of breeding and releasing Purple Emperors, to augment dwindling populations — and a barrage of letters to Forestry Commission officials pleading for the retention of some ride-side sallows.

The most famous proponent of breeding and releasing was the renowned author, wildlife artist and country sportsman Denys Watkins-Pitchford (1905–1990), who wrote under the pseudonym of 'BB' (after a grade of lead shot, which was also used to weight fishing lines).

He was a true Emperorphile, and never a collector, though an ardent angler and wildfowler. In the early 1970s, BB started to harvest Purple Emperor eggs from woods in Hampshire and West Sussex, and carefully rear the larvae in giant netted cages in his Northamptonshire garden, before releasing the adults into Fermyn Woods, near his home. Later, he found and reared local eggs, in what in butterflying circles is known as 'support breeding'. He did this for at least 25 years, often releasing as many as 25 Purple Emperors into the woods each year, assisted by his daughter Angela and his young protégé Ray 'Badger' Walker. BB wrote about what he was doing in impassioned pieces in *The Field*, *The Countryman* and the *Shooting Times*. A fascinating summary is provided in *BB's Butterflies*, edited by Bryan Holden of the BB Society.

It is likely that BB did not bring the Emperor back from extinction in these east Northamptonshire woods, as it had never quite died out, though he undoubtedly gave it a wonderful helping hand. He had a long-running struggle with the Forestry Commission over the destructive felling of sallows along the rides. In 1978, the Commission felled all the sallows along his favoured ride in Fermyn Woods. On another occasion, he mourns in the parish magazine 'a great clearance from one end of the forest to the other'. Eventually his values won through: sallows now abound throughout Fermyn Woods, and the woodland complex supports one of only four or five genuinely strong Purple Emperor populations in the country.

BB was not alone in breeding and releasing Emperors. Dr Roger Clarke, a retired GP, did similar work in Bernwood Forest during the late 1960s and early 1970s (and showed me how to look for Purple Emperor larvae in August 1970). However, BB's main contribution to the conservation of the Purple Emperor was through getting the butterfly valued by country landowners and sportsmen, via his articles (he wrote for the *Shooting Times* for 60 years). Many country landowners today are proud to have this butterfly on their land. This is BB's true legacy.

I initially discovered the Purple Emperor in BB's stupendous book *Brendon Chase* (1944), which was read to me and a dormitory full of other 10-year-old boys by an inspired housemaster in the junior house of Christ's Hospital school in June 1964. It is a fantastic yet somehow wonderfully plausible tale of three brothers who decide not to return to boarding school at the end of the Easter

holidays, but to run away to a great forest, Brendon
Chase. There, they go feral for an entire summer and
autumn, living off the land. They are serenaded by
Nightingales, climb a giant fir tree to peek inside a
Honey Buzzard's nest, and encounter, at the zenith of
the book, the Purple Emperor. I am eternally grateful to
BB, and am by no means alone.

Heslop's and BB's writings inspired many butterfly
enthusiasts, and spirited some of them away from
collecting. One such convert is my dear friend Ken
Willmott. Ken was one of the first butterfly enthusiasts to
reject collecting and turn to photography, ecological study
and conservation. In the early 1970s he started to study
the Purple Emperor in earnest, primarily during extended
lunch breaks from his job as a print setter in Leatherhead,
Surrey. He produced a newsletter, sharing his experiences
with like-minded people, including myself. Bookham
Commons, a cluster of wooded and grassy common lands
close to Leatherhead, the most wooded of which is called
Bookham Common, was his main study site. His findings
are summarised in a booklet published in 1990 by the
British Butterfly Conservation Society, now Butterfly
Conservation, entitled *The Purple Emperor Butterfly*.

At Bookham, during the mid- and late 1970s, Ken
discovered two sets of trees – 'master trees', as Heslop
calls them, or 'territories' in Ken's language – on hillocks
within the woods, where males spar each afternoon while
awaiting the arrival of females in need of their services.
Those territories are still in full use today, despite the
comings and goings of various individual trees. These

study sites enabled Ken to clarify male territorial behaviour. More importantly, he studied the egg-laying habits of the elusive females, and was the first to describe the 'rejection drop' flight, which occurs when a mated female is accosted by an amorous male unwilling to take 'no' for an answer. Ken's findings, and his published data in a detailed report produced for what was the World Wildlife Fund (now the World Wide Fund for Nature) in 1987, will be regularly referred to in this book. Essentially, Ken's work provided a much-needed ecological focus, unconstrained by any desire to collect specimens.

Towards the end of the 1990s, Liz Goodyear and Andrew Middleton, working in Hertfordshire and then (old) Middlesex, and Ashley Whitlock and myself, working in Alice Holt Forest, Hampshire, independently developed the technique of looking for male territories in woodland high points into an effective survey method, inspired by the topographically-positioned territories at Bookham Common. We developed a sound survey technique for locating this evasive, canopy-dwelling butterfly – at least in woodland on undulating or sloping ground.

Unfettered from fears about collecting, we were able to teach others this methodology, primarily by encouraging people to learn from visiting known territories where male activity could be observed. This revolutionised Emperoring, as it quickly became known, and paved the way to a great many new sites being discovered, including in counties in which the butterfly had long been thought to be extinct. Gradually it became apparent that this is not a rare butterfly, but one heavily suppressed by prejudice against its larval foodplant, sallows, and one that is significantly under-recorded. Liz

and Andrew rediscovered it in Hertfordshire, where it
was thought to be long extinct, and went on to find it to
be widespread in and around woodland almost
throughout the county. They then rediscovered it in the
old and highly urbanised Middlesex.

Until the twenty-first century there was an assumption
that the Purple Emperor was a rare butterfly that could
be seen only in some large southern oak forests. This
was part of the mythology surrounding the butterfly.
It meant that people flocked to a few well-known
localities, with bird-twitcher mentality, including Bentley
Wood in Wiltshire (Heslop's old heartland), parts of
Chiddingfold Forest on the Surrey–Sussex border,
parts of Bernwood Forest on the Buckinghamshire–
Oxfordshire border, and parts of Alice Holt Forest in east
Hampshire. Bentley Wood fills up at weekends, with
crowds loitering around the car park waiting for Purple
Emperors to descend.

However, in recent years a large number of other
Purple Emperor localities have become known, and
many of them also fill up at weekends, especially when
field meetings of Butterfly Conservation branches and
local natural history societies arrive. On a fine weather
day on a weekend in early July, it is likely that well over
a thousand people are scouring the English woods in
search of Purple Emperors, most of them hoping to
photograph the insect.

On 13 July 2005, Sussex naturalist and Emperorphile
Neil Hulme and I met beneath a Purple Emperor 'master
tree' in the gloriously named Dogbarking Wood, West

Sussex, where I had first sought the Emperor back in 1967. It was as if we had been brought together by divine purpose, and that we had always known each other and had no secrets. We instantly formed a partnership centred upon a mutual desire to establish the Purple Emperor as Britain's Premier Butterfly, with a degree of zeal matched only by the male butterfly itself. The Emperor has since spurred us on, from exuberance to overexuberance, and beyond. More usefully, we have sought to popularise this insect, the experience of which had previously been the privilege of rather a select few.

Since 2006, enormous media interest has been generated in the Purple Emperor. During the period 2006 to 2018 it probably eclipsed all other British butterflies in broadcast and print media coverage. Hulme and Oates's party piece, The Emperor's Breakfast, has been staged on TV four times, including on *Countryfile* and *The One Show*. In this act of gross eccentricity, a selection of baits is laid out in the forests, on plates on trestle tables covered in pristine tablecloths, with replica plots and empty 'control' plates as a nod to scientific methodology. Baits include fresh fox scat, various runny smelly cheeses, wine, and Hulme and Oates's trademark oriental shrimp paste. It's a hoot, but it does take this wonderful butterfly to new audiences, and we have conveyed some serious conservation messages on the back of the wonderment – plus the crucial message that butterflies are not boring.

In 2007 the Purple Emperor became the first of the British butterflies to acquire its own website and blog, *The Purple Empire*. This was set up by my old school friend Derek Longhurst. Derek originates from the village of Dial Post, on the east edge of Knepp Castle

Estate in West Sussex, but emigrated to Western Australia at the start of the Thatcher era. He is fully Aussified in all things, save one, and set up the website to keep him in close contact with the sole aspect of England still dear to him – the Purple Emperor. Today, *The Purple Empire* functions as a lively blog, which is vibrantly active during the butterfly's flight season, though it receives postings all year round. On this blog, anything goes: the more fervent, the better. There are currently also two Purple Emperor WhatsApp groups, one more extreme than the other.

Unshackled from the mistrust, secrecy, mythology and downright skulduggery which bedevilled old-fashioned butterfly collecting, and empowered by modern information exchange culture, Emperoring has entered a new and glorious era. This is the must-see, must-photograph butterfly for all wildlife photographers, and a top 10 wildlife experience for UK nature lovers. Indeed, the Purple Emperor season is a time of unrestrained fun and wonderment.

During the early 2000s, Fermyn Woods, near Brigstock in east Northamptonshire, became firmly established as *the* place to see Purple Emperors, developing one of the largest populations in entomological history. By 2009 people were flocking there in numbers, so much so that in 2012, while gathering evidence to present to a public inquiry into a proposed wind farm development close by, I estimated that 2,000 to 2,500 day-visits were made to these woods by people seeking Purple Emperors, mostly during the 10-day period early in the flight season when the butterfly was emerging in large numbers. Eventually the wind farm proposals were withdrawn.

Fermyn Woods, collectively, are part of old Rockingham Forest, and consist of a network of woods, large and small, on gently rolling boulder clay country running east from Corby down towards Oundle and southwards towards Wadenhoe and Thrapston. Most of these woods are owned by the Forestry Commission (now Forestry England), but some are privately owned (and are mainly closed-canopy broad-leaved woods with little sallow). Much of the Forestry Commission woods were clear-felled and replanted with Norway Spruce during the mid-twentieth century, though several blocks of broad-leaved woodland were retained, becoming dense native woodland. The spruce grew well for a while, then stopped growing and started to die – as is their habit on heavy clay soils. The Forestry Commission cleared most of the ailing conifers away during the 1980s and 1990s – and then did something remarkably bold, and commonsensical: they left the land to natural regeneration. Sallow is, of course, a pioneer coloniser species in such situations, though in time it is outcompeted by other, slower-growing trees that grow much taller – in these woods, Ash, Field Maple and English Oak.

Fermyn is rather a two-trick wonder. First, the Purple Emperor occurs there in surprisingly good numbers, primarily because it now contains some 250 hectares of sallow-rich habitat. Sallows are orders of magnitude more numerous here than they were in BB's day, not least because Forestry England no longer has the resources to weed them out, or the inclination. Secondly, for some curious reason Emperor males visit Fermyn's ride surfaces remarkably frequently, at least during the first few days of their lives, to feed on indelicacies such as dog excrement, fox scat, damp patches, and the various baits put down for them by Purple Emperor aficionados. When so ensconced, males offer excellent photo opportunities, such that one sees groups of five or more photographers prostrate on the ride photographing an obliging Emperor, and 20 or more people staked out along a short stretch of ride. Great Chattenden Wood must have heaved in a comparable manner during its heyday in the 1870s and early 1880s. Some naturalists may find Fermyn Woods rather overfull, but the site is so large and the butterfly so well distributed that it is possible to find yourself a quiet corner, your own piece of paradise, even at weekends. It is important that people are able to experience intense one-to-one experiences with this butterfly.

Sadly, the Purple Emperor population in Fermyn Woods may already be on the wane, due to 'nature conservation'. During the winters of 2017/18 and 2018/19 much of the main ride system was widened, in a Back from the Brink nature conservation project that focused on other butterflies. Blackthorn tangles were retained for the rare Black Hairstreak butterfly, but hundreds of sallows were felled, and hundreds – possibly thousands – of Purple Emperor larvae were subsequently fed into biomass boilers, along with the cut small-bore timber. BB's blood would have boiled. Incredibly, BB's favourite ride – known as BB's Ride – which had become badly overhung and desperately needed reopening, was left, neglected. It will be interesting to see how many of the cut sallows are allowed or able to regenerate. Although the work was well intentioned, and in many ways desirable, it suggested that the Purple

Emperor population was not deemed a significant feature of the woods and hints that this butterfly may no longer be prioritised in conservation work here.

Encounters with the Purple Emperor are at their richest at Knepp Wildland in West Sussex. Two decades ago, this 465-hectare block consisted of intensively farmed dairy and arable land, albeit with oak-lined hedges and some unimproved laggs (damp shallow combes, with relict meadowland). Realising that farming was neither economically viable nor environmentally sustainable on the estate's heavy Weald clay soils, and inspired by the profound reasonings of the Dutch ecologist Dr Frans Vera, the owners, Charlie and Issy Burrell, boldly decided to take the land out of mainstream agriculture and allow it to develop into wood pasture (also known as pasture-woodland), grazed by free-ranging longhorn cattle, deer, Exmoor ponies and Tamworth pigs. The story is lucidly told in Issy's book *Wilding* (2018), penned under her maiden name, Isabella Tree. Sallows quickly colonised the abandoned arable land, and by 2009 the Purple Emperor had colonised from Southwater Woods, a mile to the north. Vegetation surveys in 2015 determined that there were 214,251 square metres of dense sallow scrub and 304,221 square metres of open sallow scrub in the Southern Block, which constitutes Knepp Wildland. Nearly all these sallows are hybrids, some veering towards Goat Willow, and many towards narrow-leaved varieties (for more on sallow taxonomy, see Chapter 9).

By 2013 it was clear that an unusually large population of Purple Emperors was developing at Knepp. Two years later, Neil Hulme and I determined that the Knepp population was larger (or, more accurately, denser and more visible) than the population at Fermyn Woods. In 2014 the estate began running Purple Emperor safaris in the main (southern) block, by then called Knepp Wildland, led by Neil and myself, on best behaviour. These ventures have been massively successful (and surprisingly fortunate with the weather), offering unforgettable experiences within the natural world. The estate is also making money from its camping and glamping site, which attracts an increasing number of Emperorphiles during the butterfly's flight season. In addition, it currently generates some £120,000 worth of high-quality organic grass-finished meat annually.

Knepp is a work in progress, an open-ended experiment in process-led nature conservation under a naturalistic grazing system; that is, one that allows large herbivores (hare, cattle, ponies and deer), and crucially pigs, to behave naturally and drive the land's ecology within broad parameters, as they would have done in the so-called wildwood, before humankind tamed the land. There are few, if any, deliberate interventions and no tight objectives. The aim is simply to accept the vegetation structures and associated biodiversity that free-ranging grazing animals produce. The Wildland is, effectively, New Age pasture-woodland, a modern version of a habitat formerly common over much of Britain. The Purple Emperor has merely colonised the early successional scrub phase. How long a sizeable population will last here is anyone's guess, as no older versions of Knepp exist – previously, farmers and foresters would have cleared the sallow growth away.

At Knepp, Purple Emperor males spend their mornings searching for females around the sallow thickets, at least during the first half of the flight period (they take the mornings off later on). Each afternoon throughout the season, cloud and wind permitting, they establish and defend territories on the leeward side of the old, dense-leaved oaks that line the former field margins. Neil and I have given (largely humorous) names to the most popular of these territories. In 2015, a Purple Emperor transect was established along a green lane that bisects the Wildland. This route is walked weekly during the Purple Emperor season, on warm, non-windy afternoons, with Emperors occurring within an imaginary 50-metre box being diligently counted (other butterflies are ignored, as entomological riff-raff).

The female Purple Emperors skulk around the sallow brakes, mainly during the middle part of the day. Unlike at Fermyn Woods and other Forestry England woodlands with gravelled forest rides, Purple Emperors (of both sexes) do not frequently descend to feed on the ground at Knepp. Instead, they feed primarily from sap bleeds on the numerous veteran (centenarian) oaks, imbibing fermented sap (this might explain why the Knepp males, and indeed some females, are so aggressive – they are inebriated). However, it seems that the males are now starting to feed from the ground more frequently, following the infilling of rutted stretches of track with rubble to assist the Wildland safari vehicles, and given the increasing abundance of organic animal dung.

At present, the Purple Emperor is more visible at Knepp than anywhere else in the UK, because Knepp is not a traditional forest with narrow rides, but former agricultural land offering broad, open vistas. Elsewhere, sightings of individual Purple Emperors are timed in seconds; here they regularly last minutes. However, Knepp is not the place to obtain photographs of males feeding on the ground. Instead, enthusiasts can photograph them from below, basking high on oak foliage, or feeding on oak boughs.

Above all, Knepp has altered our understanding and perception of the Purple Emperor, finally debunking the myth that this is a forest butterfly which naturally occurs only in low numbers, and which spends hours sitting around doing precisely nothing. Here, at last, the Purple Emperor is revealing its true self. Knepp Wildland offers great hope for the future, indicating that the Purple Emperor does not need to be restricted to ancient woodland and legally protected wildlife sites, but can flourish where farming relaxes its grip.

Butterflies fascinate us, perhaps none more so than the Purple Emperor. That fascination develops into deep affection that expresses itself in diverse ways, including a strong desire to act − to capture, experience, understand or assist. For many, doing nothing is not a realistic option, especially when faced with unoccupied, suitable-looking habitat which is considered unlikely to receive natural colonisation. It all comes down to where we, as individuals, feel we can best make a difference. The Emperor, of course, insists on a degree of servitude and readily exploits human weaknesses, and should take the blame for any human actions deemed inappropriate.

As previously mentioned, since the late 1950s butterfly enthusiasts with certain skills and leanings have been breeding and releasing Purple Emperors back into the wild. Initially this consisted of topping up known populations, to mitigate for the impact of poor weather or adverse habitat management, but in recent decades new populations have been established, mostly on the edge of the butterfly's known range (which is itself vague and fluid).

Breeding Purple Emperors in the numbers necessary to establish new populations requires huge skill, which I for one lack. The usual technique is to catch a gravid (egg-carrying) female – which is no easy task, requiring dexterous use of a large net on the end of a long pole – and then persuade her to lay eggs in captivity. The female needs to be contained in a fine-netting sleeve placed over a branch of suitable sallow foliage and out of hot sun. She will need feeding. Some butterfly breeders (or simply, 'breeders') force-feed their females, morning and evening, by carefully uncurling the proboscis (tongue) with a pin. Others place cotton wool pads containing fructose solutions in the sleeve, which need to be kept moist. How well an individual female feeds determines how long she will live, and how many eggs she will lay. The record seems to be held by a female reared by ace breeder Colin Wiskin, which lived for nearly four weeks and laid a staggering 439 eggs. Most breeders would be delighted to get a hundred eggs out of a female. I haven't dabbled in this art since

the 1970s, and had the habit of releasing the females
back into the wild after a day or so, out of respect and
trepidation – quite frankly, I'm frightened of hurting
them. Consequently, I never obtained more than 25
eggs, but never wanted more (nowadays, I rear two to
five Purple Emperors each year, from eggs or young
larvae rescued from unrealistic situations and doomed
to perish, simply to act as a barometer of what is
happening in the wild and to keep me in near-daily
contact with the insect of my dreams; I release the adult
butterflies back where they came from).

Enabling the Purple Emperor to mate in captivity is a
considerable skill. Apparently only four people currently
have that ability. According to Colin Wiskin, captive-
bred males need to be at least six days old before they are
capable of mating, and are at the peak of their prowess
around day 10. One of Colin's captive males paired seven
times, taking a day off in between each pairing – a
veritable alpha male. Colin states that the females only
commence laying eggs six days after mating. This, I
believe, contrasts strongly with their practice in the wild,
where females appear to commence laying the day after
mating. At one stage I was told that to 'hand pair' Purple
Emperors you need to cut the male's head off, to
persuade him to open his claspers. I hope that's untrue –
a part of Emperoring mythology – as it would constitute
a decidedly dark art.

Because Purple Emperors spend some 11 months in
the immature stages, rearing them in large numbers in
captivity is labour-intensive, requiring several dense-
leaved sallow bushes carefully caged or netted with fine
rot-proof nylon netting. It is crucial to keep predators

out, notably earwigs, wasps and flower bugs, and of course birds. If environmental conditions are wrong, many first instar (L1) larvae perish, and getting larvae through mild winters is tricky (one highly experienced breeder, Derek Smith, finds it almost impossible to rear the insect after moving to mild Torbay). Surviving larvae require a great many large leaves during their main growing period of late April to early June. They also require sun in May and shade in late summer. Failure to provide adequate leafage leads to undersized adults (I pride myself in producing large Emperors). Also, overprotected larvae and pupae will produce adults before wild individuals emerge, having developed in warmer, drier environments. Releases of out-of-sync captive-bred adults undoubtedly explain some, if not all, sightings of Emperors made well in advance of the true flight season.

Perhaps the oldest introduced population, and the longest surviving, is at Cotgrave Forest, to the south-east of Nottingham. The butterfly was originally established here in the mid-1960s, but some topping up appears to have taken place. Strangely, this has only recently become known as a Purple Emperor site, now supporting a sizeable population.

In recent years, the Purple Emperor has been successfully introduced to woods in Suffolk, Essex, Warwickshire and Lincolnshire, in areas from where it was thought to be absent. These introductions, which have been frowned upon by many conservationists, having been dubbed 'unofficial', have been hugely successful and have taught us much about the butterfly.

At Theberton Wood, a small, isolated wood near Saxmundham in Suffolk, Purple Emperors were released annually between 2001 and 2004, having been bred locally by the late John Quinn. By 2009 the butterfly had spread to sallow carr woodland at the back of the nearby RSPB reserve at Minsmere, and by 2011 it had reached 10 kilometres to the south, to North Warren Nature Reserve, on the north edge of Aldeburgh. Since then, the butterfly has continued to spread to small, isolated woods across an open landscape dominated by intensive agriculture, though apparently at least one of the Emperor's servants has been actively translocating it to the Halesworth area, and recent surveys spearheaded by Liz Goodyear and Andrew Middleton have found it to be established elsewhere in Suffolk anyway. I visited Theberton in 2009, 2014 and 2016, during which period the wood itself increased in suitability, due to the careful management of sallows by an inspired Forestry Commission manager.

In Essex, the butterfly was introduced to the Marks Hall Estate, north of Coggeshall, by conservation-minded owners in the early 2000s. It is doing well there, though it was probably already present, or in the process of colonising. One of the main sales outlets for commercial butterfly breeders nowadays is private landowners wishing to bolster existing populations or establish new ones.

In Warwickshire, approximately 150 adults were released into Ryton Wood, a nature reserve to the south-east of Coventry, and another 70 or so into nearby Wappenbury Wood, by Derek Smith in July 2004. These butterflies emanated from stock originally derived from Alice Holt Forest in Hampshire. The butterfly had last been recorded in the Coventry area in 1943, though at least one local expert, Roger Smith, felt that it could have survived all along. A sizeable population quickly developed, and spread to the adjoining Ryton Pools Country Park and a nearby brownfield nature reserve, where sallows were developing apace. In 2004, Derek also released 80 Purple Emperors into Oversley Wood, a 100-hectare remnant of Shakespeare's Forest of Arden near Alcester, close to the Worcestershire border, managed by the Forestry Commission (Forestry England).

Since these two releases, the Purple Emperor has spread to at least 22 tetrad squares (squares of 2 x 2 kilometres) in Warwickshire, probably assisted by some natural spread from Northamptonshire to the east and Oxfordshire to the south-east. The extent to which the releases masked natural spread is debatable – we will never know. However, it shows that Warwickshire wants to be Purple and that introductions, whether 'official' or 'unofficial', may have a positive role to play in ensuring the future of this butterfly.

In 2014 and 2015 a small team of breeders, inspired by the highly experienced Martin White, successfully established a population in and around Chambers Farm Wood, a Forestry England wood in the Lincolnshire Limewoods a few miles east of Lincoln. The initial release consisted of a large number of final-instar larvae. The butterfly became so well established, in a wood whose rides are lined with highly suitable sallows, that no further releases were deemed necessary. On 6 July 2018, an impressive 50 individuals were counted in Chambers Farm Wood by Dennis Dell and companions, suggesting it supported one of the largest Purple Emperor populations in the country. Local expansion

took place, such that in 2018 the butterfly was seen on
the south-west edge of Lincoln. At the same time,
though, it was being discovered at other woods to the
south in Lincolnshire, suggesting a period of natural
spread northwards. Perhaps Chambers Farm Wood
would have been colonised naturally anyway? One of
the few facts Dr Martin Warren and I managed to
establish in a review of butterfly introductions in the
UK, published by the World Wildlife Fund (now World
Wide Fund for Nature) in 1990, was that many successful
introductions (of UK species) coincided with, and
confused, periods of natural spread.

It appears that no introductions have been attempted
way outside the Purple Emperor's known range – just
causal releases, of small numbers. In a way that is a shame,
as much could have been learnt that might be of
relevance to the impending need for many British
butterflies to move north due to climate change.

The rights and wrongs of all this are complex. Releases
certainly mask natural spread and population trends, and
so distort biological recording and monitoring; and
landowners and managers with conservation inclinations
or remits can suddenly find themselves facing a demand
to alter management plans in favour of a new arrival that
has appeared on their land clandestinely. It is a challenge
for biological statisticians and conservationists to get
their heads around these issues, and many records of
Purple Emperors in far-flung places are simply dismissed
as bred-and-released specimens, rather than considered
as bona fide wanderers.

Alternatively, we could flip the coin over, sunny side
up, and try to view these issues more positively. The

butterfly breeders, so long maligned, may possess skills and knowledge essential to the future of many of our less common butterflies, given that climate change could necessitate the translocation of poorly mobile species to developing habitat in northern Britain. The Purple Emperor may, however, be capable of moving north itself.

Standing advice to those considering introducing Purple Emperors to a new location is, simply, determine whether the butterfly is already there, or likely to colonise naturally; fully consider the implications of a release on site management, monitoring and recording; and, if you decide to proceed, inform the site managers and Butterfly Conservation (anonymously if needs be).

The legal side of all this is not simple. The Purple Emperor is (probably rightly) not a fully protected species, though it is one of 21 species of British butterfly afforded some 'protection' under trading restrictions introduced by the Wildlife and Countryside Act of 1981 and included in subsequent legislation (the Countryside and Rights of Way Act of 2000). Basically, butterfly traders require a licence from the Department of the Environment (DoE), and to obtain such a licence they simply need to reassure the DoE that stock being offered for sale has been bred in captivity in perpetuity. It is not for me to say that this is daft, but it can be said that the Wildlife and Countryside Act inadvertently drove a schism between butterfly breeders and other butterfly enthusiasts – all of whom are ardent conservationists.

More significantly, it is illegal to remove butterflies, in any life stage, and any other taxa, from a Site of Special

Scientific Interest, or to release them there. However, the relevant government agencies, primarily Natural England for the Purple Empire, seem to lack both the resources and the political inclination to take any action. Additionally, removing or introducing Purple Emperors (or other wildlife) is contrary to Forestry England and National Trust bylaws (which are highly similar), and the bylaws of some local authorities, but there seems to be little if any will or capacity to pursue prosecution in such matters.

This all leads us to the questions of where does the Purple Emperor occur, what was its past distribution, and how is it faring now? How rare is it – or isn't it? Do we rightly know?

CHAPTER THREE

The Purple Empire

Status and distribution: historical and current overviews,
and maps — Overall assessment

The Purple Emperor is almost certainly undergoing a
period of dramatic expansion in the UK and in other
parts of northern Europe (e.g. Denmark, Finland,
Holland and Sweden), albeit after suffering a long period
of contraction almost throughout the twentieth century.
However, at the same time there has been a massive
upsurge in recording effort, enabled by the breakdown
of the assumption that this species is, always was and
always will be a great rarity, as well as by the development
of a new survey method — looking for male territories —
and by the increase in recording stimulated by Butterfly
Conservation and the Butterflies for the New
Millennium project. The increase in recording effort has
transformed knowledge of the Purple Emperor in several
of the English counties in which it was long known to
occur, notably in Berkshire, Buckinghamshire, Essex,
Hampshire, Hertfordshire, old Middlesex, Oxfordshire,
Sussex, Suffolk and Wiltshire. Many butterfly enthusiasts,
working in particular counties, have become very fired
up about this butterfly.

The distribution map for the period 1945–50 drawn
by Heslop and featured as Plate II of *Notes & Views of*
the Purple Emperor suggests a broad band of Purple
Empire running east from Wiltshire, through

Hampshire and the northern half of the Isle of Wight, and into West Sussex, then swirling north through west Berkshire, much of Oxfordshire and Buckinghamshire, and up into Northamptonshire and Lincolnshire; plus a smaller belt running north from north Somerset into the Forest of Dean and up into Herefordshire; an isolated band in Suffolk and Norfolk; and an outpost in mid-Kent. Missing from Heslop's map are Devon, Dorset, East Sussex, Surrey (incredibly, and erroneously), Middlesex, Hertfordshire, Essex, and much of (eastern) Berkshire and Buckinghamshire. Apart from the Surrey *lapsus* it was probably quite an accurate map for the era. The butterfly was undoubtedly seriously suppressed by the prejudice against sallows (and willows generally) that flourished after the establishment of the Forestry Commission in 1919 and, especially, during the 'Dig for Victory' ethos of the Second World War.

The earlier distribution maps offered in butterfly books by Edmund Sandars (1939) and E B Ford (1945) are more speculative. Sandars's book, which was my boyhood butterfly textbook, depicts a concentration of Purple Emperors in Lincolnshire and an absence from the Home Counties; Ford's suggests a rare denizen of the western Weald, the New Forest, central southern England, Northamptonshire, Suffolk and Norfolk, the West Midlands and north Somerset.

The Millennium Atlas of Butterflies in Britain and Ireland, for the recording period 1995–99, shows a concentration of sites in Wiltshire, Hampshire (excluding the New Forest), West Sussex, Surrey, west Berkshire, west Buckinghamshire, Oxfordshire and east Northamptonshire, plus a small number of sites in east Devon and west Somerset, Hertfordshire and mid-Kent.

Since *The Millennium Atlas* period, either the butterfly has infilled considerably within its central southern England heartland, and expanded northwards and eastwards from there, or it has proved to be distinctly under-recorded during *The Millennium Atlas* recording period, or both. I like the latter theory, though with Purple Emperors proof and disproof are difficult. Whichever is the case, the differences between *The Millennium Atlas* distribution map and the current map are spectacular.

The latest map (overleaf, for 2017) shows a distribution enhanced by successful introductions in Warwickshire, Suffolk and Lincolnshire, with associated spread from release sites, and a trail of rediscoveries or recolonisations in Hertfordshire, Middlesex, Essex, East Sussex, (East) Dorset and Gloucestershire, plus considerable infill in each of the butterfly's core range counties.

The only county that appears to have dropped off the map is Devon, where the butterfly's status is in abeyance. Since this map, Purple Emperors were discovered or rediscovered in three more counties in 2018 and 2019 Leicestershire, Staffordshire and, almost certainly, Worcestershire.

Currently (September 2019), the Purple Emperor is known to occur in 27 modern counties: Bedfordshire, Berkshire, Buckinghamshire, Cambridgeshire, Dorset, East Sussex, Essex, Gloucestershire, Hampshire, Hertfordshire, Kent, Leicestershire, Lincolnshire, Middlesex, Norfolk, Northamptonshire, Nottinghamshire, Oxfordshire, Rutland, Somerset, Staffordshire, Suffolk, Surrey, Warwickshire, West Sussex, Wiltshire and Worcestershire.

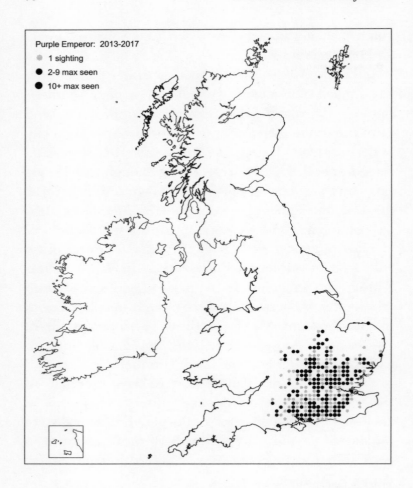

Its distribution in some of these counties requires further clarification. The butterfly may well also occur in a few others (notably Devon and the Isle of Wight, and quite possibly south Yorkshire).

Overviews of the history, current status and future prospects for the Purple Emperor in all counties where it currently occurs, and where it has occurred historically, are given in the Appendix, structured county by county

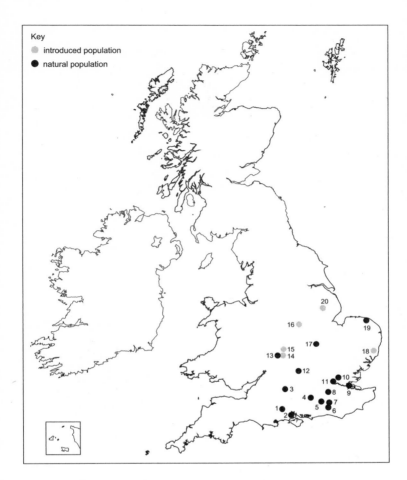

PURPLE EMPEROR LOCATIONS

1. Bentley Wood and Whiteparish Common, Wiltshire
2. New Forest, Hampshire
3. Savernake Forest, Wiltshire
4. Alice Holt Forest, East Hampshire
5. Chiddingfold Forest, Surrey and West Sussex
6. Knepp estate, West Sussex
7. Southwater Forest: Dogbarking, Dragons Green, Madgeland and Marlpost, woods
8. Bookham Common, Surrey
9. Great Chattenden Wood, Kent
10. Epping Forest, Essex
11. Hampstead Heath, London
12. Bernwood Forest, Oxfordshire
13. Heart of England Forest, Warwickshire
14. Oversley Wood, Warwickshire
15. Ryton Wood, Warwickshire
16. Cotgrave, Nottinghamshire
17. Fermyn Woods, Nottinghamshire
18. Theberton Woods, Suffolk
19. Sheringham, Norfolk
20. Chambers Wood, Lincoln

within administrative regions — just read the accounts
that are relevant to you. See also the section on mobility
in Chapter 4 (p. 91).

The big question about the Purple Emperor is just how
under-recorded it is. Scarcely? Modestly? Moderately?
Significantly? Massively? Almost totally? We do not
know, but at present those of us who study the butterfly
are veering towards the 'significantly' and 'massively'
categories, and we do not dismiss outright 'almost
totally'. One County Butterfly Recorder commented,
early in 2019: 'I cannot keep up with the spate of new
records of this butterfly!'

Something massive is happening with the Purple
Emperor, and it is happening right now. Throughout
entomological history (which runs back to *c.* 1800) the
butterfly has only been consistently present in around
half a dozen counties. However, over the last three or
four decades it has reappeared, or been rediscovered,
sometimes spectacularly, in at least 18 counties from
which it was deemed to be long extinct.

Traditionally, most localities for the Purple Emperor
were traditionally kept secret, to prevent other collectors,
and   the   much-despised   entomological   dealers
(professional collectors, who sold specimens), from
muscling in. The butterfly was cloaked in secrecy, and
consequently became shrouded in mystery: knowledge
and mythology became blurred. It was deemed a great
rarity. We chronically misunderstood the Purple
Emperor, and our obsession with catching and pinning it
meant that our relationship with it was badly skewed.

Think of the humble Comma butterfly, a one-time rarity now found over much of England, Wales and southern Scotland, and which is appearing in Northern Ireland. Just over a hundred years ago it was all but restricted to the Welsh borderlands, plus scattered weak populations in South East England, but it began to expand during the 1920s and has recently exploded. Like the Purple Emperor, it is not dependent on a single larval foodplant and it occurs diffusely, at low population density: the most Commas I have seen in a vista is seven, in 55 years of butterflying. Also, like in the Purple Emperor, the males establish territories which can be used annually for several years. However, unlike the Purple Emperor, the Comma is a ground dweller and regularly visits flowers; it is therefore much easier for us to encounter. Imagine, then, a wandering, almost nomadic butterfly, albeit much larger than the Comma, which lives predominantly in the tree canopy, does not like flowers, and which we see mainly through narrow fissures in its treetop world.

The old North Wales records, which I have not researched in any detail, speak volumes: if genuine, they hint of a butterfly able to exist in mountain valleys in high-rainfall areas, and probably breeding on sallows growing along boulder-strewn rivers – as happens in the Pyrenees (where summers are warm, but stormy). Either that, or they tell of a serious wanderer, capable of turning up anywhere. No one has looked for the Purple Emperor in Wales in recent years.

Likewise, no one has ever searched for His Imperial Majesty outside his known historical range. The South Lakeland valleys and the region around Silverdale in

north Lancashire hold much suitable-looking habitat.
Certainly, this butterfly-rich area was well frequented by
butterfly collectors from the late Victorian era into the
1970s, and is almost haunted by today's butterfly
photographers. But no one has looked for Purple
Emperors here, not even me. Diffuse Purple Emperor
populations prone to feeding on oak sap and loath to
descend to woodland rides could easily have been
overlooked throughout entomological time, not least
because the techniques for spotting this butterfly differ
markedly from those deployed with all others.

The suburban and urban records, which are all from
the modern era when people began to look skillfully
and in earnest, also speak volumes. Like the Comma, the
Purple Emperor is quite capable of surviving in suburban
environments, as it too is a mobile insect whose
foodplants are relatively common.

The message from this assessment is simple: look and
you may find. Ask questions of this butterfly, and do not
be enslaved by the assumptions we consider to be
knowledge. Do not conform to the patterns of this
world, the Emperor doesn't.

CHAPTER FOUR

Introduction to the adult stage

General considerations − Beauty and the Emperor's wings −
Aberrations or colour variants − Emerging from pupae −
Longevity − Mobility and dispersal − Timing of the flight
season − A second brood? − Levels of abundance − Mortality

The two sexes of the Purple Emperor are so different in
terms of character and behaviour, and in their degree of
visibility to us, that it is best to place the bulk of the text
on the adult stage into separate chapters on the showy,
more active males (Chapter 5) and the more seclusive
females (Chapter 6). There is, of course, much overlap,
for example in feeding behaviour and in the weather
conditions favoured for activity. Many of the more
generic aspects of adult activity will be discussed here.

For decades, centuries even, our interest in butterflies
was centred on the colours, shapes, patterns and shades
of the adult butterfly, the 'imago'. They were elusive
items of beauty, to be pursued, captured and treasured.
Their life cycles were of secondary interest to most
so-called entomologists, and ecology and conservation
were right off the radar. All that has effectively changed
since the mid-1970s, with interest in butterfly ecology
and conservation now strongly to the fore, and butterfly
enthusiasts diligently recording and monitoring
butterflies. With some species, though, we are still playing
catch-up and setting the baseline, not least with the
Purple Emperor.

The iridescence of the male Purple Emperor's wings attracted most interest, and still does. Nothing matches it among the British fauna. The female Purple Hairstreak possesses a tiny patch of quality purple iridescence, the intensity of royal blue on the wings of the Large Blue matches the equivalent spectrum of the Emperor's wings, and a pristine male Adonis Blue will shimmer an electric light blue which rivals the lightest tones of the Emperor's colour spectrum. But as for the rest, they are transient beings; forget them.

Humankind has long been obsessed by beauty, and by its pursuit. We approach beauty from all perspectives, through the arts and sciences, and through mathematics and reasoning, seeking to define and rationalise it. We are hardwired to it. I know not why, but the search for beauty seems to be an integral part of the human condition. A contemporary exploration of the human need for nature's beauty is articulated brilliantly by Dame Fiona Reynolds in her 2016 book, *The Fight for Beauty*. We seek the rare, the precious and elusive, all of which are borne upon the Emperor's wings.

The male Purple Emperor does beauty big time, and he knows it. He does not only use it to seduce, to win over coy females, but also to vanquish rival males. His shimmering iridescent hues render the Purple Emperor Britain's lone tropical-looking butterfly. Depending on the angle of view and the angle of the light, a single flick of his wings can take the observer through a spectrum from dense black through Tyrian purple, royal blue and several hues of turquoise, and back, often to the audible click of those dark-edged wings. At times, it seems as though the white hindwing band and forewing spots, and the reddish-pink ocelli (circle markings) and anal angle (bottom body-side) markings at the rear of the hindwings, are functioning on different levels, or planes, especially when the butterfly is flying. Make no mistake: this butterfly is all about deception, trickery and illusion.

But we only see the Emperor's colours on the rare and brief occasions when he descends to the woodland floor, usually to feed on something foul, and perchance to bask briefly nearby. That juxtaposition, of exquisite butterfly on a canine deposit (or worse), is a mighty metaphor for our relationship with beauty, and with nature.

The male's colours and immense beauty are actually best seen from several metres above, on the rare occasions when we are able to look down on *HIM* from on high, even though he then loses his bat-like size. I have only done this from a mobile elevating work platform (MEWP or 'cherry picker') and when looking down on males patrolling the tops of streamside sallow bushes from halfway up a steep valley slope (in the Pyrenees, and in combes in the East Hampshire Hangers). Then, he appears as a male tropical *Morpho* butterfly: a living storm of flickering, radiant light blues which seems too brilliant for this country, and perhaps for this whole febrile world. This means we seldom see the full glorious majesty of the Purple Emperor, and are all too often being sold woefully short in terms of our experience of the butterfly. We need to up our ambition.

The sad thing, of course, is that those electrifying colours fade as the butterfly ages, as the fine

light-refracting scales wear off over time; so that an old Emperor, viewed from above, scarcely flickers or shines. Instead, he has turned brown with age, though still possessing a faint mauve-purple aura, which tells of a now largely bygone glory. The bulk of specimens in butterfly collections appear like this – brown vestiges and sad parodies of the real thing.

We need some hard science to rationalise all this beauty. Fortunately, a 2011 paper in the *Journal of the Optical Society of America* on the iridescent features of the males of the Purple Emperor and Lesser Purple Emperor (*Apatura ilia*), which occurs over much of continental Europe, explains that the iridescence is observed only within a fairly narrow angular range (in both species), far narrower than in, say, the iridescent *Morpho* butterflies of the tropics. Peak reflectivity occurs at around 380 nanometres on something technical called the Colour Wavelength Measurement Scale. This is actually within the ultraviolet (UV) range, beyond what our vision can see.

Crucially, the paper suggests that the iridescence is more likely to be connected with intrasexual communication between males than with intersexual communication and attraction between males and females. Indeed, the paper states that the males undoubtedly use 'beauty as a weapon'. That is the most fascinating, and pertinent, sentence ever written about Purple Emperors – Heslop would have loved it. The paper also argues that the exhibitionist males may stand out like sore thumbs to the females, and adds that they are actually clad in ultra-purple, not ordinary purple (ultra-purple functions well within UV range, which begins at around 400 nanometres). Insects can, of course, see within the UV range – we can't.

Also crucial is the finding that the intensity of reflected light makes these two Purple Emperor butterflies highly visible to their own species but considerably less visible to other animals, with the males appearing dull brown from almost all directions – good camouflage for forest insects. Interestingly, the scales of the white wing markings seem designed to scatter light within a forest environment.

In all butterflies, the scales are positioned rather like overlapping roof tiles. In *iris* and *ilia* there are two types of scale: cover scales, which have a denser construction, and ground scales. The cover scales are responsible for the iridescence, the ground scales for the brown base. The cover scales wear off more readily, which is why old males appear brown.

The female has no need of the heady transient beauties of this world. She seeks to detract attention, not attract. She does not want to flatter or deceive, but to avoid, and to fade far away into the forest dim, where she may go about her business without being unduly molested by flashy, sex-obsessed males.

She is a giant creature of shadow and darkness, with her leaden wings broken up by bands and spotting of creamy white. When freshly emerged, she is a study in charcoal, in various intensities of grey, black-edged, though with a dusting of ochreous scales along the leading (front) edge of her forewing. The tawny ocelli in the bottom corner of her hindwings, which both contain a black 'false eye' centred with powder-blue scales, draw the human eye more than they do in the male: it says to predators 'attack me here', on the part of the wing that matters least. She too will brown with age, as her black scales rub away.

There is awesome beauty, too, on the underside of the Purple Emperor, where both sexes are remarkably similar (so much so that I am regularly uncertain whether I am looking at *Himself* or *Herself,* as the male and female are called by Purple Emperor aficionados). The underside is a meditation in rich reddish-browns and silvery-greys, punctuated again by the white band and spots, plus areas of blackening, and much silver towards and on the legs and body. The underside of the White Admiral is similar, and would perhaps be lovelier were it not for the false eye marking off-centre in the Purple Emperor's forewing.

This eye is haunting, and piercing, possessing a flame-orange iris with white highlights and a fearsome black pupil dusted with pale blue. Neil Hulme likens this to the eye of the most vicious of all our raptors, the Northern Goshawk. The male Purple Emperor would appreciate that comparison. Often, when settled with wings closed, the Purple Emperor tucks the forewing down behind the hindwing, particularly in windy weather; but if disturbed, the forewing will be raised to reveal what appears to be the eye of a predator, perhaps peering through foliage, but ready to strike. Most biologists would call this a defence mechanism; I call it the butterfly's nuclear deterrent.

We must also not ignore the Purple Emperor's compound eyes (tiny independent light-detecting units enabling a wide angle of view and great movement detection). If I was to personify Mother Nature, she would have those dreamy green-swept, browning eyes, all-seeing and all-evading, which tell of a depth of detection and perception far greater than ours. And the butterfly's dark-haired body, concealed and protected, and the dark, flame-tipped antennae all hint of secrecies, senses and sensing beyond our perception and comprehension. This butterfly – this insect, this animal – transcends mere human beauty and understanding.

Every now and then the patterning on the Purple Emperor's wings differs from the norm, mainly in the form of reduced white bands and spots. These colour forms, also known as aberrations or variations, are, by and large, similar to those of the White Admiral.

Aberrations are exceedingly rare in the wild. I have seen 15 Purple Emperor colour aberrations, of which I have managed to photograph four (had I been a collector I would probably have netted six), plus various distant and unconfirmed possibles and several unduly large specimens. Heslop saw about 10 colour aberrations, most of which are in his collection, and Stockley just two. A further indication of just how rare they are is provided by the fact that only two aberrations have been recorded by Ken Willmott in countless hours of observation over 40 years of study at Bookham Common, a locality which regularly produced White Admiral aberrations.

Butterfly collecting in Britain was heavily focused on obtaining these colour variants, so much so that the pursuit of aberrations dominated butterflying during the first half of the twentieth century. Pride of place in any collection, of course, would have gone to any aberration of the Purple Emperor, though aberrations of the Large Blue and Swallowtail would also have been highly treasured.

Some butterfly breeders have endeavoured to breed Purple Emperor aberrations in captivity, and many of the specimens of aberrations in museum collections in the UK and in continental Europe result from such experiments. These aberrations have been produced by temperature-shock treatment to the freshly formed pupa, suggesting that frost or extreme heat during a crucial phase in the pupation process might explain the appearance of these aberrations in the wild. In which case, extreme temperatures at the end of May and the beginning of June may be what trigger aberrations of the Purple Emperor.

Two generations of the Gulliver family acted as paid guides to collectors during the collecting heyday in the New Forest. They also bred aberrations for sale. Their specialism was to place freshly formed pupae of the White Admiral down their garden well (above water level), to cool them down in order to produce the much sought-after 'Black Admiral' aberrations, known as ab. *nigrina* Weymer and ab. *obliterae* Robson & Garner. This was quite a good little earner for them. They would have made a fortune had they done it with Purple Emperors.

A number of Purple Emperor aberrations (colour, pattern and size variants, described by specialists) are figured in British and European butterfly textbooks (see References and further reading). Some 35 named aberrations are listed and described (at least in part) on the UK Butterflies website. This list is derived from an unpublished piece of work by two museum taxonomists, A C Goodson and D K Read, who viewed all the major museum collections of European butterflies in order to describe the British aberrations, but only produced a draft report, typed, with handwritten annotations and a scribbled foreword which ends, 'Good reading and hunting!' They then retired, leaving behind an unfinished masterpiece.

The differences between many of the named European aberrations of the Purple Emperor are so slight that it would be impossible to identify many accurately from photographs; a specimen would be needed. Also, it would be impossible to tell the dwarf-sized aberration ab. *iridella* Cabeau and the giant form ab. *maximinus* Heslop simply from photographs. The latter (named by Heslop) looks like a typical specimen, only it is too large to fit on a standard 3.5-inch setting board. That means that this aberration can only be determined by attempting to set a netted specimen. That is typical Heslop.

At times the same aberration has been described by two different authorities, and given two different names. Thus, ab. *immaculatus* Esper is the same as ab. *tatrica* Cabeau, with Esper and Cabeau being the authorities (taxonomists) who named them. Also, and most importantly, Frohawk confused what is ab. *lugenda* Cabeau with ab. *iole* Schiffermüller. This led to decades of blurring and confusion. The original specimen of ab. *iole* was destroyed when a museum was burnt down during the Austrian Revolution of 1848. Apparently, it lacked any vestige of whiteness. All specimens of so-called ab. *iole* that have subsequently been examined have possessed some white, normally two pairs of small white dots near the forewing apex. The nearest to true ab. *iole* is a male Heslop took in Bentley Wood in 1969, which resides in Bristol Museum. Perhaps *iole* is a myth, though I personally would count Heslop's specimen as a genuine ab. *iole*.

Just to add to the confusion, it would seem that the 'ab. *iole*' male figured in the frontispiece of Richard South's classic work on British butterflies might be ab. *bureana* Cabeau. It is certainly not ab. *iole*, and has too many white spots to be ab. *lugenda*. The specimen needs re-examining (a task that cannot be accomplished from a low-quality photograph).

The majority of Purple Emperor aberrations captured or photographed in England in recent decades are specimens of ab. *lugenda* or ab. *afflicta* Cabeau. The latter has more white spots, and vestiges of the white bands, which are entirely lacking in ab *lugenda*. Several of these are figured (as photographs) on the UK Butterflies website. I have photographed three ab. *lugenda* specimens myself, two males and a female, and one ab. *afflicta*, a male. In Latin, *lugenda* means 'mournfulness', and *afflicta* means 'damaged' or 'wretched'.

Less frequent is ab. *iolata* Cabeau (formerly called ab. *semi-iole*), in which the white bands and spots are significantly reduced. This equates to ab. *obliterae* (or ab. *semi-nigrina*) in the White Admiral, the commonest aberration in that species. I have seen only two specimens of ab. *iolata* and have seen photographs of only two others from recent years. It is rare.

On the other hand, I doubt that ab. *maximinus* is at all rare, especially in the Weald where I see giant males (probably equating to Heslop's ab. *maximinus*) almost annually – but verification requires me to kill them, which I will never do. They can be confused with ordinary females, which are almost invariably larger than normal-sized males.

The hotspot for Purple Emperor aberrations is Fermyn Woods, where aberrations have been recorded in almost each of the last 16 years. In 2012, at least seven distinct aberrations were photographed there. That the worst summer for weather and butterflies of my lifetime produced so many Purple Emperor aberrations rather beggars belief, but does fit in with the theory that they were triggered by cool temperature shock, as most of June 2012 was cold and (very) wet. In 2019, at least five (and possibly as many as 10) aberrations of the *afflicta* and *lugenda* varieties were recorded in Fermyn Woods, and two (an ab. *lugenda* and an ab. *iolata*) were photographed in Bernwood Forest on the Buckinghamshire–Oxforshire border. All of these aberrations may have been stimulated by cool nights in early June that year.

Additionally, in recent years Purple Emperor aberrations have been seen in Alice Holt Forest in Hampshire, Bentley Wood in Wiltshire, Bookham Common in Surrey, Chiddingfold Forest in Surrey and Sussex, Cotgrave Forest in Nottinghamshire, and Madgeland Wood in West Sussex. Curiously, only a single definite aberration has been seen at Knepp Wildland, despite the size of the population there and the intensity of observation: an extremely pale, almost yellowish, female seen laying eggs on 1 July 2016; the white markings were normal; she may equate to ab. *thaumantias* Cabeau (Neil Hulme and I have also glimpsed black-looking Emperors at Knepp, but lost them before positive identification could be made).

The theory that Purple Emperor aberrations in the wild result from temperature shock on freshly formed pupae is challenged by the fact that the localities which have produced most aberrations over the years, Bernwood Forest and Fermyn Woods, have long histories of captive breeding and releasing, suggesting genetic modification in those races – in which case these aberrations could simply be genetic. It remains to be seen whether aberrations appear in recently established populations which have resulted from the release of captive-bred specimens, in Essex, Lincolnshire, Suffolk and Warwickshire.

As an identification tip, when seen in silhouette from below, the absence of the prominent white bands in most Purple Emperor aberrations can be quite distinctive, but much depends on the angle of view and the intensity and angle of light. Quite often, though, these markings do not immediately show up on normal 'type' specimens in extremely dull or very bright conditions, especially early or late in the day when sun angles are low. You need to look twice, or thrice even, before proclaiming an aberration. Also, the undersides of most aberrations, when visible, appear distinctly reddish-brown, and almost red in bright light.

People who are able to provide proof of having encountered one of these highly prized aberrations in the wild are entitled to membership of *The Iole Fellowship*, an excessively exclusive disorganisation that requires fellows to look down their noses at mere mortals, get plastered on the anniversary of their encounter with an aberrant Emperor, and to wear the much-coveted ab. *iole* badge (there is also *The Golden Emperor*, an 18-carat gold badge, 10 of which have been minted; only three have ever been awarded, one of them posthumously – to I R P Heslop). These badges have been produced by Sussex Emperorphile and Knepp Wildland naturalist Paul Fosterjohn.

People who breed Purple Emperors find that they emerge from the pupa at all times of day and night, though with a peak in mid-morning. The process is quite simple: the pupal case cracks around the head and the V-shaped tongue casing, and the adult insect clambers out, all body and legs, with tiny, limp and stunted wings, and wobbly antennae. It immediately hangs head-up from the pupal case (or occasionally after clambering on to the leaf bearing the pupal case) and begins to pump fluid into the wing veins. The wings steadily expand over about half an hour, depending on the temperature (which

is influenced by wind speed). But the butterfly must then
stay still, waiting for the wings to dry out and harden,
before it is able to fly. This may take three or four hours.

During this period of waiting, the butterfly is
extremely vulnerable to predators and, I think especially,
to damage by wind and rain. There are a number of
records of damaged specimens being found on the rides
beneath sallows. I saw one myself, a crippled male, along
the main ride in Fermyn Woods in 2014, and managed
to locate the vacated pupal case some 8 metres above.
That male had been blown out of the tree.

We do not know how long individual adult Purple
Emperors live. The standard way of determining this is
by catching and individually marking freshly emerged
butterflies, releasing them, and then catching (or
otherwise positively recording) them again. Capture-
mark-release-recapture work (CMRR), or 'mark-and-
recapture', as it is more commonly called, can also
determine mobility (or dispersal) and, with the aid of
statistical modelling packages, population size.

The current CMRR technology involves netting
butterflies, and marking the wing undersides by means of
fast-drying, oil-based felt-tip pens. Done properly, it neither
harms nor inconveniences them – especially the large and
robust species. With Purple Emperors, two-figure numbers
can easily be inscribed in the broad white band on the
hindwing underside, or large colour-coded dots placed
within those white bands. With the latter method, much of
the essential 'recapturing' can be done remotely, by focusing
binoculars on perched, marked specimens.

However, CMRR is scarcely practical with our canopy-dwelling species – four species of hairstreak and, most notably, His Imperial Majesty, the Purple Emperor. You cannot net enough individuals, especially early in their lives, and end up making insufficient recaptures (unless you had a large team thoroughly covering a relatively compact site, for a month, and using several of the modern equivalent of Heslop's high net, on carbon-fibre poles some 10 metres in length and costing around £2,000 each – if we can find a sponsor, we'll do it).

I have experimented in CMRR with the Purple Emperor, though, by releasing marked bred specimens, and also by netting and marking some wild males. Unfortunately, out of 30 recently emerged specimens that I and a companion marked (21 males, 9 females), only one, a female, was ever recorded again – seven days later in the same glade in Alice Holt Forest, in 1977. I was also involved in a mark-and-recapture experiment, led by top Catalan scientists, in the eastern Pyrenees in 2019. Unfortunately, the Purple Emperor population there had inexplicably collapsed – had we done the work a year earlier we might have marked in excess of 50 specimens and learnt something highly valuable.

Equally unhelpfully, only two of all the distinct aberrations that I know of have been seen on more than one day (two male ab. *afflicta* specimens which were seen in the same parts of Fermyn Woods on separate days in 2011 and 2019). It is worth emphasising here that news of a Purple Emperor aberration on the wing rapidly attracts butterfly photographers, especially in Fermyn Woods; aberrations are ardently sought out, generating mark-and-recapture information.

Distinctly damaged specimens, particularly territorial males which have been pecked by birds or, more likely, torn by high winds while at roost in the treetops relatively early in their lives, should provide 'ready-marked' specimens. We do indeed see such distinctively damaged specimens, mainly in windy flight seasons, but they are rarely seen on subsequent days, and their wing condition can of course deteriorate further, rendering them unrecognisable. It is only very old males with distinct wing wear that are recorded more than once, suggesting that they have become somewhat sedentary with age.

These fragments of information – please don't call them data – may suggest that Purple Emperors are either very short-lived, or highly mobile, or both. We simply do not know, but ask most butterfly experts and they will tell you that Purple Emperor males will live for 10 to 15 days on average, and the females a little longer. That is supposition; there is no evidence – apart from in captivity, where specimens are force-fed, put to bed at night, and protected from rain, wind and predation (though subjected to different stresses). The supposition is based on CMRR work conducted on similar-sized butterflies of other species, notably those of the same family, the Nymphalidae, but which are not canopy dwellers.

My own guess, for what it is worth, is that the bulk of males live only for about a week, though a few may live for up to three weeks, while many are very short-lived – hardly surprising given the kamikaze nature of freshly emerged Emperors. I cannot offer comment on the females, having seen so little of them. Being less active, they may live slightly longer, as is the case with the females of other British butterflies that have been properly studied. I am, though, convinced that this is a highly mobile species, individuals of which traverse tracts of landscape.

We need a scientific or technological breakthrough here, to enable mark-and-recapture work. Replicating the female pheromone perhaps represents the most realistic chance at present. This has already been done with a number of butterflies and moths. The males would, in theory, be easily attracted to what is called a pheromone lure. The area of most scientific interest is, I think, the issue of the insect's mobility, rather than its longevity.

The Purple Emperor's mobility is hinted at in an intriguing note in *The Entomologist* journal for 1919 by a butterfly collector called F G S Bramwell. Bramwell was deep-sea fishing some 3 kilometres off the West Sussex coast when he was buzzed (dive-bombed) by a male Purple Emperor. He surmised that it had come from France, and reports that it headed off towards Brighton. I do not dispute Bramwell's assessment that the insect was French, and consider him fortunate, as any self-respecting Sussex Emperor would have caused sufficient agitation for the boat to capsize, while a Sussex female would have casually dismasted the vessel and cast him adrift in the English Channel.

In addition, there is a scatter of records of Purple Emperors from the Channel Islands, particularly from Jersey. These are thought to be of individuals that have wandered across from Normandy and Brittany, where the butterfly is considered to be widespread and nomadic. Also, a note in *The Entomologist* magazine for 1916 tells that one was collected while resting on the piles of Bournemouth Pier. These records, plus a plethora of sightings in strange places on land, well away from wooded terrain, suggest that individuals of this species are capable of significant movement, and that the Purple Emperor may at times cross the English Channel as a vagrant or even as a short-haul migrant.

The number of records of Purple Emperors, males especially, in strange places is simply astounding. Pride of place on the twenty-first-century list is the male rescued from the departure lounge of Gatwick Airport. In recent years, males have also been recorded from several supermarkets (most recently, Tesco at Earley, a suburb of Reading, which contains much suitable-looking habitat, Tesco at Whiteley in south Hampshire, Tesco at Gunwharf Quays in Portsmouth, and Waitrose in Andover, Hampshire); Boots the Chemist in Petersfield, Hampshire, and in Haslemere, Surrey; and an impressive array of public houses with silly modern names (e.g. The Frog Inn at Skirmett in the south Chilterns), various garages, farms, liveries, private houses, greenhouses, wheelie bins, a christening at Winchester Cathedral, and at least two village schools, two public schools, a headmaster's study and one prison.

Additionally, the Butterflies for the New Millennium database (which contains 8,613 records, up to 2017) includes records from over 50 gardens, six golf courses (including an incident at the fourth tee at Silverstone Golf Club, Buckinghamshire), three churchyards, three garden centres, two nursing homes, a hospital, a borstal, a trout farm, an airfield, a crematorium, a racecourse, a conference centre, the lido at Ruislip, the National Film Archive at Berkhamsted, a Ministry of Defence ammunition dump, the Royal Military College of Science in south-west Oxfordshire and, best of all, in July 2013, the swimming pool at Cliveden, Berkshire, out of which the young Christine Keeler had emerged in early July 1961, to inflame a cabinet minister and spark off the infamous Profumo Affair which ostensibly led to the collapse of the government of its day. Missing from this illustrious list, at least for the time being, is The Purple Emperor pub at Harlow in Essex.

Not to be outdone, on 11 July 2007 a female Purple Emperor was found squashed on the pavement at Bell Yard, just off Fleet Street, close to the Royal Courts of Justice in central London. The specimen is now in the Natural History Museum. She had been seen flying around low trees in a nearby treed square two days previously. This event occurred before Purple Emperors were included in costly 'butterfly confetti' for releases at lavish weddings and other social events (the practice has generated a plethora of false sightings as far away as Belfast, where in July 2014 a male was recorded on the butterfly transect at Minnowburn, a wooded valley on the city's western edge, only to be traced to a wedding release). Never mind what this particular female was doing in central London and what chaos she generated in the nearby legal chambers; how far had she travelled?

It is my belief that the Purple Emperor is a highly mobile butterfly, regularly traversing large areas of landscape, rural and suburban, and even at times urban – and seascapes too. It pushes limits, as many insects do. When source populations are strong and weather conditions permit, both males and females seek out new habitat patches, which can develop surprisingly quickly and can be short-lived; the butterfly has to track them, in order for the species to survive. Males also have the habit of setting up territory on the leeward side of clumps of tall trees on wooded high points, often some distance from woodland and far away from sallows (1 kilometre is not uncommon), in both rural and suburban landscapes. I never cease to be amazed at how itinerant the males are at Knepp.

The Purple Emperor's recent spread in Holland is particularly impressive. There, it has to traverse large tracts of seriously hostile terrain, rural and urban, where sallows and willows are scarce or absent, to colonise large but highly isolated wildlife sites, where the dominant sallow is the unfavoured Grey Willow. In Holland, there is little in the way of urban brownfield land where sallows can flourish, as redevelopment takes place there instantly, and verge mowing is conducted even more regularly than it is in the UK; and yet this butterfly is leaping from site to site in Holland. Railway corridors, where some sallows are tolerated, may be the only feature connecting suitable pockets of habitat and therefore assisting the Emperor's spread.

The butterfly's conquest of Sweden is even more impressive. Having spread throughout Denmark, it entered Sweden in 1983 and by 2003 had established thriving populations along the southern coastal area. It has recently reached Stockholm. Additionally, independent expansion in the Baltics led to the Purple

Emperor's return to Finland in 1991, after a 50-year absence.

My conclusion is that we have been underestimating this butterfly's mobility terribly, and its powers of colonisation. We considered it to be only locally mobile, easily hopping from copse to copse in well-wooded landscapes, often by means of treed hedges. That is the impression given by Professor Jeremy Thomas in *The Butterflies of Britain & Ireland* (2014). He ascertains that within its core range, of central southern England, the species may breed almost wherever suitable sallows grow. I would like to concur, but I would add that the Purple Emperor may not be consistently or uniformly present in many (or most) of those myriad habitat patches, as there are years of plenty and seasons of paucity, and periods of expansion and contraction, as Heslop's writings indicate.

Think of a giant matrix of sallow-rich habitat patches flaring up and dissipating over tracts of landscape so large it is hard to say where one tract ends and another begins, and what constitutes a genuine gap. Then, view those individual habitat patches as light bulbs: some glow for long periods, representing longer-term Purple Emperor breeding areas on nature reserves, but most blink only for short pulses; and, of course, all the time new bulbs are being added, while others are being extracted. This is called a metapopulation. Think blinking lights, albeit with purple bulbs. That is what the Purple Empire looks like. But we can perhaps go further: other butterflies establish colonies or metapopulations; the Purple Emperor establishes an empire.

As the tale of Knepp Wildland demonstrates, the Purple Emperor can be a remarkably early coloniser.

Heslop probably knew that this was the case, back in the 1950s, but never articulated it. But he did provide us with his theory of 'observation threshold'; that is, the population density above which this intermittently active canopy-dwelling species can be seen. Of course, much also depends on habitat structure – Knepp is an unusually open habitat, where the butterfly is more visible than in most other localities. Also crucial are flight season weather, which impacts on activity levels, plus observer numbers and skills, and population size, as the males are only fully active in the presence of rival males.

Heslop states that the earliest the Purple Emperor has ever appeared in the UK was Midsummer Day, 24 June. However, despite his profound knowledge of British butterfly literature, which he studied assiduously while residing in Nigeria, this is not quite true. The earliest affirmed UK record is held by the supremely hot summer of 1893, when a boy from Marlborough College, Wiltshire, captured a male in nearby West Woods on 10 June. There is also an annoyingly vague report in an entomological periodical for that year stating that the butterfly was on the wing in the New Forest 'by early June'.

There are records in the old Biological Records Centre butterfly database (now the Butterflies for the New Millennium database) from 24 May 1894 at Hartsholme, near Lincoln, 30 May 1938 at Petworth in West Sussex, and 5 June 1918 at Tenbury Wells in Worcestershire. Those were all hot summers. Some of those early records may, though, be of larvae, which have transposed into adults within the recording system; others may simply be date or species errors – typos. All these records need double-checking. Colin Pratt, in his *A Complete History of the Butterflies and Moths of Sussex* (2011), states that early males have occasionally appeared during the second week of June in Sussex, but gives no specific dates (and does not mention the 1938 Petworth record).

The Midsummer Day 'record' stood for many years, 1893 apart, though it was equalled on several occasions, notably in 1976. Then, on 23 June 1989, on the hilltop at Woolbeding Common, outside Midhurst in West Sussex, I was buzzed by a freshly emerged male. I journeyed home in jubilation, only to find that Ken Willmott had seen one the previous day at Bookham Common.

But Ken's new record did not last long. Climate change was already kicking in, and the flight seasons of most of our butterflies are now commencing and ending earlier and earlier. In 2011 the Purple Emperor was observed at Bookham Common on 13 June, by Ken Willmott's deputy, Rob Hill. On 3 June 2018, a male was photographed feeding on something unmentionably foul in Oaken Wood, a Butterfly Conservation reserve in Chiddingfold Forest, Surrey. Unfortunately, there are grounds to believe that this might have been a specimen reared in captivity (which often emerge earlier). That year, the first definite wild specimen was seen on 13 June, at Castor Hanglands National Nature Reserve in Cambridgeshire. The modern era is producing odd early records in most years, nearly all of them from inexperienced observers. Some of these may be of bred specimens, and some may be misidentifications, illusions or figments of the imagination, not least because the Purple Emperor is a master of the art of deception.

In recent years, the battle for the first Purple Emperor of the season has been a contest between Bookham Common and Knepp Wildland. At both, the butterfly now regularly appears in mid-June. These are so-called 'early' sites, with the latter supporting an unusually large population, but I suspect that Great Chattenden Wood, in the sunshine epicentre of Gravesend in Kent, may be even earlier. Much depends on recorder effort, and on diligent reporting. Currently, the official record for the earliest UK Purple Emperor in modern times is held jointly by the freshly emerged male which was seen feeding on a canine deposit (before being flushed up by a mountain biker) at Bookham Common by Rob Hill late in the morning of 11 June 2017, and by another seen at Botley Wood, south Hampshire, on 11 June 2019. These records will, I am sure, also be short-lived, and a May Purple Emperor seems inevitable.

Whereas many observers seek out the first Purple Emperor of the year, few, if any, look for the last – they have moved on to other butterflies, such as the Brown Hairstreak and the downland blues. Consequently, late Purple Emperors are poorly recorded. The all-time latest record seems to be one seen by Heslop on 16 September 1962, at the end of what he calls an 'unprecedentedly late' season. As stated in *Notes & Views of the Purple Emperor*, it seems likely that the Emperor also lingered into mid-September in 1956, when Stockley found an egg in a Sussex wood that could not have been laid more

than a week previously. In 1977, after another late flight
season, a female was seen in Alice Holt Forest on 2
September, and a freshly laid egg was found.

There are also late records in the Butterflies for the
New Millennium database: from Selborne in Hampshire
on 2 September 1997, Dunsford in Devon on 2
September 1986, and Coolham, near Knepp in West
Sussex, on 31 August 1972, a late year. All these records
need double-checking, if that is still possible. Oddly,
the Selborne 1997 record is not mentioned in the
Hampshire & Isle of Wight Butterfly Report for 1997,
which gives the year's final sighting as 9 August, near
Romsey.

In common with those of many other British
butterflies, the Purple Emperor season is now
commencing, peaking and ending a week to 10 days
earlier than of yore, regularly starting in mid-June,
climaxing at the end of June or in early July, and finishing
by August. A scan through the Butterflies for the New
Millennium database shows that the vast majority of
modern records are for the period 21 June to the end of
July. There are surprisingly few August records from the
present century, and very few after the first week of that
month. That represents a major shift, as until 1989 the
pattern was for the first males to emerge in early July, for
numbers to peak during July's second week, and for the
last stragglers to be seen during the second week of
August. There were, though, early years, such as 1970 and
1976, when the butterfly appeared in late June. I can
remember Baron de Worms remarking that '*iris* is quite
often out in late June'. There were also late years when
the butterfly did not emerge until after mid-July. In 1977,

after an appallingly cold and wet June, the Purple Emperor did not begin to emerge in any numbers before the start of July's fourth week.

As with other butterflies, there are 'early' and 'late' districts and localities. The areas around the Weald (including east Hampshire and south Surrey) and Oxfordshire currently produce the earliest adults on the Purple Emperor blog. My guess is that Kent should also be 'early'. In 2019, there was a ring of early sightings (in middish-June) around the M25 corridor.

Conversely, the butterfly appears several days later in Norfolk, Northamptonshire, Nottinghamshire and north Wiltshire. Heslop knew that the Purple Emperor season started and ended later in his beloved Wiltshire than in Sussex. Savernake Forest in Wiltshire, one of my study sites, regularly records the last UK sighting of the year. By and large, the bigger populations produce the earliest adults, and often the last, but that may be because these sites are more closely monitored.

The books say that the Purple Emperor season lasts for six weeks. For once, they are actually correct – almost – though it is not quite that simple, as at sites supporting small populations the butterflies are visible for only about three weeks – Heslop's observation threshold theory is at play (see p. 96). There are sites supporting sizeable populations where the flight season appears to be relatively short, most notably Fermyn Woods, where the season seems to last for only about four weeks (though this may simply be because butterfly recorders do not work the tail end of the flight season there). At Knepp, most of the last few flight seasons have lasted a full six weeks, though the heatwave of

2018 curtailed that season down to five heady weeks and the 2019 season there lasted for a staggering seven weeks (probably because many sallows came into leaf late that year, as the trees flowered unusually profusely in response to stress generated by the 2018 drought, causing some larvae to feed up unusually slowly, and even more to perish).

The books say that the Purple Emperor only has a single brood each year, throughout its European range. However, second-brood specimens have been accidently reared in captivity on a number of occasions. These are celebrated in entomological journals as far back as 1894. These specimens have emerged in mid-autumn, usually in late October. Dr Dennis Dell bred the Purple Emperor outdoors in lowland Switzerland for 19 years. For the first 16 years all specimens emerged on time, but he inadvertently produced second-brood specimens during his last three years of breeding. This leads to speculation that climate change may stimulate the butterfly into producing second-generation adults, by speeding up larval development.

Colin Pratt briefly mentions that wild-bred second-brood specimens have occasionally been seen in Sussex, notably at the end of September 1933, after a hot summer, though I can find no other reference to wild second-brood specimens in the old entomological literature. However, a genuine wild second-brood Purple Emperor, a female, was seen in woods on the Wiston Estate, near Ashington in West Sussex, on 9 October 2005, by a reliable recorder, David Geoghegan. That year, there was a hot fortnight in mid-July, which would have speeded up egg development, followed by a fine August and an unusually warm and dry autumn, which could have accelerated larval development.

Neil Hulme, Ashley Whitlock and I have since looked for second-brood specimens after hot summers, in Alice Holt Forest and at Knepp Wildland. We feel it is just a matter of time before other second-brood specimens are recorded, not least because of the manner in which other, reputedly single-brooded species are starting to produce second-brood specimens in the wild. It was a trifle surprising that none were recorded during the autumn of 2018, after a record-breaking hot summer in which the butterfly emerged early and second-instar larvae were observed in the wild as early as 20 July. However, the bulk of August that year was cool, which may have prevented the butterfly from double brooding, and only I looked in earnest.

Remarkably, on 20 November 2019 a female Purple Emperor was observed, low down and close up, in privately owned woodland north of Milton Keynes, Buckinghamshire. This was after a poor August and during a long, wet autumn. With Purple Emperors, expect the unexpected.

Heslop, in *Notes & Views of the Purple Emperor*, defines 'abundance' in the Purple Emperor as being where one might see a hundred apparent individual Purple Emperors (previously unrecorded individuals) during a 10-day period at the height of the flight season, with at least one day on which 20 are seen. That definition inspired me, as my first study population, in and around the woods known as Southwater Forest, West Sussex, comfortably reached that standard, and at times exceeded it. I suspect Heslop had set the bar too low, but perhaps populations were lower in his time?

The populations in Fermyn Woods and Knepp Wildland, where an experienced observer can comfortably see in excess of a hundred apparent individuals in a day and perhaps a thousand in 10 days, are an order of greater magnitude. Those two populations are beyond Heslop's wildest dreams, though it is apparent from the old literature that the Purple Emperor did occur in comparable numbers in the distant past, in places such as Great Chattenden Wood.

The nonsense here, of course, is that whereas Heslop's one hundred–plus in 10 days criteria might be appropriate for species that readily occur at low density in the UK, like the Purple Emperor and Duke of Burgundy, and perhaps even the Comma, it would be grossly inapplicable for species that readily occur in profusion, like the Chalk Hill Blue, for which Heslop's 20 individuals on a peak season day would constitute a puny and highly vulnerable colony. Also, and obviously, Heslop was talking about apparent individuals, rather than a lone butterfly making 20 appearances on patrol.

Stockley, in *Notes & Views of the Purple Emperor*, tells of a Sussex wood where the Purple Emperor was 'very common' during the period 1947–54, such that over 70 individuals were seen on a peak day in 1953 and the females were regarded as a hedgerow butterfly, as numerous as the Gatekeeper. R W Watson, who knew

Heslop and Stockley well (the photograph of Heslop, Hyde and Stockley in the back of *Notes & Views of the Purple Emperor* was taken in his garden), told me that it was a site where sallows abounded among young conifer plantations and which also encompassed abandoned fields choked with sallows.

Incredibly, there are few other quantitative statements on Purple Emperor numbers in the published entomological literatures, or in Heslop's diaries. No one thought about counting butterflies until the Butterfly Monitoring Scheme was developed at Monks Wood Research Station during the early to mid-1970s.

Today, most of the better-known Purple Emperor localities meet Heslop's abundance criteria. Each county within the core area of the Purple Empire holds a handful of such sites. Many other localities fail to reach the Heslopian abundance threshold because of a lack of systematic and quantitative recording.

The bar has been raised, I think through better tolerance of sallow bushes in and around our woods, and through the advent of quantitative butterfly recording. At present, there are two 'super league' Purple Emperor localities, Fermyn Woods and Knepp Wildland – both these populations are of relatively recent origin, notably the latter. In addition, I would argue that any site where a moderately experienced butterfly recorder can see 50 apparent individuals in a day represents a top national site, by current standards. But perhaps the bar has been raised since Heslop's day because we have got better at Emperoring?

The main problem of course is visibility, or rather, lack of it. As Heslop so accurately states: 'The floor of his world is forty feet above our heads, and it is only through seams and fissures in that floor that our world and his come into contact.' But there are secondary problems, of recorder skill and recorder bias. This is not a beginner's butterfly, and most people wishing to see it visit a small number of well-known sites. Few seek out pastures new, though that is changing now. They are missing out, unnecessarily, and I would direct them to Chapter 7, 'Looking for Purple Emperors'.

We cannot extrapolate any of this into estimates of population size (i.e. the number of individual Purple Emperors at a given site). There are a couple of papers on this subject in the entomological journals, including one by Heslop. They are meaningless, though of interest as mathematical exercises. Hard science is needed here, through statistical analysis of good-quality mark-and-recapture or tracking data.

Another factor hindering our ability to estimate population size is the issue of what constitutes a population, or a colony. In reasonably wooded or tree-covered landscapes it is hard to determine where one colony ends and another begins. This suggests that the Purple Emperor largely occurs within metapopulations (clusters of interrelated colonies over a landscape), on account of its mobility, wherein butterflies are regularly moving from habitat patch to habitat patch, colonising new sallow growths as they develop and dying out locally as sallows are felled or die. This is effectively what Professor Jeremy Thomas is describing in *The Butterflies of Britain & Ireland*.

Even in the two super league localities of Fermyn Woods and Knepp Wildland, it is very rare to see more than four Purple Emperors together at once. This is in part because of the butterflies' gross intolerance of each other, but it does illustrate its general scarcity. For many years my personal maximum was seven in a close vista. This I managed seven times over seven years, before eventually breaking into double figures in 2018. At present, there are to the best of my knowledge only four people alive today who have encountered vistas of double-figure Purple Emperors in the UK: Messrs Dell, Hulme, Oates and Willmott. Heslop never managed more than six. The Butterflies for the New Millennium database (to 2017) shows records of double-figure counts from a mere 34 sites (13 in Berkshire, Buckinghamshire and Oxfordshire, five in Northamptonshire, four in Surrey, three in each of Hampshire, Sussex and Wiltshire, and one in each of Cambridgeshire, Suffolk and Warwickshire).

Death comes to us all, even a life form as confident and fearless as the Purple Emperor. The body is designed to fail, though with butterflies, of course, the continuum continues in a never-ending cycle: the species merely retreats into its egg stage, and begins again.

On many occasions over the years, beginning in late July 1975, I have watched aged male Purple Emperors embark on their final flight: they head sunwards, though weakness causes them to sink gradually lower and lower, until they crash-land randomly among the grasses, and meet their end among the realm of the spider and ant. Often this happens during the mid- or late afternoon

period. In 2019 Neil Hulme photographed a dying female being consumed by wood ants. She was beyond rescue.

But those Emperors are the fortunate ones, who have lived long and fruitful lives, and have worn themselves out, literally. Freshly emerged males are utterly fearless, taking on speeding vehicles and coming off the worst, and embroiling themselves in the likes of wet cement, melting tarmac, creosote and dairy slurry. They simply do not recognise danger, or failure. The females seem to have more sense about them, often ending their lives along a sunny sallow edge.

Much has been written in the butterfly books about birds being major predators of Purple Emperors, but

there is precious little evidence for this. The only records
are of observations of strikes by the rapidly declining
Spotted Flycatcher and single incidents involving a
Kestrel and a Hobby. Heslop, and other authorities, claim
that the Jay is a significant predator of adult Purple
Emperors. Heslop may have rather had it in for this bird,
having been a keen country sportsman.

Birds are held responsible for the distinct tears, deemed
to be peck-marks, that are often seen in Purple Emperor
wings. However, the incidence of tears or peck-marks
correlates strongly with windy seasons, and in particular
with stormy nights. I suspect that the majority of this
damage is incurred while the butterflies are at roost, and
is effectively storm damage.

Certainly, adult Purple Emperors can be massacred by
heavy rain and strong winds, especially at night when
the males are at roost high in the treetops. Take the
examples of the 2009 and 2010 Purple Emperor seasons,

when the butterfly emerged in excellent numbers, then flourished for a while before its numbers were reduced by at least 50 per cent by autumnal gales in mid-July, around St Swithin's Day (as described in *In Pursuit of Butterflies*, 2015). It is clear that nocturnal gales and deluges do untold damage to adult populations of this insect, and severely reduce the number of eggs that the females lay.

CHAPTER FIVE

Beauty as a weapon: the male Purple Emperor

*Male ego – Times of flight, and night flight – Young males –
Ground feeding and tongue cleaning – Fox scat and worse –
Shrimp paste, bananas and human sweat – Tree sap and feeder
trees – Honeydew – Nectar and herbaceous plant sap – Local
diet preferences – Sallow searching and oak edging – Male
aggression – Clash and chase – Interaction with other winged
insects and with birds – Possible explanations for territorial
behaviour – Changing and maintaining territories – Territory
types, and a summary*

Adult male Purple Emperors are ultra-special, and they
know it. It is them rather than the aloof and secretive
females that captivate us. But do not be blinded by their
beauty, as they would wish us to be; the males have the
mentality of one of J R R Tolkien's orcs.

In character, one would hope that the Purple Emperor
could be compared to the better-behaved Roman
emperors – Claudius, Constantine or Diocletian,
perhaps. The opposite would be nearer the truth: think
Caligula, Commodus and Nero. This butterfly is utterly
amoral.

One sees far more of the male than of the female, not
because they are more numerous but because they are
far more active and salient. The male ego ensures that he
keeps a high profile. If you breed the butterfly in captivity
the sex ratio comes out at around 50:50, but the males

are probably two or three times more active than the females, as are those of other British butterflies.

The male Purple Emperor goes through various behavioural phases during the stages of his life. In brief, he does different things at different times of life, at different times of the flight season, and in different weather conditions. Much depends on population density, and the presence or absence of rival males and of females in need of male services. Habitat structure, the landscape matrix and weather conditions are major drivers and suppressors of activity. These factors create a three-dimensional matrix cube of possibilities, most of which I think I now understand.

Until recently it has been difficult to predict what Emperor males are going to be up to, and when – and this partly explains our ongoing fascination with this enigmatic species. Heslop's writings here are unclear and, in places, misleading. But our perception and understanding of this butterfly changed when two sites with genuinely large populations developed during the present century, Fermyn Woods and, more recently, Knepp Wildland. Previously, I would be happy to see 30 apparent individuals in a day, and 300 day-individuals (the total of all the apparent individuals seen on each day) in an entire, exhausting season. In 2018, I saw over 300 apparent individuals on a single day at Knepp, and some 2,500 apparent individuals in all – and wrote down each and every one (my butterfly diary for 2018 is 92,000 words long – almost as long as this book). These two sites enabled me and other observers to break through the problems posed by small sample size and dead time (standing around for hours waiting for something to happen – when, in fact, one was simply in the wrong place). Knepp, especially, was a major breakthrough, as the Purple Emperor is so much more visible there, in what was previously an open field landscape, rather than the more normal closed-canopy woodland with narrow rides and uniform, vertical-wall wood edges. This book would not have been possible without Knepp's revelations.

In a nutshell, the males are highly active during the first half of their adult life, but become afternoon butterflies as they age, with old males becoming active for only three or four hours, after midday. Early on in their lives, perhaps for the first week, males want to be active for 12 hours a day, weather permitting, though they will be in different parts of their domain at different times of day, again weather permitting. Throughout their lives they exhibit hedonistic, narcissistic and anarchistic tendencies.

It took me about 45 years to determine the times of flight in *Apatura iris*, partly because Heslop's two essays on the topic sent me into a labyrinthine cul-de-sac, through inaccuracies, but mainly because of the aforementioned problems posed by small sample size: we see so little of this butterfly. Also, and vitally, it is easy to be standing in the right place at the wrong time (see also Chapter 7).

The male Emperor himself is actually a very active butterfly, as long as the weather permits and so long as there are other males around, or a good chance of needy females turning up. If he's all alone at a party, so to speak, he can sink into abject lethargy, especially in hot weather. Perhaps he's got a low boredom threshold. Heslop relates watching one lone male for a 10-hour vigil, during which time the butterfly was active for a mere 10 minutes. I have had many comparable experiences, but only in places where population levels were very low, and mainly late in the flight season, when the butterfly is winding down. When there is little aerial biodiversity activity up in the canopy, as in poor weather or in dismal summers, the males can be almost soporific. They need winding up.

In typical high–summer weather, early season males tend to become active after 8.30 am, after warming up in the early morning sunshine high in the oaks (or equivalent) where they roost. In hot, anticyclonic weather they become active from around 8 am. Conversely, in cool weather, and especially after chilly summer nights, they may not become active until 10.30 am, or even 11.00 am. As the season progresses, males may not appear at all during the morning, suddenly arriving on their territory around 1 pm. They behave increasingly like ageing rock stars (think of a certain member of the Rolling Stones …).

During the first week or so of their lives, and the first half of the flight season, males assiduously search for freshly emerged females over and around sallow bushes during the morning. During this period they explore the shrub–layer canopy, and may visit the ground to feed. In late morning they wander over the high canopy, seeking to establish afternoon territories. These three aspects of male behaviour are explained further in this chapter.

Male activity can be suppressed by heat on hot afternoons, when the temperature exceeds 24 degrees Celsius. They can become lethargic from 2.30 pm to 4.30 pm, becoming active again when the day begins to cool off. Again, much depends on male density, and on how early or late it is in the flight season, as fresh males tend to keep going no matter what. In hot weather during the second half of the flight season, males can become fully quiescent, moving only if disturbed by a close-flying bird or the like. Yet during the sustained heat of 2018, males showed little sign of heat suppression at Knepp Wildland, almost certainly because there were so many of them around that they were constantly on guard. Instead, they moved to north-facing edges, and remained fully active there, out of the heat and glare of the sun, participating in what butterfly folk call 'shading'. Several even went shading low down in thick outgrown hedges, where they tangled with male Commas and Red Admirals. With Purple Emperors there are exceptions to most if not every rule: expect the unexpected.

At night, Purple Emperors roost in trees, the males favouring oaks. In cool weather males may go into roost just after 5 pm. More normally, they retire around 6 pm. However, on days when the temperature has exceeded 24 degrees Celsius, and during the first two-thirds of the flight season, they indulge in an impressive evening flight which peaks in activity between 6 pm and 7 pm, and which may persist up to 8 pm, or later, providing the evening is still and warm. The evening flight is, though, highly localised, with males disputing possession of warm, sheltered foliage bowls along west-facing wood edges, where the lowering sun lingers long and there is no wind chill. In other words, they gather in warm spots, where the sun's heat lingers longest. Often, evening activities are close to, or around, feeder trees (see p. 128), notably oaks with sap bleeds. They regularly join in with the evening flight of the Purple Hairstreak, a butterfly of the oak canopy which is quiescent during the heat of the day but conducts its courtship and mating during the evenings, peaking in activity between 6.30 pm and 7.30 pm on calm, warm high-summer evenings.

Eventually male Emperors go into roost in leaf sprays high up in the canopy, out of any wind, in both sun and shade. Most seem to roost on leaf undersides or even the underside of twigs, but it is hard to observe this clearly (by day, they perch exclusively on leaf uppersides). Some other British butterflies roost similarly, notably the Purple Hairstreak and the High Brown Fritillary, which is critically endangered in the UK. I once read a short but delightful description of Emperors and High Browns squabbling while going to roost high in the New Forest oak canopy, back in the 1890s.

Heslop, in *Notes & Views of the Purple Emperor*, states that he regards occasional night flying as a recognised feature of this species, especially in very hot weather when the moon is full. There are indeed a number of records of Purple Emperors being attracted to lights at night, and to moth hunters' lamps, alongside other butterflies from the family Nymphalidae, notably the Red Admiral and Painted Lady. *The Butterflies of Sussex* (2017) cites the example of a male being attracted to a house light close to the summit of Black Down, near Haslemere, at 10.30 pm on the thundery night of 27 July 2013, during a heatwave. I myself almost certainly saw males flying near Dragons Green, West Sussex, during a sheet lightning storm in the early hours of 8 July 1975.

On the night of 16 July 2013, I saw Purple Emperors flying at night in Fermyn Woods. I had been out to dinner at a friend's house, and flushed two males off the tracks through the woods while driving back to the forest cottage I was renting, at around 11 pm. I stopped, and then saw two bat-like figures flitting around the moonlit oaks – only they were butterflies. The temperature was around 20 degrees Celsius.

The intense heatwave of early July 2018 lured me out on two hot, moonlit nights at Knepp Wildland, when I was staying in a tepee on Knepp's glampsite. On the first occasion I quickly found myself surrounded by the Wildland's free-ranging herd of longhorn cattle, and on the second, the Tamworth pigs. Butterflying in the dark, surrounded by animals, is not easy, but I did see large butterfly-like shapes crossing from oak to oak, black against a light night sky. I decided to leave this aspect of the Purple Emperor's behaviour to someone younger, fitter and more competent, took a stiff drink and sank Lethe-wards.

Heslop writes about 'pioneer males', the first males to emerge at the start of the flight season. These he considers to be high flyers, often flying well above the treetops, in stark contrast to their habit during the main part of the flight period. I regret that I have no evidence to support his theory, rather the reverse; a shame, as it would be quite glorious to look for males patrolling at speed 25 to 60 metres up in the azure sky, as Heslop advised.

Instead, I often see early season males exploring low over scrubland and hedges.

What is clear, and Heslop would agree, is that males on their initial flights are capable of doing anything – and I mean anything, including conducting kamikaze assaults on moving vehicles. Freed of the shackles of caterpillarhood and the imprisonment of the pupal stage, and regally winged, they explore randomly and brazenly, high and low, checking things out. Heslop rightly states that these early flyers are highly inquisitive and ridiculously fearless. One of the first males of the 2016 season attacked me, rather violently, down the Green Lane at Knepp, before dispensing with me with a single flick of his well-earned wings. I strongly suspect that these Day One males are quite capable of covering large expanses of terrain – dispersing, in other words – but I can offer no concrete proof, yet. They probably know that they are not quite ready for breeding and that there are few, if any, females around. Heslop, too, suggests that they are great explorers.

Eventually, most Day One males settle down, usually on a favoured territory, where they indulge in classic afternoon male territorial behaviour (see later in the chapter). Many of us see our first Emperors of the year on a known territory, in canopy gaps where their ancestors have been seen in previous years – but simply because that is where we look for them.

Early in the morning of 26 July 1971 I saw my first low-flying Purple Emperor, a male swooping lower and lower over a stretch of ride beside a forest gate. Being a teenager at the time, I did the silliest thing I could possibly have done: I charged at it with my butterfly net, in a Geronimo moment, and of course missed. It was an aberrant specimen of electrifying light blue, and pristine. The vision haunts me still. I should have hung back and allowed the butterfly to settle, make itself comfortable, and start to feed. Then, I could have netted the butterfly, or perhaps have picked it up. It was coming down to feed on some excrescence on the woodland floor. This *lapsus* hits me every time I pass the eastern entrance to Madgeland Wood – but I never made that mistake again, and hope that others learn from this tale.

Many, and quite possibly most, males descend to the woodland floor to feed (termed 'grounding') in their first few hours of adult life, or at least, the first few days. This is apparent by their pristine or near-pristine condition. Most of the (several hundred) males I have observed feeding on the ground were in their first five days of life. Sightings of grounded older males are rare, and consist largely of males in their final hours.

Although the science is seriously but predictably lacking, it appears that male Purple Emperors need to take on board some particular minerals in order to get themselves into breeding condition. Research on other larger butterflies, notably some swallowtails and the Monarch, has shown that caterpillar diet tends to be low in sodium. Sodium aids reproductive success in male butterflies, and can be transferred to the female during mating to help egg survival; research has also found that Monarch butterfly caterpillars that feed in the salt splash zone of roads develop stronger flight muscles. Another theory, backed by some scientific evidence, holds that these extra chemicals (sodium, or whatever) boost male pheromone levels. One of the People of Purple Persuasion, a Cambridge biochemist no less, is working to determine which chemical(s), or volatiles as he terms them, the male Emperors are seeking when they feed from substances on the ground.

Males normally descend to the rides between the hours of 10 am and noon, but early in the season there is a secondary pulse of 'groundings' during the late afternoon and early evening period, between 5.30 pm and 7.30 pm. Additionally, during the first week or so of the flight season the odd freshly emerged male can be encountered down on the ground during the heat of the day, especially around 2 pm. In very hot weather males may start to descend at 8 am and may have ascended by 10.30 am. During the heatwave of late June and early July 1976 males (and some females) were descending to breakfast in the rides of Alice Holt Forest between 8.15 am and 9.15 am. The earliest I have encountered a grounded, feeding Emperor is 7.30 am and the latest (in daylight) is 9.45 pm, both in very hot weather.

Individual males can feed for considerable periods of time, around an hour, though ground-feeding bouts normally last for 15 to 30 minutes. Much depends on how successful an individual male is at finding adequate sustenance, whatever that may be. Often a male will fail to settle properly, but will hop nervously from spot to spot, probing.

Quite often a male will cease feeding, and fly up into the nearby bushes or lower branches for a few minutes before descending for a second bout. This is not rest time but tongue-cleaning time, the equivalent of beak-wiping in birds, with the proboscis being carefully cleaned on a soft leaf. Purple Emperors will also often need to clean their tongues after feeding on sap bleeds. I am convinced that this tongue-cleaning behaviour explains many, if not most, sightings of Emperors supposedly feeding on the secretion of aphids on leaves known as 'honeydew'. These butterflies are not feeding; they may even be regurgitating, having overdone things. Also, tongue cleaning is at least partially explained by the butterfly's common habit of feeding on dusty sections of hardcore along a woodland ride, rather than on areas of obvious moisture.

Males almost invariably feed on the ground with their wings closed, though they may bask open-winged for a while, between feeding bouts, particularly when feeding in the shade. Heslop advises us to look out for the 'shark's fin' shape of a grounded male. I am rubbish at this, as my eyes are constantly scanning for Emperors in flight high up. I spot the distinctive, motionless shape of a feeding Emperor too late, and off he flies in disgust, up and away. One of these days I may manage to almost tread on a grounded Emperor without exclaiming 'Bugger!' loudly. The problem, of course, is at its worst when the butterfly is feeding head-on or tail-on to you, and is virtually invisible. *Apatura iris* was discovered in one Buckinghamshire wood when the owners inadvertently drove over a feeding male. Needless to say, the Purple Emperor is now ardently conserved there.

If you want to watch an Emperor when it swoops down, seeking to feed, the thing to do is freeze – do not allow him to see you move, or he will be off. This is

incredibly hard to do, but it is vital to suppress one's
adrenaline when he is coming down, and to wait for the
yellow tongue to become fully ensconced in some
indelicate viand. With some types of coarse fish you have
to wait for the float to disappear right under the water
before you raise the rod to strike. The same principle
applies to feeding Emperors.

Male Emperors feed on a diversity of naturally occurring
substances on the woodland floor. Fresh fox scat, the
deposit of the omnivorous Red Fox, is a firm favourite,
accounting for 37 per cent of my observations of ground–
feeding males. I have recorded as many as four males
feeding on a single scat (Fermyn Woods, July 2013).
When it comes to fox poo, the bigger the better is the
rule, with heaped piles of thick deposits positioned as
territory markers being a firm favourite. Neil Hulme
calls these heaps 'gorilla's fingers'. I must confess to
having cycled around the Fermyn Woods rides early in
the morning to mark out, manoeuvre, or even gather the
previous night's scats, to assemble them into a giant bait,
and once attempted to explain this to a bewildered dog
walker. Scats become unattractive to the butterfly after a
couple of days.

At Knepp Wildland, the butterfly started to descend
to feed more regularly on the ground after predator
control ceased, in 2015, and the fox population increased
greatly (to the demise of an overnumerous rabbit
population). Prior to then, fox scats were decidedly rare
at Knepp, and very few Emperors were seen feeding on
the ground.

Dog deposits are also popular, accounting for 23 per cent of my recorded feeding observations. Interestingly, records of Emperors feeding on cow pats ceased during the early 1980s, until the advent of modern organic cow pats; perhaps this was due to the avermectin group of wormers? It may be that some bovine veterinary products are deemed unacceptable by the butterfly. At Knepp, where organic cattle roam, several records of Emperors feeding on cow pats are made annually. Strangely, though, there have been no observations of Emperors feeding on pig manure there, though Heslop gives examples of this being a highly attractive food source. This may simply be because the Knepp Tamworth pigs seldom dung along the open tracks, but scatter it off-piste, where we seldom venture.

Other forms of animal dung which have attracted feeding Emperors are rabbit droppings, brown hare droppings, deer pellets (Roe Deer, Fallow Deer and, at Knepp Wildland, Red Deer) and, once, hedgehog scats.

Heslop bemoans the Emperor going off decomposing carcasses, particularly dead rabbits, which were successfully used as bait by Victorian butterfly collectors. He states that dead animals became unattractive to the butterfly during the first half of the twentieth century and laments, in his own inimitable style, that the Purple Emperor is no longer 'identifiable with the mephitic in odour'. Likewise, the butterfly seems to have gone off petrol, which was an attractant until the advent of unleaded types.

I once observed two Purple Emperor males feeding on the rotting carcass of a Roe Deer which had drowned in a disused ex-military cesspit (Lasham Wood,

Hampshire, 1982). Pride of place – for grossness – goes to the Emperor observed feeding contentedly on the fresh carcass of a dead bull high up in the Catalan Pyrenees in early August 2018 (the grossness wasn't caused by smell, which hadn't quite kicked in at that stage, but by the profusion of flies, and their ominous buzz).

In stark contrast to what is stated in most butterfly textbooks, I have seldom observed Emperors, of either sex, imbibing from the edges of puddles or larger waterbodies (fewer than 10 observations in 50 years). Often, the butterflies are not feeding from anything obvious to us, at best a slight dampness – urine perhaps (though they do not seem to favour human urine, and they have been tempted with it often enough; mostly male). Maybe it is best that we do not know what they are actually feeding on, but moisture is clearly not an essential requirement.

Often, the butterfly is attracted to minerals contained within the ride surface, especially on standard forest 'roads', covered with gravel hoggin or Carboniferous limestone chippings. At Knepp, it is attracted to sections of the estate tracks which have recently been filled in with rubble. The first Emperor I ever saw feeding on the ground was probing away at a piece of brick along a section of woodland track which had recently been filled with rubble (Dragons Green, July 1973). Needless to say, Purple Emperor males are seldom encountered down on grassy rides, doubtless because the minerals they seek are absent or inaccessible.

The male Purple Emperor also seems to have a fatal affinity with cement mixers. This was first noted by

Heslop back in the early 1950s. Most recently, in 2018 three (deceased) males were removed separately from a cement mixer working on a house extension in Warwickshire. Moist lime is presumably the attractant.

Finally, for there is a need for finality here, Purple Emperor males are encountered almost anually in houses somewhere within the Purple Empire, in search of sustenance. The classic locality for this feeding activity is the forestry cottages in the south-west corner of Bentley Woods, opposite Blackmoor Copse. Heslop and subsequent writers chronicle the near-annual invasion of this row of cottages since they were built in the late 1950s. Major General 'Kit' Lipscomb, who took over from Heslop on the Blackmoor Copse Nature Reserve Committee, states that at least six males entered the cottages in 1969. He quotes, in *The Entomologist's Record* for 1970, one housewife bemoaning: "'They were always coming in" … she was keeping her windows shut on sunny days to keep them butterflies out.' They are still regularly recorded there today. One wonders what chaos they have caused.

Baiting for Emperors became fashionable again at the start of the present century, having died out in the post-Heslop era. Neil Hulme and I started the revival, after I had been inspired by the ace Japanese butterfly photographer and devotee of worldwide members of the Apaturidae, the late Yasutaka Murata. Yasutaka discovered that oriental shrimp paste worked as bait for males of oriental species of emperors and successfully trialled it with the Purple Emperor in England. I first met him in Alice Holt Forest on a broiling day in July 2006, when in a short period he successfully baited down a pristine male using a sliver of shrimp paste he had smuggled through customs at Heathrow Airport.

Inspired, Neil and I indulged in various flights of fancy, using different brands of shrimp paste. Unfortunately, the best variety we discovered – something foul called Hau Loc, from a district of that name in Vietnam – got banned by the EU as being unfit for human consumption (the EU had rather missed the point). Experimentation soon got out of hand, with esoteric baits such as pickled mudfish and something vile called tiny shrimp. Neil soon discovered that shrimp paste bait is most effective in dilution, as a thin soup, when poured out in places along bare woodland rides early in the morning. He began cycling around the rides on a folding bicycle, bearing jeroboams of diluted shrimp paste. Others followed suit. Today, entire lengths of gravelled rides in Fermyn Woods are dotted with drying puddles of bait during the peak Emperor season, and the heady aroma of shrimp paste hangs heavy along the rides on hot still mornings. Heslop would approve. The poor Forestry Commission threatened to put up notices of prohibition. We threatened to bait the notices.

Not all modern baits work. Bananas and banana skins are regularly deployed along woodland rides in Emperor season, presumably inspired by observations of owl butterflies (*Caligo* species) feasting on overripe bananas in butterfly houses. Bananas are copiously deployed in Bentley Wood. However, I know of no single instance of a Purple Emperor feeding on banana, let alone on a shrivelled, blackened skin. It is yet another piece of nonsense that has entered Emperoring mythology, and I doubt that this book will kill it off. Of course, some butterfly photographers turn their noses up at the very idea of baiting for Purple Emperors, regarding it as akin to using a worm to catch Brown Trout in a chalk stream, but it is a sure way of photographing Purple Emperors other than on excrement.

It must be confessed that Purple Emperors are attracted to human sweat. The less I say about this penchant, the better. Suffice it to say that Neil wears filthy, sweat-drenched trousers throughout the Purple Emperor season, in order to generate 'trouserings' – incidents when males settle to imbibe Lord-knows-what from a person's trousers.

Curiously, baiting scarcely works at Knepp Wildland, despite the size of the Purple Emperor population there. This may in part be due to the quantity of animal dung lying around there, but is probably more to do with the fact that Purple Emperors there, of both sexes, feed primarily on sap bleeds on the numerous veteran oaks. Our time would be better spent drilling bespoke sap runs in oak trunks during early spring, when the sap is rising.

The Purple Emperor is a high-energy butterfly. Just because it seldom (if ever) resorts to flowers does not mean that it does not need to feed regularly, and from high-energy sources. Emperors feed as frequently as the most flower-bound Meadow Brown; it's just that we seldom see it happening – because we are not looking properly, and because of the volume of branch, bough and leafage in the way.

As discussed in Chapter 2, Heslop experimented with a wide range of baits, until eventually he realised, as his co-author Roy Stockley calmly states in *Notes & Views of the Purple Emperor*, that '*Apatura iris* is principally a tree-feeding insect', preferring sap runs and perhaps, when available, honeydew.

At Knepp Wildland, and at most – if not all – localities with old oaks, both male and female Emperors feed primarily from sap bleeds and runs. Heslop, rightly, devised the term 'feeder tree' for a tree featuring sap runs or bleeds and favoured by the butterfly. English or Pedunculate Oak is very much the preferred tree, but Ash, Beech and other broad-leaved trees are occasionally utilised, including weeping cut stumps of Silver Birch or Downy Birch. I know of no instances of the Purple Emperor feeding from conifer sap (or any other British butterfly, apart from the Red Admiral and, once, near St Andrews in Scotland, the Grayling).

Large sap runs, with distinct treacle-like flows, are rare — apart from in the wake of great storms, such as those of October 1987 and January 1990. They remain as dark stains for many years, long after they have dried up and ceased to attract insects. Several species of beetle and fly breed in these sap runs, and a whole host of invertebrates feed there as adults.

Small sap bleeds — consisting of indeterminate bubbles of often whiteish sap — are relatively frequent, especially in the oak-dominated Weald. Unfortunately, they are hard to spot. Most are fairly high up on secondary branches, rather than low down on main trunks or on major branches. Purple Emperor aficionados are not clued in to looking for them. At Knepp Wildland, in the region of 10 per cent of the many hundred veteran oaks produce observable sap bleeds in any one summer. These bleeds are best located by spotting and following the distinct zigzagging flight which Purple Emperors (both sexes) indulge in when they can sense a sap flow, before flying into the tree canopy. Even then, the butterflies are hard to spot when settled and feeding, since they almost invariably feed with closed wings, usually motionless, and because of branches and foliage blocking the view. Often one spots them flying off in disgust, having been disturbed by Hornets feeding there.

On oaks, sap bleeds usually last for a week or two, but some may persist for a whole Emperor flight season, while others prove to be ephemeral features. A good sap bleed will attract males and females for an entire season. Occasionally, a branch will produce bleeds for two or three consecutive years, especially on diseased or ailing trees. These ace 'feeder trees' will be used by Purple

Emperors daily, from mid-morning through to early or even late evening, and become focal points for activity, especially during the second half of the flight season, wind permitting. The most Purple Emperors I have seen together on a sap run or bleed is a paltry six, though there are records of as many as a dozen.

Although Ash dieback disease, caused by the fungus *Hymenoscyphus (Chalara) fraxineus*, is starting to produce an abundance of stressed or dying Ash trees throughout the Purple Empire (and beyond), it looks as though these diseased trees are not attractive to the Purple Emperor, lacking sap bleeds. The diseased trees seem to dry up, and retreat into themselves.

The butterfly books state that Purple Emperors, of both sexes, feed regularly on honeydew. I have already cast some doubt upon this claim, and will now dispute it fully.

Many tree-feeding aphids are quiescent in high summer, when the quality of the phloem sap is poor. In spring, when the trees are actively growing, and again in autumn as leaves senesce, the phloem is rich in amino acids and sugars, so that aphids such as the Common Sycamore Aphid can occur in huge numbers, producing large quantities of honeydew. Strangely, I know of no observations of Purple Emperors feeding on honeydew on Sycamore, conifers or willows, which all readily support dense colonies of aphids. I have, though, on two occasions witnessed male Purple Emperors feed on the copiously sticky leaves of Small-leaved Lime, another tree renowned for its tree aphids

(Boulsbury Wood, west Hampshire, and Webb's Wood, north Wiltshire).

The Common Oak Aphid, which favours English Oak, can be present in large numbers during the Purple Emperor season. As with other insects, it has boom years and years of scarcity, and its populations yo-yo up and down from week to week, or even day to day. It feeds primarily on the underside of leaves. Like many tree aphids, it flicks its honeydew away, so that some of the excretion is likely to land on the upperside of leaves below. Much is washed away in rain, as it is water-soluble, but some is protected by foliage above. In hot, dry and windy weather the leaves can become coated in dust, and aphid secretions harden in hot, still weather. In both those situations, honeydew is rendered unusable.

All this suggests that, at best, the supply of honeydew on oak leaves is intermittent, episodic and unreliable. Also, there is a big question mark over why the butterfly does not use other aphid-favoured trees if it is so keen on honeydew, and why it doesn't feed on oak leaf undersides, where most honeydew is likely to be present. Most years I do see Purple Emperors, notably females, probing the uppersides of oak leaves, but only briefly, and seldom with any obvious degree of satisfaction. The sole exception here was the long hot summer of 1976, when there was a superabundance of aphids and their ladybird and hoverfly predators. There were many reports of Purple Emperors (apparently) feeding on honeydew that year.

Over the years I have seen more Purple Emperors feeding on sticky Ash buds than on tree honeydew, alongside Red Admirals, White Admirals, Speckled

Woods and Purple Hairstreaks, and, later, the Brown
Hairstreak. Strangely, though, this habit seems to have
gone out of fashion with all these butterflies in recent
seasons, apart from the Brown Hairstreak, even in Purple
Emperor landscapes where veteran oaks are rare; this
change predates the onset of Ash dieback disease.

Purple Emperors very rarely take nectar from flowers.
I have only witnessed this twice. In both cases, Sweet
Chestnut flowers were utilised. Most instances of Purple
Emperors seen 'nectaring', to use the common
butterflying term, are momentary, resulting from
butterflies wandering over open ground testing various
substances with extended proboscises, probing almost
randomly, and sampling ground-prostrate flowers.

However, each year there are two or three reports of
Emperors, of either sex, feeding on garden Buddleias.
These records mostly involve old individuals, and those
in the process of dispersing. Most records are from towns.
Individuals can spend significant amounts of time
feeding on Buddleia flowers. So, at times the Purple
Emperor can behave like a normal butterfly.

Additionally, in the eastern Pyrenees, Purple Emperors
of both sexes readily descend to feed on the distinctively
large buds of the Woolly Thistle. These individuals are not
feeding on nectar, but on sugary sap oozing from flower
buds which have been attacked and damaged by an
assortment of large beetles and weevils, primarily large
weevils from the genus *Larinus* (*L. carlinae* and/or
L. turbinatus, which are both thistle feeders). I have counted
as many as 20 Purple Emperors feeding on damaged

Woolly Thistle heads in a 30-minute circuit of a 1-hectare meadow near Llanars, Catalonia, alongside several other species of butterfly, notably the Comma, Red Admiral and White Admiral. In the UK, Woolly Thistle is primarily a plant of cattle-grazed dry grasslands, but it does grow in and close to several Purple Emperor localities on chalk, including in Savernake Forest. As yet there are no records of the butterfly feeding on Woolly Thistle sap in England, but nobody has looked. It may be, though, that there is a shortage of suitably large invertebrate attackers of Woolly Thistle buds — I have noted little substantial damage to Woolly Thistle buds here.

Heslop was on to something massive when he devised the hypothesis of 'sweet and sour localities', districts where certain food sources are favoured by the Purple Emperor. His writings did not develop his thinking much, which is a shame as there certainly are places where particular food sources are apparently preferred over others. Much probably depends on the availability of oak sap, resulting from the frequency of veteran oaks. In such places, oak sap is the primary food source for adult Purple Emperors, of both sexes. In large woods where older oaks are absent, the Purple Emperor descends more readily to feed on food sources along the rides. This, Neil Hulme and I believe, is the principle reason why the butterfly (males especially) feed so readily on the rides in the Fermyn Woods complex in Rockingham Forest: there is a shortage of oak sap there.

Neil and I go further, holding that males (and females) are decidedly more aggressive in parts of the Purple Empire where old oaks are frequent and where oak sap is the preferred food source. The Northamptonshire Emperors are effete weaklings in behaviour when compared to their aggressive counterparts in the Weald. Certainly, there is a strong correlation between male aggression in *Apatura iris* and veteran oak frequency.

There are also localities where the Purple Emperor seldom descends to the ground, including the Southwater Woods complex in West Sussex, where I first studied the species.

Young male Purple Emperors spend considerable amounts of time searching for females among the breeding grounds, particularly during the mid-morning to early afternoon period. They fly in a swooping manner over the sallow crowns and along scrub edges, often hovering in front of certain sprays, perhaps where female pupae are located. They are looking for freshly emerged virgin females in need of mating. I term it 'sallow searching'. They do this a lot during the first half of the flight season, but cease when the female emergence is complete. In some years the end of the sallow-searching season is quite abrupt, as if a switch has been flicked, but more normally it takes place over three or four days, until the later-emerging males have wearied of it. Much depends on the population size. Once they stop sallow searching, the males cease to be active during the mornings and become creatures of the afternoon and evening. At Knepp, the switch is flicked around day 20 of the flight season (with day 1 being the day of the very first sighting).

Incredibly, sallow searching went unrecognised until the early years of the present century. Heslop never picked up on it, nor did the meticulous Ken Willmott, as the structure of the habitat at his main study site, Bookham Common, rendered it difficult to observe there. I overlooked it for years too, though my diaries clearly indicate that I observed it in the copses around Dragons Green in the early 1970s (and certainly in 1973).

This oversight probably occurred because Purple Emperor breeding grounds are often rather diffuse, a matter of the odd sallow scattered among other low-growing trees or dotted about in the landscape. Also, it is difficult for us to spot sallow-searching males from the narrow woodland rides from where we observe most of our Emperors. The penny dropped, for me, in the early 2000s, when the main ride in the Straits Inclosure of Alice Holt Forest was lined with sallows in perfect condition for the butterfly, and Emperors could be watched frenetically searching the crowns of these and other low trees. Vistas of four searching males were seen.

Sallow searching was even more salient in Fermyn Woods, where I studied Emperors from 2005 to 2017. Sallows occurred in distinct blocks bordered by broad ride, where the butterfly's population was considerably larger than elsewhere, and the butterfly more visible. Then, during Knepp's glory years of 2014–18, when the young sallow stands were so open that one could readily observe what was going on over and around them, it became clear that loose groups of males were spending the late morning period systematically searching the sallow crowns, plus the crowns of other shrubs and low trees mixed in among the sallow thickets – so ardently that one rather felt for the hapless females. During the late June and early July period of 2018 it was possible to count up to a hundred males engaged in this activity on a one-way route walk during the main three-hour period of indulgence, with three of four individuals regularly appearing in a vista. One morning I counted 60 sallow-searching males in an hour. They seemed to be roaming around in loose packs. Of course, they squabble if they meet up, but only briefly, as their minds are on other matters. Sallow searching is also prevalent in the best Buckinghamshire locality, a privately owned wood in the north of the county where the rides are copiously lined with sallows.

The vast majority of pairings and positive-looking courtship flights that I have observed (more than a

hundred) have resulted from sallow-searching males
flushing out virgin females. I am convinced that this is
the main mate-location strategy in *Apatura iris*, at least
away from undulating landscapes where sallows and
Purple Emperors occur diffusely and where hill-topping
activity occurs around 'master trees' (see later, p. 148).

Early in the flight season, sallow searching can occur
at just about any time of day, even way into the evening.
Often it is carried out by males in the process of changing
or establishing a territory, but territorial males regularly
drop down to fly over any adjoining sallow stand just to
check it out, before reascending.

A variant of sallow searching is 'oak edging'. This term
describes the male's habit of flying along the edges of
stands of tall oaks (or Beech) adjoining areas of sallow-
rich scrub. They do this to flush out perched females,
who have forsaken the scrub, perhaps in order to avoid
the males. Females spend much time perched relatively
low down (about halfway up) on the oaks, and on other
broad-leaved forest trees, but the males know and exploit
this habit. Oak edging is a common behaviour in some
localities, most notably in Fermyn Woods and the best
Buckinghamshire locality. It is incorporated into sallow-
searching and normal dispersal behaviour, by ever-
opportunistic males.

As revealed in Chapter 1, Purple Emperor males have
long been renowned for their territorial aggression up
in the tree canopy during midsummer afternoons. They
are not alone among butterflies in displaying strong
territorial traits, but among the British and wider

European species their levels of belligerence are unrivalled – and they revel in it. We have yet to explain it scientifically; a scientific paper in *The Entomologist's Record* (2010) by R J C Page on territorial behaviour and mate location is disappointingly inconclusive – equivalent of football's nil-nil draw without a shot at goal – due to low sample size.

The male of another of our aristocratically named butterflies, the diminutive Duke of Burgundy, is, in human terms, a vicious little thug of a beast. The males gather in loose aggregations, in sheltered spots which warm up early in the morning (without ever becoming too hot). There, they settle on low stems or leaf blades, and launch themselves at anything small and dark that enters their airspace. Virgin females gravitate towards these 'lekking' grounds and are instantly and unceremoniously mated – to anthropomorphise, the male doesn't even ask the lady's name. In between such events, male Duke of Burgundies battle among themselves for aerial supremacy, spiralling furiously upwards together to heights of 5 or 6 metres before suddenly separating and dropping back down. This happens repeatedly. It is highly entertaining. They squabble with other dark butterflies, notably with pugnacious males of the Brown Argus and their arch rival, the male Dingy Skipper. Some Duke of Burgundy males are more active, more worked up, than others, and can be labelled alpha males. These achieve the most pairings. You would not want your daughter or sister to associate with a bloke with the moral compass of a Duke of Burgundy, let alone with one that has the attitude of a male Purple Emperor.

The male of the Purple Emperor excels in dastardly antics. Of the species on the British butterfly list, only the pioneer immigrant males of the Painted Lady can compete with him for territorial aggression. This is remarkable, as these worn, grey pilgrims have endured a long and arduous journey to get here. They are highly worked up, and will fight spectacularly with territorial Emperors. Home-grown Painted Lady males, however, do not display such behaviour, but behave tamely, as garden butterflies, sipping nectar.

The Emperor squabbles mostly with the Purple Hairstreak, which can put up a good fight at times but is often summarily dismissed. Occasionally, males of the Brown Hairstreak enter the Emperor's airspace late in the Emperor season. They too can offer some brief but impressive resistance, before being dispatched. Bolshie males of the high-summer aristocratic nymphalids, the Comma, Red Admiral and White Admiral, tend to perform their own aerial dynamics well below the Emperor's radar, out of his airspace, and altercations between him and them are consequently rare, though when they occur the Emperor is invariably triumphant. The Silver-washed Fritillary does fly high, often venturing over the Emperor's oak canopy, but it is not an aggressive butterfly and does not retaliate, wisely making a quick exit.

The only resident British butterfly that may be able to take on the Emperor properly is the Swallowtail. The male is slightly larger than the Emperor in size and can become highly territorial. However, Swallowtails usually fly at lower levels, perching on prominent bushes just above reed tops. Moreover, the Emperor has yet to be discovered in the Norfolk Broads, the Swallowtail's only British haunt, though I am confident that it will soon colonise the Broads, if it is not already there, and that it is only a matter of time before severe altercations can be witnessed in the Broadland tree canopy. I for one will be booking a front-row seat, egging the Emperor on – not that he needs any encouragement. I have seen territorial males of the continental subspecies of the Swallowtail, *Papilio machaon gorganus*, take on the Purple Emperor. These were good fights, but the Emperors proved more agile and far more malicious, and the Swallowtails came off worse, beating a hasty retreat, physically undamaged but with bruised egos.

The Emperor reserves his full aggression for rival males. To anthropomorphise wantonly, these guys seriously hate each other. Think Liverpool versus Manchester United, add Celtic versus Rangers, add Scotland versus England at anything; multiply all that by πr^2 (which you diligently learnt at school but never used), and double it again for good measure – and you're approaching the degree of vitriolic rivalry exhibited by male Purple Emperors.

Standing orders for Emperors on territory are: 'Attack at once. No quarter.' Not bad for an insect lacking a sting or a bite, let alone the full battery of weaponry it thinks it possesses. And if a bunch of inebriated male Emperors were to gather outside a city club late on a summer night, their chant would be similar to the grand conclusion of the Millwall football club supporters' anthem: 'No one likes us – we don't care!'

When an incoming Emperor male enters occupied airspace, the resident male – who may have been sitting tight for ages on an oak spray – immediately launches himself at the intruder. They circle around each other two or three times, before ascending up into the ether, spitting fire and brimstone at each other, in a high-speed chase. This behaviour has been termed 'clash and chase' by Liz Goodyear and Andrew Middleton, though 'intercept, circle and chase' might be more apt. In human terms, the first word of their verbal engagement will begin with the letter F, before the conversation deteriorates into the grossly ineffable. Sometimes, several spats occur before one male is displaced and moves on. They may ascend out of human sight, before returning separately.

Usually, one of the males quickly returns to assume control of the cherished canopy gap, and the loser moves humbly on – often to generate trouble elsewhere. To the human observer below, it would appear that the male-in-residence usually wins. However, observations I have made from a cherry picker, from above, where it is easier to identify individual males, indicates that the incomer regularly wins, especially early on in the flight season.

Incidentally, when males come in to land on a leaf spray, they approach at speed and then perform a last-second backward flip, to settle facing outwards, ready to take off again and intercept. That I gleaned from observing them from above, and confirmed by watching super slow-motion film footage.

A brief cautionary tale can be offered here. Several years ago, some kindly soul gave me a rather crude and thoroughly plastic lifesize model of a male Purple

Emperor. This was placed on the dashboard of my car, where it took up territory above the air vent slot, driver's side. Two years later I was given a second specimen. This I placed at the passenger end of the 1-metre-long air vent slot.

At the first sharp corner, the newcomer invaded the hitherto immobile resident male's territory. A frightful altercation took place, at the end of which the incomer was unceremoniously precipitated down the air vent, where it remains to this day, unextractable. Such is the degree of rivalry between male Purple Emperors.

Male aggression knows no bounds in the Purple Emperor. They do not merely launch themselves at other butterflies, or other living creatures – any drone flying close to a male territory will be instantly intercepted (possibly to the butterfly's demise, if the propeller blades are not caged), and males have been seen launching themselves at low-flying military aircraft, though the downdraught of helicopters is too much for them. I swear I once saw a male launch at Concorde, which used to fly over the middle of Alice Holt Forest at 4 pm daily; and more than once I have seen males launch at low-flying Hercules aircraft, albeit somewhat belatedly and tentatively.

More normally, winged insects, such as bumblebees, Hornets and larger horseflies and hoverflies, are regularly seen off. Esoteric invertebrates such as snakeflies (Raphidioptera, probably *Phaeostigma notata*) and the Sabre Wasp are on my personal 'hit list'. Basically, anything larger than a worker wasp is vulnerable to violent assault. As already remarked, however, Hornets regularly displace ageing Emperors from sap bleeds, though fresh males are less easily disturbed.

Dragonflies and high-flying damselflies are regularly intercepted. I have witnessed some fine tussles with hunting hawker dragonflies, male and female, including the Battle of the Emperors – the Purple Emperor versus the Emperor Dragonfly. Technically, taking on a large dragonfly such as the Emperor Dragonfly or the Golden-ringed Dragonfly is a high-risk strategy, as you're attacking a carnivore, but I have yet to see *iris* come off worse in these clashes, and some large woodland dragonflies, notably the Southern Hawker, are actually more inquisitive than aggressive.

Male Emperors regularly launch themselves at birds entering their territory, pursuing them at speed and with malicious intent. Mostly, the birds ignore them. The following notable birds have been attacked by male Purple Emperors in the UK during this century:

Small birds	Crossbill (Savernake Forest), Siskin (Alice Holt Forest), Lesser Spotted Woodpecker (Dogbarking Wood, West Sussex) and Redstart (Great Chattenden Wood, Kent)
Medium-sized birds	Cuckoo (Knepp), Green Woodpecker (various localities), Great Spotted Woodpecker (various localities) and Turtle Dove (Knepp)
Large birds	Common Buzzard (various localities), Northern Goshawk (Savernake Forest), Hobby (Bookham Common), Raven (Alice Holt Forest and Savernake Forest), Red Kite (Fermyn Woods and Savernake Forest) and White Stork (Knepp, 2018)

The assault on a Hobby was a mistake by an individual Emperor which I choose to gloss over, as was an attempt by an old male Emperor to evict a whole family of Spotted Flycatchers from an outlying copse of Alice Holt Forest in 2002. Suffice it to say that both Emperors went down in a blaze of egotistical glory. However, at Knepp Wildland individual Spotted Flycatchers are regularly forced out of the oak canopy, to change feeding location – the Emperors gang up on them.

The White Stork incident was remarkable in that this must have been the first time an Emperor has launched itself at a White Stork in Britain since the medieval period – then, we ate all the storks (or they fled in terror before hordes of violent Emperors). Knepp is co-hosting the reintroduction of this magnificent bird to the UK, hence the 2018 assault on a supposedly pinioned bird which had flown out of its pen and had unwisely attempted to soar over one of the most violent male territories in the Wildland, a territory known as *Two Fingers*.

The birds most commonly seen off by irate Emperors are Blue Tits, Chaffinches, Chiffchaffs, Collard Doves, Great Tits, Jackdaws, Nuthatches and Wood Pigeons, but there are local specialities too, such as Stock Doves in Savernake Forest. Tits are a firm favourite, leading Neil Hulme to coin the immortal term, essential to anyone serious about Purple Emperors, 'de-titting'. Perhaps there is some atavistic hatred of tits, given that these birds are serious predators of hibernating Purple Emperor larvae.

Best of all was my last sighting of the male Red-backed Shrike that hung around in one part of Knepp Wildland during the 2017 Purple Emperor season. I last saw it being hotly pursued by a Purple Emperor, albeit by a female, *Herself* no less.

The overwhelming question, of course, is why behave like this? Why such extreme levels of aggression – why bother? Are they invertebrate psychopaths? Biologists will argue that the answers lie in the stark biological fact that the butterfly is the mature reproductive stage of a complex metamorphosis, and that all male butterflies are hell-bent on mating, and with getting themselves into, and then maintaining and demonstrating, breeding condition, and with occupying the physical situations that offer the highest chance of a mating. They are, in a nutshell, sex-obsessed. Perhaps, then, these highly territorial males are the alpha males, in prime breeding condition, jostling for pole position in the mate-location stakes?

What blows some of that thinking out of the water is the paucity of observed pairings resulting from territorial behaviour, in contrast to the number of observed pairings resulting from sallow searching, oak edging and general exploration. The fact that females astutely avoid male territories, and canopy gaps in particular, can easily be explained away by arguing that such females are already mated. Certainly, mated females normally avoid male territories like the plague, flying low through them, well below the male radar. On occasions, however, mated females do visit territories, seemingly on purpose; perhaps this is to make sure males are present in case they may be needed for second matings later on, or to keep them on territory and deter them from sallow searching, thus enabling the females to get on with the business of egg laying?

The alternative explanation is that these highly aggressive males are actually losers, who have failed to find a virgin female through searching the sallows, and who are ardently keen to receive the odd unmated female who needs to fly into canopy gaps to find a mate. Perhaps these territorial males are not in prime breeding condition and are, in effect, desperate – and are taking it out on each other, and on other life forms (and military hardware)? Whatever, they are extremely loath to take 'no' for an answer.

Liz Goodyear and Andrew Middleton believe it may be that territories are especially important in landscapes in which the butterfly only occurs at very low population levels, and/or where sallows are so scattered that sallow searching is rendered unviable. However, one does not see less territorial behaviour where populations are high because of the extent of male rivalry.

Technically, I have observed enough of all this activity, and for long enough, to have formed a valid opinion. Yet, I have not. Our thinking may be too limited here, or too constrained by modern scientific mindsets. Could it simply be that these pugnacious territorial males are, for want of a better term, thoroughly inebriated – too much fermenting oak sap – or at least highly tanked up on sugars? This thinking is backed by the fact that males are far more aggressive in landscapes where veteran oaks, with associated sap bleeds, are numerous, notably in the Weald. It may simply be a matter of diet.

Or, perhaps there may just be some form of deep psychological or even metaphysical dimension to all this, something way beyond the ken of modern biological science? True understanding of this (seemingly appalling) male behaviour may be some way off. The butterfly remains ever an enigma; only don't mess with it, especially the Wealden males.

Observations from cherry pickers, and in open habitat at Knepp Wildland where males are far more easily observed, indicate that individual males regularly move on and change territories, particularly during the first half of the flight season. Our problem, of course, is that we see the same territory occupied from day to day and are unable to separate male from male, and so assume that just a single male is present, day in, day out. One, nicknamed Brian, was seen for about 10 days running in a particular territory near Bucks Horn Oak in Alice Holt Forest, in 2006. He had no distinguishing features, such as distinctly pecked forewings, and may well have been several Brians. It may be pertinent that weather conditions remained stable throughout that supposed tenure.

Experience at Knepp suggests that an individual male may change territory three or four times in an afternoon. Knepp, though, is a site with a great many territories close by and with an unusually large population, and associated high levels of interaction and displacement. In other sites, such as Alice Holt Forest, I determined that a single male may maintain a territory for much of the day.

Older males, late in the season, certainly attempt to maintain the same territory, day after day. But by then their energies are waning, the population is in decline, and these ageing blokes are optimistically hoping for old females in need of a second mating to appear. It may be far easier for old males to maintain a choice territory late in the season, due to the lack of competition.

Also, it may well be that in low population density situations, where sallows and Purple Emperors are dotted about diffusely over large areas of landscape, the males spend much of their lives in high-point territories and seldom, if ever, go sallow searching. This is what Andrew Middleton and Liz Goodyear believe to be the case over much of the East of England region, where the butterfly seems to be subsisting at very low population levels.

By the 1830s, Purple Emperor populations had become renowned for favouring individual trees, or even branches, from year to year. As previously stated, Heslop termed these trees 'master trees', which he says are almost invariably oaks, and which all males must visit during their lifetime. He does not, however, suggest how many of these focal points exist per acre, hectare, square kilometre or square mile, or how many males can be seen around them at any one time (*Notes & Views of the Purple Emperor*, his other published articles and his diaries suggest four or five maximum). At one point, early on in his musings, Heslop states emphatically that the Purple Emperor will desert a locality when the master tree is felled. Thankfully, that is untrue: the males simply move elsewhere, only the butterfly enthusiasts fail to locate them.

Somehow, the concept of the master tree became part of entomological thinking, though remaining gloriously

nebulous. Ken Willmott's work at Bookham Common, a
wooded hilltop on gently sloping land, provided greater
clarity. In the mid-1970s Ken discovered, by happy
chance, two places in the wood where males assiduously
gather every (suitable) afternoon throughout the flight
season, from the first to the last day. These are sheltered
hilltop glades, totalling about an acre in ground area,
where prominent oaks and some other trees (Ash and
Hornbeam) grow. Crucially, surrounding tall trees, which
are densely leaved, provide shelter from winds below
Beaufort scale 5 ('fresh breeze') from just about all
directions. The preferred trees here are in sheltered high-
point situations.

One of these stations, at Mark Oak, is the highest
point on the common. There, males perch on, and
perform antics around, a loose group of tall Turkey Oaks
towering above a dense Hazel canopy. There are tall oaks
to the west, which provide shelter from prevailing winds
but which do not appear to be used by the butterfly. In
strong south-westerly winds, some Emperors are
displaced downwind to a more sheltered glade a little to
the north-east. There are some sallow bushes used for
breeding close by, but the main breeding grounds are
several hundred metres downslope.

The other location, near the wood edge, by Hill
House Farm, is less obvious, and is some distance from
sallows, but is again well sheltered in most wind speeds
and directions. The arboreal structure of both of these
spots, which Ken terms 'territories', has changed over
the years, due to conservation thinning work (mainly to
remove invasive Sycamore trees), and the Turkey Oaks at
Mark Oak are difficult to observe at present, due to

recent Hazel growth, but the Purple Emperor has consistently used these territories for over 40 years. These places offer sheltered canopy gaps some 18–25 metres up. It is these sheltered gaps that attract the males. At both sites, several trees are used for perching, and not just oaks, with individual trees being used in different weather conditions.

There is in effect a cluster of individual territories present at both sites; so 'territory clusters' or 'cluster-territories' might be a more appropriate term – like the 'sacred groves' of various ancient human cultures. Male Purple Emperors here are effectively indulging in a sophisticated form of the hill-topping tactics exhibited by the males of various nymphalid and swallowtail butterflies in warmer countries, in which they gather on rocky or grassy summits for courtship and mating. It is a well-known mate-location strategy, which immigrant Red Admirals and Painted Ladies exhibit in the UK. With Emperors, though, the hilltops (or, more normally, hillocks) are wooded – call it arboreal hill-topping – and the behaviour is often hard to observe.

In the excellent Purple Emperor season of 1983 Ken watched, mesmerised, as 11 males chased each other high over the Hill House Farm territory, the lead male of which was of the ab. *lugenda* type. That was the highest number of airborne Purple Emperors I know of being seen in a vista – ever – until Neil Hulme saw a shimmering knot of 14 at Knepp Wildland on 2 July 2018.

Ken is so wedded to Bookham that he never seriously ventured in search of sheltered arboreal high points elsewhere. I met him there in 1995 and, inspired, set out

to find male territories, or master trees, or whatever you
want to call them. I had some grounding, having found
my first master tree, as I then called it, near Dragons
Green, back in 1971. It was a clump of three Silver Birch
trees that grew above a canopy of Hazel and sallows,
close to a long line of planted Yew trees beside the
wayleave of a pylon line. The trouble was that it was only
occupied intermittently, and it took me decades to work
out why: it was a secondary, or overspill, territory, used
when populations were high (as in 1975) or when males
had been displaced from a line of slope-crest oaks to the
south-west by winds. It irks me that I never searched
that oak line, as it is now a blindingly obvious hotspot,
but the adjacent rides were overhung and observation
would have been difficult. The Silver Birches blew down
in the Great Storm of October 1987, and the wood then
lost its sallows. But I did search elsewhere within those
woods between Southwater and Billingshurst, and found
a series of individual territories in linear glades along the
road separating Marlpost Wood from Madgeland Wood,
and around three veteran oaks standing at the cross-rides
on the summit of Dogbarking Wood. The latter site has
been in (modest) use since at least the mid-1960s, when
it was discovered by N T Fryer, a naturalist-master from
Christ's Hospital school.

The thing that held me back from understanding
male territory behaviour was the Straits Inclosure, an
80-hectare block of even-canopy oak woodland on
level ground in the south-westernmost part of Alice
Holt Forest, where I have studied Emperors since 1975.
There were no master trees, territories, cluster-
territories or whatever there, or at least none visible to

the diligent eye. Worse still, the males largely disappeared from the wood around noon, only to reappear there in early evening. In the 1976 heatwave I thought that they simply slumbered their way through the afternoon, knowing that male activity can be suppressed by heat. Eventually I cracked it with the assistance of Ashley Whitlock: males were flying north-eastwards out of the wood in the late morning, crossing the road, flying over a bungalow called 'Woodlands' and disappearing into the main forest! Better still, they came back in the early evening, via a slightly different route. They were quitting the flat lands of the Straits Inclosure and disappearing into the sloping ground of the main part of Alice Holt Forest, where they went hill-topping. Some males may have been journeying for nearly a kilometre. A few were also flying out of the wood westwards, uphill, to assemble along the edge of the East Hampshire Hangers. A few, though, were hanging out during the afternoons along the leeward side of the wood, depending on wind speed and direction, but only the odd one tried to set up territory around tall oaks within the wood. Despite intensive searches around taller oaks, we could find no consistent territories in the entire wood.

In the early 2000s, Ashley and I searched for territories all along the prominent ridge that forms a spine along the east edge of Alice Holt Forest before cutting into the forest and heading north. We found about a dozen territories along the ridge top, and a few more have since come to light. Some are along the wood edge, including in gardens cut out from the old forest and in a decommissioned car park in the central forest, by

Bucks Horn Oak. Some of these territories are cluster-territories, in permanent use, as at Bookham; others are single territories with sole occupants; and some are used only in certain weather conditions. Most attract more than one male, and so offer spectacular observations of sparring males.

Straits Inclosure is not unique in lacking consistent master trees or territories. Most of the Fermyn Woods complex of old Rockingham Forest in east Northamptonshire stands on near-level ground. Again, Purple Emperor males show little interest in establishing Bookham-style territories here, although they do aggregate for afternoon shenanigans over the tall poplars at Lady Wood Head, with shelter from the west provided by tall Corsican Pines across the ride, and also around a prominent Turkey Oak on sloping terrain in Harry's Park Wood, Brigstock. Males also establish afternoon territories around some individual trees within the woods, with one large and prominent sallow being occupied each afternoon. Sallow searching is definitely the main form of mate location throughout these woods.

In Fermyn Woods, and elsewhere where lines of tall oaks adjoin areas of sallow–rich scrub, the males also indulge in 'oak edging'.

Likewise, in Bernwood Forest and other woods on more level ground in Oxfordshire and Buckinghamshire, Purple Emperor territories are few and far between, and are often transitory or seasonal. Dennis Dell and Mick and Wendy Campbell searched hard, finding good territories around slope tops but virtually none on level ground, even when the tree canopy was uneven. In the main block of Bernwood Forest, there is but one consistent known territory, on the northern edge of Waterperry Wood.

For 20 years Liz Goodyear and Andrew Middleton have spent the bulk of each July systematically surveying for Purple Emperors in Hertfordshire and Middlesex, and latterly in Cambridgeshire, Essex, Suffolk and Norfolk, simply by searching for male territories at high points and in wood-edge canopy gaps. Often, they are viewing from afar, across fields, scanning the wood edge for activity through binoculars. Their findings have radically overhauled knowledge of the butterfly in the region, moving it from 'rare' or 'extinct' to 'widespread'. They too struggle with finding territories on flat terrain.

Knepp Wildland took Purple Emperor male behaviour into a new, clearer dimension. At last we had a genuinely large population in a relatively open habitat dotted with several hundred veteran oaks, growing in broken lines along outgrown hedge systems, and occasionally as singletons or in small copses, close or adjacent to huge thickets of sallows. The terrain is largely flat, or flattish, so genuine hill-topping does not occur. Since 2013, over a hundred individual territories have been identified. Some are cluster-territories in daily use (winds permitting), but most are canopy gaps between neighbouring oaks which are occupied by one or two males at the most.

Crucially, Neil Hulme and I have found that leeward oak edges are utilised by Purple Emperors; in other words, that the males (and indeed females; see Chapter 6) are distributed by wind, and assemble leeward. In a west wind, east-facing oak edges are occupied, and so on. Being a relatively exposed site (as opposed to conditions in typically dense woodland), some of Knepp's territories scarcely function in wind speeds in excess of Beaufort scale 4 ('moderate breeze'). In any wind, the butterflies are active only on the leeward side of the trees, even if that is the shady side.

In our exuberance, Neil and I named and mapped these territories. Thus, Knepp Wildland hosts *The Benny Hill Show*, *The Brexit Negotiations*, *Gratuitous Violence*, *Lady Chatterley's Lover*, *Mindless Violence*, *Posh Totty*, *Pride and Extreme Prejudice*, *The Serial Offenders Institute* and *Skinhead Ally*. One or two are so politically incorrect that I dare not mention them here. For those of a nervous disposition, there are the more modest *Match of the Day* and, quite plainly, *The Avenue*, and all the territories along the Knepp transect route have plain numbers as well. In 2019 we determined that all unnamed territories should simply be called 'The Backstop', instantly creating over a hundred Backstops.

Oak is favoured by territorial males throughout the Purple Empire, because its dense foliage provides more shelter than most other trees – if densely leaved – and because it can offer sap bleeds. Stag-headed and weakly foliated oaks are used only if there is tall and dense leafage windward. In Savernake Forest, giant Beech trees, some 35 or 40 metres tall, are utilised, around the tops of which Emperors seem as small as Purple Hairstreaks. Elsewhere, Hornbeam, poplars, Sycamore and Wild Service Tree are chosen and I have even recorded Tulip Tree in use (Blacknest Copse, an outlier of Alice Holt Forest). Contrary to many people's expectations, conifers are readily used, providing there is sufficient shelter from wind. The insects have no problem in perching on conifer needles. Several of the Alice Holt Forest territories are conifer-based, and there are others elsewhere, mainly involving Corsican and Scots Pines. There is an excellent conifer territory in Oversley Wood, Warwickshire, where Emperor numbers are closely monitored. There is also a well-known territory based on Corsican Pines in Finemere Wood, Buckinghamshire. In effect, males will utilise almost any type of tree providing there is sufficient foliage to offer calm perching situations and non-turbulent airspace. This might eliminate only Aspen, whose foliage is ever in perpetual motion, even on the stillest of days.

But male territories always have sallow (or willow) somewhere within their catchment area, so to speak, though catchments may perhaps be vast. Territories are upslope of, but not necessarily in close proximity to, breeding grounds. Many a suitable-looking situation proves unoccupied because of the absence of sallows downslope or within suitable commuting distance (generally less than half a kilometre).

Abroad, there are records of Purple Emperor males genuinely hill-topping, occupying bare rocky outcrops. Recently, a male was seen aggressively hill-topping some 2,500 metres up in the Andorran Pyrenees – well above the tree line. I have been assaulted by a violent hill-topping male some 1,500 metres up in the Catalan Pyrenees, which tried to knock me off a 100-metre rocky pinnacle called the Roca de les Bruixes (Witches' Rock). On steeply sloping ground there, the males also establish territories on the walls and roofs of buildings (a water tower is regularly used in East Anglia).

In summary, on sloping or uneven terrain Purple Emperor males establish territories in arboreal high points where there are sheltered perching points and tranquil airspace, with the shelter normally being provided by dense foliage to the windward side. A variety of trees are used, though English Oak is favoured because of the ability of its thick foliage to calm the air, although Beech is almost as able to do this. Some daily migrations occur, with males moving significant distances up to the territories after spending the mornings sallow searching (during the first half of the flight season) or simply lazing the time away (in the second half). It appears, though, that many males do not indulge in these antics in even-height woodland on level terrain, though some may make daily migrations to more suitable locations, and a few may establish territories along wood edges. Some territories are small, attracting single or twin occupants, while others are cluster-territories where several males perch on different trees and interact with each other. Sallows may be close by or some distance away, downslope, but within a territory's catchment. We are dealing with a highly mobile, almost nomadic, butterfly, the tenacity and mobility of which have both been seriously overlooked.

So, we have seen that the males are aggressive and fearless beyond the point of absurdity, on account of their awesome sex drive. Watching them in their territories has almost certainly made us underestimate how mobile they are, and their territorial activity is so riveting that it makes us ignore the females. Clearly, the females have much to contend with, not least because they may only need to mate once (or twice), and to them are charged the all-important tasks of laying eggs to ensure the insect's survival, and dispersing in search of new habitat. We can anticipate that the females are radically different to the males, in terms of character and behaviour.

CHAPTER SIX

The Empress: a life apart

*Feminine issues – Telling females from males – Times of
flight – Avoiding males – Maiden flight, courtship and mating –
Rejection drops, or tumbledowns – Feeding time – The
complexities of egg laying*

The two sexes of several British butterflies were originally
described as separate species, because they differ so
greatly – for example, the Brown Hairstreak and Silver-
washed Fritillary. The male and female of the Purple
Emperor are certainly distinct, though the key
characteristics are not always evident to the distant
viewer. *Herself* is usually larger and certainly lacks the
magnificent iridescence of the male. Her colours change
with age. A fresh female is dark chocolate-brown or
charcoal-grey, depending on angle of view and intensity
of light, but she will lighten considerably as she ages,
becoming mid-brown.

In terms of character and habit, the two sexes are even
further apart, and have differing mindsets. People who
breed Purple Emperors find that, on release, the males
immediately fly off and upwards at speed but the females
sit tight on a leaf, often for hours. At times it seems that
they almost live in different dimensions. That feeling is
supported by the extent to which mated females seek to
avoid the over-amorous males. From the point of view
of the mated female butterfly, the male of the species is
an infernal nuisance, to be avoided at all costs once the
essential nuptials have been completed.

Mated (or gravid) females spend considerable amounts of time sitting around, gestating eggs and avoiding pestilential males. In the heatwave of 2009, I went past the four-hour barrier while watching a perched female at Bentley Station Meadow, a Butterfly Conservation reserve on the edge of Alice Holt Forest. Then, suddenly, she upped and offed, over the oaks, and was seen no more. I was perhaps fortunate; a couple of birders observing from a bird hide recently watched one particularly recalcitrant female sitting in an Ash tree for six hours, at Calvert Jubilee Nature Reserve in Buckinghamshire. That is *Herself* all over, a veritable minx.

Even worse for observers, the Empress often flies low through dense woodland, weaving a way through the lower canopy, away from our sightlines, avoiding the males. In woodland consisting of tall oaks and a Hazel understorey, they often fly below the oak foliage and above the Hazel canopy – which makes them incredibly hard to see, unless you purposefully hunt them down. At Knepp, I regularly see females meandering through the branches, well below the male-infested canopy.

Standing orders for the Purple Emperor females are, simply: 'No cooperation. Zero tolerance.' That attitude is applied to all life forms, including *Homo sapiens*. This means that the Empress is incredibly hard to study, far harder than the Emperor.

With nearly all British butterflies, the key to cracking the species' ecology is to follow the egg-laying females. That trick scarcely works with a small number of our species, most notably the Purple Emperor and, for some reason, the Heath Fritillary in its moorland habitats on Exmoor (where I have encountered a single egg-laying female in 27 years of annual survey work). Even the arboreal Purple Hairstreak is more cooperative, as the females can be seen laying a fair percentage of their eggs low down on oaks during the second half of their flight season.

Confession: I find the two sexes of *Apatura iris* increasingly difficult to tell apart. This is doubtless in part due to deteriorating eyesight but also, I fear, to high levels of non-cooperation by *Herself*, at least when I am around. Size provides at best only a guideline, as there are large Emperors and small Empresses. Colour is unreliable too, for the male's purple is rarely visible to us, as we see most of our Purple Emperors from far below, and we are often looking into the sun – at momentary sightings of distant, dark butterflies making off at speed. More significantly, it is hard to sex Purple Emperors by behaviour as, quite often, what you thought was a perched male, fairly high up on an oak, suddenly transposes into a female when it flies off. Non-cooperation again. An additional complication is provided by the male's habit of perching on sallow foliage during pauses in sallow searching. Furthermore, the females can at times be aggressive, including towards birds and even towards Emperor males, and us; so it is not always possible to sex a Purple Emperor simply by belligerent antics.

The best ways to tell the two apart are to look, firstly, for the broader hindwing of the female, and secondly for the more pointed forewing tip of the male. The width of the white band on the underside of the hindwing can also be diagnostic, being broader in the female – if it is showing properly. However, quite often it is hard to make these distinguishing features out, as all too many sightings of the Purple Emperor are sudden, brief and distant flurries of activity. The only times that I can readily sex Purple Emperors are when males and females are feeding together on oak sap bleeds, when a female is laying an egg, when looking at a male from above and marvelling at the purple iridescence, and when males are clashing and chasing. Also, females do not roost high in the oak crowns as the males do, but lower down on the oaks and in the shrub-layer canopy, including on sallow.

It is unusual to see a female before 10.30 am, apart from in extremely hot weather. Most of my early morning sightings have resulted from males flushing perched or basking females out from the scrub canopies where they spend significant amounts of time doing next to nothing. In such circumstances the disinterested female gets the hell out of it quickly, and the male flies off to generate chaos elsewhere.

Mostly, females become active in the late morning, usually from around 11.30 am. Their activity peaks from 1 pm to 3 pm, when they are engaged in egg laying. In hot weather they tend to have a siesta from around 3.30 pm until after 5 pm, followed by a pulse of activity around feeding sites. In fact, the majority of my observations of females feeding on oak sap bleeds, which they strongly favour, have taken place between 3.30 pm and 6.30 pm.

On warm, still and bright evenings females may be active until around 8.30 pm, albeit locally and intermittently, especially along sheltered west-facing oak

edges and in the vicinity of feeder trees. In cool, showery weather their activity may be confined to warmer, brighter spells during the early afternoon period.

I suspect that some females may be active on warm, still nights under a full moon. I have seen moonlit shadows on such nights, in Fermyn Woods and at Knepp Wildland, though of course it is impossible to sex the butterfly under such conditions. Early one morning I found a freshly laid egg on a spray I had examined the previous evening (as there was a first-instar larva close by, which I was monitoring). The night was warm and moonlit, and I strongly suspect that the egg was laid during the night. The Northamptonshire surgeon J H C

Phillips, who taught BB much about the Purple Emperor and was an associate of Heslop, was convinced that females lay eggs on warm, moonlight nights.

Neil Hulme and I suspect that the males inadvertently suppress female activity, and hinder egg laying, in the Purple Emperor and in a great many other British butterflies. Now, this is difficult to prove or disprove; at best we can merely demonstrate probability, or possibility, so treat this as a hypothesis in need of vigorous scientific testing.

The males of other butterflies on the British list certainly suppress female activity, with mated females cowering away from over-amorous males. In mid- to late morning the Cambridge-blue males of the Chalk Hill Blue swarm and shimmer over the swathes of short turf rich in the larval foodplant, Horseshoe Vetch, that form the butterfly's breeding grounds, searching for freshly emerged chocolate-brown females. In the process, they hinder or even prevent the egg-laying females from accessing the breeding grounds until later in the day. That may pose no real problem in sunny anticyclonic weather, but in weeks when convective cloud cover develops day after day, after bright starts, it may be highly significant, reducing the annual egg lay. The males of the Marsh Fritillary behave similarly on the calcareous grassland sites where I have studied that species, with the females needing to sneak in under the male radar in order to lay their eggs. As previously mentioned, Duke of Burgundy males gather in lekking areas, which would also be important breeding grounds if they were not infested with males – no mated female worth her weight in eggs would venture into such a maelstrom. Perhaps this sort of male activity encourages emigration in females, and is an important dispersal mechanism.

Neil and I have seen enough of the Emperor and the Empress to believe that the same issues affect the Purple Emperor, in a big way, depending on population density. Crucially, the bulk of egg laying is conducted at precisely the time that males are most active in their territories, when the males are otherwise engaged. Also, male avoidance may well explain why the females fly so much lower than the males (except when males are sallow searching), living much of their lives purposefully below the male radar.

One would like to think that the Purple Emperor indulges in an elaborate, intricate and polite courtship ritual which would put bowerbirds to shame. The truth, though, is very different, with courtship being kept to a bare minimum. To put it bluntly, the females need to get wedded, bedded and egging as quickly as possible – anything less would represent a distinct biological disadvantage.

The maiden flight of the virgin Empress is described as being 'erratic' by several authors, including Heslop and Willmott. It is certainly quite distinctive, and markedly different to the even-keeled, controlled, steady and powerful flight that females subsequently adopt. The key difference is that mated females fly in a direct, unwavering manner, usually close to tree or shrub foliage and sometimes at speed, with regular wingbeats; on the other hand, virgin females constantly dip, rise, waver and alternate, careering about within an unusually broad flight corridor, and with irregular wingbeats. Later, they only fly in this way, and then briefly, when they have come off oak sap bleeds and appear, to the human eye, to be somewhat inebriated. Virgin females are worth following, for they will quickly be intercepted by a male.

As stated previously, I have witnessed well over a hundred courtship flights, plus a larger number of brief and inconclusive affairs in which the pair quickly vanished from sight. That's a large sample by Purple Emperor standards. The majority of definite courtships began when a sallow-searching male flushed a perched female out of the understorey canopy or from along the middle foliage layer of an oak edge (or equivalent). A receptive female then leads her suitor in a short follow-my-leader flight, with him following from a distance of about half a metre, up into the treetops at an angle of about 45 degrees. This flight usually lasts less than a minute. The White Admiral does something similar, though the follow-my-leader part lasts much longer and is less urgent, with the male often copying the female's movements.

The Empress will then settle in a topmost spray, wings closed. The male will land beside her, and immediately try to join with her, from sideways on or slightly from below, end to end. The speed of joining depends on how still the foliage is, and whether she has been fortunate enough to acquire just a single suitor. Here, problems arise, for Purple Emperors need still and stable foliage for quick joining and successful pairing, and a female may have to move to another, more sheltered situation – with her over-amorous suitor desperate to get on with it.

A virgin female may attract more randy males than she can cope with, and have to deal with an unwelcome mass courtship situation. At 3.45 pm on 25 June 2018 in a part of Knepp Wildland known as Oak Field, Dennis Dell and I spotted a female flying erratically westwards along an oak line infested with males. She hoovered up males as she progressed, both singletons and sparring pairs. Then, she blundered into a major and particularly violent territory called *The Bay of Assassins*, where three males were squabbling. She then panicked, understandably, and careered north along an outgrown Blackthorn hedge, followed by a shimmering bundle of nine – repeat, nine – males, each one of them ardently intent on mating with her, but the whole group giving the impression of an amorphous iridescent balloon. Our vision vanished around the back of a veteran oak. Incredibly, we failed to locate the pairing, which would have been advertised by unsuccessful males trying to muscle in, suggesting that the group had moved on a fair way. It was the most wonderful thing Dennis and I have ever seen, though it didn't do our blood pressure any good; the episode exceeded the worst excesses of TV's *The Benny Hill Show*, and we felt extremely sorry for the female – and ashamed of our own gender. A week later, Neil Hulme watched what he described as a 'bundle' of 13 males in pursuit of another hapless female nearby. Like Dennis and I, he was so convulsed by the shimmering vision that he failed to locate the inevitable resultant pairing.

Mating takes place in the treetops, in the very zone regularly patrolled by males. Consequently, mating pairs are regularly pestered, and at times interrupted, by lone males trying to oust the incumbent male and muscle in. Neil and I have seen a fair bit of this at Fermyn Woods and Knepp Wildland, and I have also witnessed it in Alice Holt Forest. In fact, homing in with binoculars on a high spray in front of which a patrolling male repeatedly hovers, or suddenly crash-lands with frenetically dithering wingbeats, is the best way of locating mating Purple Emperors, though like so many techniques it only works at sites supporting large populations. Mating pairs normally sit quite still, with their wings closed (one or even both partners will open their wings to bask if weather conditions are relatively cool or cloudy).

Occasionally, mating pairs are blown out of the treetops by strong winds. This explains most sightings, and photographs, of Purple Emperors *in copula*. I have

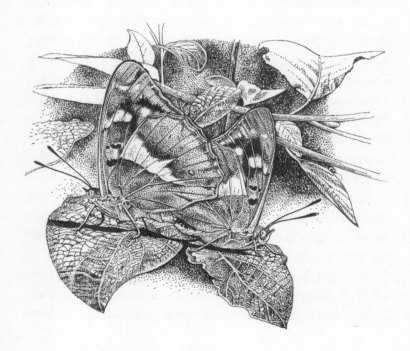

been shown photographs of blown-out pairs stranded on the ground at Ashtead Common in Surrey, Chiddingfold Forest in Surrey/West Sussex, Fermyn Woods in Northamptonshire, and on a vehicle tyre at Porton Down, Wiltshire. Roy Stockley, in *Notes & Views of the Purple Emperor*, describes watching a pair being blown out of the treetops in windy weather on 5 July 1952, with the female subsequently carrying the male. The only time I have seen a mating pair in flight was at Knepp Wildland in early July 2018, when a female carried her mate back up into the high oak canopy after they had been flushed out of the treetops by other males, on a calm late afternoon. The pair had dropped down in a successful effort to lose these unwarranted attentions. This incident took place close to a major territory.

I have witnessed 14 Purple Emperor pairings from start to finish. That is an impressive sample from this, the most scientifically uncooperative of all British butterflies. From this sample, one can conclude that the Purple Emperor mates for 3 hours and 32 minutes on average. The longest pairing lasted 4 hours 20 minutes, and the shortest just under three hours. In sexual performance, at least, the Purple Emperor by far exceeds human capability.

Crucially, nine of these pairings resulted from sallow-searching males locating receptive females, and only five from females entering male territory airspace. Of those five, two pairings involved old and worn females, for whom it must have been a second mating. This included the first pairing I witnessed, in the Straits Inclosure of Alice Holt Forest, on the afternoon of 11 July 1976, when the Purple Emperor season was well on the wane. I have also witnessed other older females seemingly soliciting a second (or perhaps even third) mating, though the outcomes were not observed. Incidentally, all these observations of actual or apparent second matings occurred in hot weather during prolonged anticyclonic conditions, and around male territories. This is important, as it suggests that territorial males are hoping to encounter females in need of a second mating (or the few virgin females that have not been found in the bushes by sallow-searching males).

Mating ends quite suddenly and the male normally flies quickly off, almost with a hop, a skip and a jump, intent on his next amorous adventure. The female tends to rest and bask close by, before making off through the branches. On 9 July 2019, at Knepp Wildland, a pair that joined in the oak tops in Oak Field at 4.26 pm separated at 7.45 pm, and proceeded to bask and then roost there, about a metre apart. A third male came in to bask and roost close by. This episode suggests that the Purple Emperor is occasionally capable of something approximating to moral behaviour.

After mating, the male of the species will be the Empress's fiercest enemy, though he lives ever in the hope that she might need his services again, and never doubts his prowess.

Mated females are regularly intercepted and pursued by overoptimistic males who are loath to take 'no!' for an answer. She will reject their advances by performing what Ken Willmott describes as a 'rejection drop', in which the mated female will reject unwelcome advances by fluttering or even dropping downwards, almost vertically, and often from 10 metres up, with her suitor circling around her, dancing, shimmering his purple hues, beseeching, pleading, entreating – and perhaps spraying her with amorous male pheromones. Her objective is to get rid of him, and the best way to do that, of course, is to puncture the male ego; in this case, by pulling out at the last possible second, and upping off and away at speed, having forced the would-be assailant to crash-land on the ground or, worse, into a bramble bush or nettle patch. It doesn't always work out that simply. Quite often the female crash-lands herself, in which case she will sit tight, with wings (and legs) firmly closed, until the male finally gets the message. Sometimes both partners land, and end up feeling pretty damn silly, and pretend that they're not there.

Ken was the first person to note this particular piece of Purple Emperor behaviour. I did not observe it until I began to study the large population at Fermyn Woods during the mid-2000s, but I now see it almost daily during the appropriate part of the flight season at Knepp Wildland and have observed well over a hundred instances. Neil Hulme and I witnessed over 50 of these rejection drops, or 'tumbledowns' as Neil calls them, at Knepp during the 2018 season alone, recording a peak of 11 instances on 2 July. Most of the tumbledowns that I have witnessed resulted from males suddenly swooping down from the oaks to indulge in a session of sallow searching and intercepting an egging female, or from females crossing a low wood-edge canopy gap, and being accosted by a territorial male perched higher up.

It may well be that pheromones are being used, with the female squirting 'I'm already mated' pheromones and the male spraying – I'd rather not say what – at her. Some hard science needs doing here, to determine the role of these chemicals in courtship and mating in *Apatura iris*. Observational evidence suggests that Purple Emperor pheromones are not particularly powerful – bad news for a species reduced to occurring at low population density. Certainly, there is no equivalent of the strong pheromones employed by large moths, such as our Emperor Moth, whereby a receptive virgin female can attract several males from distances of many hundreds of metres. Highly sophisticated mate-location strategies are necessary for a butterfly or moth occurring diffusely over tracts of highly modified landscape if powerful attractant chemicals are not in use, as appears to be the case with the Purple Emperor.

Tumbledowns are very much features of the afternoon. All my observations have taken place between noon and 5.30 pm, and mostly between 2 pm and 5 pm. The data from Knepp Wildland indicates that tumbledowns occur mostly during the third quarter of the flight season, and that they cease before the season's final week. In 2018 they were observed from 23 June to mid-July (with a late one on 21 July), peaking during the first week of July.

Tumbledowns are showy affairs, with the males displaying their full colours, flickering through the entire spectrum of purples, violets and blues. Several of the Purple Emperor safaris that Neil Hulme and I have run at Knepp have been blessed by tumbledowns occurring among groups of 20 or so attendees. The tumbling butterflies are oblivious to people, but the safari-goers are utterly delighted, as these large and spectacular butterflies dance mesmerisingly among them. Sometimes more than one Emperor is involved, which doubles the woes of the Empress and prolongs a tumbledown from one or two minutes to three or even four. If the Empress is fortunate, the two males will forget about her and go off squabbling.

Here it must be confessed that Neil and I have a trick up our sleeve: we know that most tumbledowns occur around oak sap 'feeder trees' and deliberately lead safari groups to those trees at an appropriate time. We are merely exploiting a trick that Purple Emperor males use, of lying in wait for females around feeder trees – and causing maximum chaos there.

Finally, a denial needs to be issued here: Neil and I have never once chanted the risqué rugby song 'Get 'em down, you Zulu warrior!' at a tumbledown.

Although the evidence is less extensive than with the males, I believe that females feed even more frequently than males, especially between bouts of egg laying. Like their male counterparts, they resort increasingly to oak sap bleeds during the latter stages of their life.

There is no evidence that females need to take minerals on board prior to mating. Certainly, they are seldom attracted to unsavoury substances. I know of no records of females feeding from fox scats, and precious few from canine deposits (and some – or most – of those 'records' may be of males that were not showing their purple colours, to inexperienced observers; I have been shown several photographs of so-called females feeding on the ground, which were actually males). Relatively few females have been captured or photographed on baits, throughout Purple history.

However, females do descend to the ride surfaces to feed from time to time, mainly during the first week or so of their lives or in extreme weather. Most records seem to be of females imbibing moisture, presumably dew but possibly urine, along grassy rides, or in the grassy edge of a surfaced forest ride. I witnessed a fair amount of this in Alice Holt Forest at the zenith of the long hot summer of 1976, and in Fermyn Woods during the 2013 heatwave. One rarely sees females feeding on the ground at Knepp Wildland, presumably because of the abundance there of their preferred food source, oak sap.

At Knepp, Neil Hulme and I see as many females imbibing from oak sap bleeds as males, and late in the flight season most of the Purple Emperors we see feeding on oak sap are female. They may be taking this supposedly high-octane fuel on board late in their lives in order to squeeze out a few more eggs. The habit of the males ambushing females around feeder trees has been noted previously, indicating that visiting these trees is a risky though essential business for *Herself*.

Most of my sightings of the butterfly apparently feeding on honeydew involve females, though as noted in Chapter 5 I am not convinced that honeydew is a major source of sustenance for Purple Emperors in Britain – it's just that it may be more significant for the females than for the males, particularly in habitats devoid of veteran oaks hosting sap bleeds.

Egg laying is what the Empress is all about, though she is not easily observed while placing those precious eggs. We have little idea how many eggs an Empress lays in the wild, though it is reasonable to assume considerable variation between individuals and from year to year, with much depending on weather conditions (the seasonal egg-lay total appears to be higher in warm seasons). If pressed, my guess would be that the average wild female lays in the region of 50–75 eggs, but the range here may be from nought to 150. Ken Willmott estimates 'probably in the region of 40 (min) – 100 (max)'.

Most sightings of Empresses egg laying, or in the act of oviposition if you want to use the technical term, are momentary, distant and from far below – a matter of a dark shape fluttering in and out of the tops of tall sallows. Following egg-laying females is relatively easy with most British butterflies, but with the Purple Emperor it is decidedly difficult. She will settle briefly on the upperside of a leaf, usually with wings partly open, and quickly bend her abdomen down to deposit a single egg, before scurrying off. Eggs are almost invariably laid singly, but in bouts, wherein half a dozen or more eggs are laid within a few frenetic minutes.

Although the odd egg can be laid early or late in the day – the earliest and latest recorded times are 7.30 am (by K E J Bailey, *Notes & Views of the Purple Emperor*) and 8.35 pm (myself, Knepp Wildland, 2016) – the bulk of egg laying takes place during the early afternoon period. In his detailed report to the World Wide Fund for Nature, Ken Willmott states that the vast majority of Purple Emperor eggs are deposited between noon and 2 pm, except on cool days, when few if any are laid. This is based on a sample size of 32, derived mainly from meticulous studies at Bookham Common during Ken's lunch breaks from work nearby. Neil Hulme, in *The Butterflies of Sussex* (2017), states that data collected in Sussex shows that most eggs are laid between 1.30 pm and 3 pm, adding that he holds what he calls 'the witching hour' – that is, peak egg-laying time – to be 2 pm. Heslop provides further confusion, claiming in *Notes & Views of the Purple Emperor* that 'there is fairly general agreement that the wild female lays most (but not all) of her eggs between 11.00 and 1.30 B.S.T.'. Data in my possession, derived from a sample of over 300 observations when eggs were definitely laid, suggests that around 75 per cent of eggs are laid during the period 1 pm to 3.15 pm. So, there you have it – a confusing absence of clarity, but that's *Herself* all over. To confound the situation further, it has already been pointed out that some egg laying may take place on warm, moonlit nights.

Time of day alone may not provide sufficient clarity for a true understanding of egg laying, as weather conditions must also be brought into consideration. Also, slightly different patterns of behaviour are observed in different summers. The problem for the observer, though, is that peak egg-laying activity coincides with peak male territorial activity, and we cannot be in two places simultaneously: the observer must choose between the boys or the girls, and the boys are easier to see. I suspect that Ken Willmott is very close to the truth when he surmises that females lay during the early afternoon period, with the sun at its zenith, in order to select leaves that are adequately shaded from full afternoon sunshine, on account of the young larva's vulnerability to desiccating sunlight.

Existing data does not help to determine the temperature range, and wider weather window, for egg-laying activity. Thermometer readings taken in shade at breast height, where standard measurements are taken, may only be loosely relevant to the canopy level direct sunshine temperatures which egg-laying females experience. My guess is that a minimum shade temperature of 19 degrees Celsius is necessary for egg laying, and that the activity is curtailed by heat in excess of 24 degrees Celsius.

Much has been written about the manner in which the female deposits her eggs. Some authors write about how the female 'strikes the sallow'. I have never been happy with that phrase, and neither was Heslop, who states in *Notes & Views of the Purple Emperor* that females only 'strike a tree' when homing in on oak sap. Later in the same paragraph he surmises that instances of females striking sallows are probably misidentifications of males searching for females. Spot on! I have never seen a female 'strike a sallow', and never will. No way could she enter a sallow bush at speed; she would crash into foliage. Let us expunge this misleading phrase from the Emperoring lexicon. It is a classic example of the nonsense mythology that has developed around this insect.

Instead, the laying Empress flits powerfully, warily and purposefully around sallow bushes, seeking a way into the foliage crown. Heslop, and his co-author Stockley, help us considerably by talking about the use of a 'dropping-off point'. This is because females sit on high branches close to and generally above stands of sallow bushes for some time, before descending on an egg-laying foray. In his seminal work, *Life Cycles of British & Irish Butterflies* (2019), Peter Eeles writes about females undergoing bouts of egg laying, lasting around 10 minutes, during which in the region of half a dozen eggs may be laid. That is indeed the general pattern, though it includes incidents when eggs were probably not laid. Ken Willmott also writes about witnessing frenetic pulses of egg laying, of some 10 minutes in duration, during which 6–10 eggs are deposited.

The majority of eggs are laid on isolated first-year leaf sprays directly below the canopy umbrella, in positions of moderately heavy shade – or on similar leaf sprays on the shady side of a bush. This must be to avoid exposing first-instar larvae to too much direct sunshine, which causes them to desiccate. The female may be thinking not so much about the egg, but the larva. Willmott states that females select leaves in the shadow of other branches, adding that: 'The only essential requirement appears to be that of shade, irrespective of the aspect.' I fully agree, though not simply because of the larva's aversion to heat, as shade and exposure levels also impact on leaf suitability, with first-instar larvae being unable to cope with thick leaves (as will be discussed later).

Eggs are placed at various heights, though the majority are laid out of our reach, 4 to 8 metres up. Conversely, I have also found eggs and young larvae as low as knee height (which is curious, as I have never seen an egg laid lower than 2 metres up; few people have – which begs the question of when low-level eggs are laid). Ken Willmott states that 80–90 per cent of eggs are deposited high up within the shaded crowns of tall sallows. There is a difficulty for accurate recording here as most observations of females supposedly laying are at heights where verification is extremely hard. We need to be careful about such sightings, as females often go through the motions of egg laying without actually doing so – they are frequently put off, by gusts of wind or other disturbances, and often appear to reject the leaf they have settled upon, after apparently laying. Indeed, no egg was laid in 32 per cent of the instances of 'egg laying' that I have recorded (out of a sample of over 400) – and where the exact spray has been checked. That suggests that about one-third of the time a laying female rejects a selected leaf, or fails to lay there. In addition, egg-laying data is difficult to obtain simply because females often disappear from view while depositing their eggs.

In his *Natural History of British Butterflies* (1924) Frohawk states that the female settles for eight to 10 seconds while in the act of laying each egg, though my own observations indicate that eggs can be laid in half that time. Certainly, sightings of females settling on leaves for less than three seconds are of females rejecting that leaf, even if the abdomen has bent down to touch the leaf surface.

My own observations suggest, I think strongly, that the majority of eggs are carefully placed. However, in the region of 25 per cent of eggs seem to be plastered randomly. The random distribution of some eggs may be due to stressed females – ageing, ill-nourished and underpowered individuals, or those stressed by challenging weather conditions (heat, low temperatures or wind), or those avoiding males. Alternatively, it may simply be that (some) females lay a proportion of their eggs in unusual situations to ensure that not all eggs are metaphorically placed in one basket. Thorough scientific investigation is required to determine precisely where, when, why and how eggs are laid.

With regard to position on the leaf, the majority of eggs are laid towards the leaf edge, almost exclusively so on smaller leaves. On genuinely large leaves, which fully accommodate a perched Empress, eggs tend to be laid more towards the midrib, or even on it.

It is clear that male and female Purple Emperors behave very differently, which is hardly surprising as they fulfil markedly different functions. In brief, I would describe the female Purple Emperor as being shy and retiring, though decidedly aloof and exceptionally hard to study. I would add that when it comes to non-cooperation, she may prove unrivalled among British wildlife. Having looked at both the male and female of the species, it is now time to try to issue some clear advice on how to look for these complex but intriguing creatures.

CHAPTER SEVEN

Looking for Purple Emperors

Constant vigilance, or watch the birds! – Information sources –
Leeward! – Looking for sallow-searching males – Grounded
males – Canopy gaps and wooded high points – Feeder trees
– Recording and monitoring – Access issues

The Purple Emperor is a unique butterfly, which necessitates unique viewing techniques. With British butterflies in general you look down, or along the horizontal plane, but for Purple Emperors you look up, and long and hard. This is simply because the Purple Emperor is primarily a canopy-dwelling insect, which today occurs largely at low population levels, is only intermittently active and rarely visits flowers. Of course, you need to keep an eye open for 'grounded' males as they feed on the paths, but they do this only during the first half of their flight season. Birders are used to looking up, and scanning tree foliage, and also possess the vital skill of being able to focus binoculars on fast-flying distant objects. Binoculars, and the ability to use them, including for scanning along wood edges, are the most essential piece of equipment for those wishing to see this butterfly, as most of your sightings will be distant, fleeting and from below. Anyone who goes birdwatching or has spent time fishing will have the visual observation skills and the depth of patience necessary to work (study) Purple Emperors.

There are also a few other rules for 'Emperoring', as butterfly folk call it. The practice involves a considerable amount of standing around, loitering with earnest intent, waiting for this butterfly to explode into action – and explode it will, when it feels like it. Sitting will seldom suffice, as it narrows your vista of search right down. I often carry a shooting stick or lean heavily on my long shepherd's crook. Backache is obligatory, and you can be eaten alive by clegs and mosquitoes, and frazzled in the sun. Heatstroke will at times kick in. If you find yourself flagging then utter the magic word, 'January!', and your powers of concentration and your love of summer's heat will be instantly restored. I find *Test Match Special* commentary an essential part of a day's Emperoring. Never leave your lunch or tea in the car; take it with you, and plenty to drink. No self-respecting Emperophile will visit a public house until the Emperors have bedded down for the night (and will then celebrate the day in true Emperorian style).

Crucially, you must ignore all other butterflies and yield only unto *HIM*. Don't worry, for the Emperor rewards his servants. Also, you will be surprised by the diversity and numbers of other butterflies you will see making their way up and over the trees, even species that you consider to be low-flying meadowland creatures like the humble Meadow Brown.

You never know when the Purple Emperor is going to appear, so never relax or switch off: constant vigilance is essential. In angling parlance, watch the float! Also, follow birds and insects bigger than worker wasps as they move through canopy gaps: if they stray near to a perched male he will give chase. Pigeons are especially useful here. Watch the pigeons!

Skilled drone operators may be tempted to use their gadgets to flush inactive males (and females) into action.

The males are likely to attack it; the females will skuttle off. This could develop into an invaluable survey technique for locating new Purple Emperor localities, but requires expert control, as drones will need to be flown quite close to undulating foliage, and could potentially injure the butterflies. The secret is to fly the machine slowly and move it away fast when attacked.

Experience is everything, as the Purple Emperor appears in different guises, depending on distance and angle of view, intensity of light, vegetation background and sky colour. No two encounters with this insect are ever truly alike. In time you will even learn to look out for imperial shadows passing over bare ground (in 2018, over 50 of my sightings at Knepp Wildland were derived from shadows of sallow-searching males and egging females cast on parched bare ground).

Nowadays, it is easy to find out whether the Purple Emperor is on the wing or not, and the secrecy over localities, which pervaded into the 1970s, is now gone. The key sources of information are the websites of the 15 branches of Butterfly Conservation which cover the main counties in which the Purple Emperor occurs, the Purple Emperor blog (*The Purple Empire*) and the UK Butterflies website. All these provide up-to-date information on when and where the butterfly is flying. This means there is no longer any excuse for visiting at the wrong time of year.

These websites will also offer guidance as to the stage in the flight season in which your visit is taking place. This is crucial information, as the butterfly does different

things at different times. For example, you will only see
males down on the ground during the first third of the
season, and then mainly during the morning. Once the
male emergence is complete, you will need to look
exclusively upwards – they stop coming down.

The most important word in the Emperoring mindset is
'leeward'. Butterflies, even one as strong and bold as the
Purple Emperor, dislike wind. Emperors aggregate
leeward, out of the wind. So, search east-facing edges in
a west wind, and change your modus operandi if the
wind changes direction during the day (the butterflies
will quickly move with it). In a southerly wind, this
means that you will be working north-facing edges, and
looking into the sun. In a westerly wind, you will be
looking westwards, often with harsh bright light angling
across you. Wear a hat, sunglasses or a visor – you will
need them.

So often, people are standing in the right place, but
are looking in the wrong direction, and see little, if
anything. May their numbers dwindle.

During the first half of the flight season the males
assiduously search sallow bushes in the shrub layer for
freshly emerged females, particularly during the mid- to
late morning period. This activity is more visible at some
sites than at others, for breeding grounds can be hidden
from our view. Sightings of sallow-searching males can
be brief, but much depends on how open the habitat is.
The flight pattern of searching males is powerful and

inquisitive. These searching males also inspect wood edges close to sallow stands, again seeking to flush out perched females. While doing this they fly along the middle height zone (where females perch), not along the treetops (which females avoid).

Looking for sallow-searching males is a good way of seeing Purple Emperors at many sites, and also constitutes a useful method of surveying for new sites, depending on the habitat structure. But beware: this activity ceases once the female emergence is complete and males start to age. Only look for sallow-searching males during the first half of the flight season (before day 20).

Most butterfly enthusiasts, especially photographers, search for males feeding on some nasty excrescence along woodland rides. Watch out for fox scats and other deposits! This feeding activity normally takes place over a couple of hours in mid-morning, starting and ending earlier in hot weather, and later in cool conditions. It is essentially a feature of the first third of the Purple Emperor season. So, to see grounded males (as they are known), you need to know precisely where you are in the flight season: check the websites.

Descending males swoop down from on high, changing direction in a switchback motion, as if following the route of some mountain road. They can fly fast and low along a woodland ride, searching for the scent of something tasty. If a male approaches you, play musical statues: freeze, for any movement is likely to scare him away. Celebrate later.

Males usually feed with their wings closed, with the forewing raised. Broadside on, feeding males are quite salient, so long as you are paying proper attention. Head- or tail-on, though, they are easily missed. Then, you may not notice *HIM* until it is too late, and he flies away in disgust. If he takes off, keep still, for he may want to resettle.

Once engaged in feeding, Emperors become wholly absorbed in what they are doing and are easily approached. Watch for the probing tongue, it will tell you when to approach – allow him to get his yellow tongue firmly ensconced into the feeding substance before you move in for a closer look or to take photographs. Occasionally, males become so engrossed in feeding that you can encourage them to crawl on to your finger.

Often, a male will take a break midway through a feed, flying up to a low ride-side bush to clean his tongue for a few minutes, and rest, before descending to resume feeding. Watch out for tongue cleaning, and be prepared for a second coming. Stand still, again, when he starts to descend.

Females are rarely encountered feeding on the ground, and then mainly along grassy edges. They almost invariably remain wary and difficult to approach. You won't get much cooperation out of them.

Each afternoon, throughout the flight season, males perform aerial acrobatics in and around their territories. This is one of the best wildlife experiences in the British Isles and is truly captivating. Most of this activity takes place around canopy gaps – open spaces between two densely foliaged trees, often oaks. It is quite distinctive, even when viewed from afar, and is 100 per cent diagnostic: no other British butterfly does it, at least not at that elevation (sparring Red Admirals and Commas perform at lower levels, are much smaller insects, and are less aggressive). You cannot mistake sparring Purple Emperors.

Most male territories are slightly downwind of wooded summits or on the eastern side of clumps of tall trees. Some are in quiet airspace above a glade surrounded by tall trees on summits. These stand out like church spires in the landscape, and may be visible from miles around. Check them out, even if they are outside woods. The easiest territories to find are those on wooded high points and those along sheltered wood edges. An experienced observer can identify Purple Emperors from distances of 100 metres or more. Only the Swallowtail can be seen

from further away, though it looks coffee-coloured, while
Purple Emperors appear black.

A number of male territories are well advertised in
publications and on various websites. The two at
Bookham Common are currently promoted on the
National Trust website. It is worth visiting one or two of
these renowned territories first, to get your eye in, and
develop a feel for these ultra-special places, before
venturing into *terra nova*.

If nothing is happening at a known territory, you are
either too early or too late in the season, or the weather
is too dull, or it's too windy and you need to move
downwind and find where the males have moved to, or
just a lone male is present and you need to wait for a
passing bird, or large insect, to rouse him into action.
Think about what is or isn't happening, and consider
your options.

Large and distinctive sap runs, showing as splurges of a
black treacle-like substance running down a tree trunk,
are decidedly rare. Mostly, Purple Emperors feed on
small bubbles of whiteish sap on diseased oak branches
(or occasionally on Beech or other deciduous trees). It is
hard to spot such branches, which are often hidden by
foliage (dead trees or boughs exposed to the full heat of
the sun seldom offer any sustenance to butterflies, as the
sappy oozings have desiccated). If a tree or a bough is
riddled with the borings of beetle larvae, it's past the sap
bleed phase.

Most feeder trees are discovered by spotting Purple
Emperors (of both sexes) zigzagging into the tree,

having sensed flowing sap. Watch out for that distinct
flight pattern, for a lot of activity will take place around
feeder trees, especially during afternoons and evenings.
The presence of other sap-feeding insects is often a
giveaway: look out for Red Admirals, Commas, Speckled
Woods and Purple Hairstreaks, which all readily feed on
sap bleeds, and the Hornet and other social wasps, plus
various bee-mimic hoverflies. However, most of these
small bleeds that Emperors utilise are short-lived, and
even a 'good' feeder tree may only last for a season.

Butterfly monitoring was established in the UK in 1976.
The UK Butterfly Monitoring Scheme (UKBMS),
which coordinates monitoring and produces species
trends and reports, is run by a partnership led by Butterfly
Conservation and the Centre for Ecology & Hydrology
(CEH). Most of the data is derived from butterfly
transects, in which butterflies are counted within an
imaginary 5-metre square box around a recorder who
walks a fixed route in suitable weather each week
throughout the butterfly season. A few of our butterflies
don't play ball with this method, notably the Mountain
Ringlet (our one montane species) and our canopy
dwellers, led of course by His Imperial Majesty, the
Purple Emperor. Most of the Purple Emperor records in
the UKBMS are of males feeding on something vile
along a woodland ride. The most recorded on a single
UKBMS transect is three, which has been achieved once.
The vast majority of sightings of Purple Emperors along
transect routes will be discounted, for being well outside
the 5-metre box.

Some experienced Purple Emperor observers have been experimenting with other methodology. At Knepp Wildland, Neil Hulme and I walk a Purple Emperor single-species transect, along a 2-kilometre length of oak-lined green lane. This deviates from UKBMS methodology in that our recording 'box' is 50 metres wide, the transect is walked only between 12.30 pm and 5 pm, when males are on territory, and we veer a little leeward on windy days, to avoid missing out on seeing displaced Emperors. We also only record Purple Emperors. We aim to walk this transect each week for the five- or six-week long Purple Emperor season at Knepp, spacing out the gap between our counts as evenly as possible. It works, for this location. In 2018, we counted 201 Purple Emperors, males and females, along this route.

Elsewhere, Ken Willmott has kept a record of the average number of males seen in a vista each year at the Bookham Common territories since the late 1970s. Most years are 'three years'; 'four' is quite good and 'two' is poor. Since 2005, Mike Slater has conducted weekly timed counts at the main territory in Ryton Wood, Warwickshire, counting the number of apparent individuals in a designated 10-minute search period between 2 pm and 4 pm in appropriate weather. The highest annual tally at Ryton is nine in 2018; the lowest is none, in 2012. These methods seem to work at these localities.

However, I found it difficult to obtain reliable data from the main territory in Alice Holt Forest, at the north end of Goose Green Inclosure. This is a cluster-territory, where males continuously move about, changing trees, leading to issues with double-counting.

Also, vistas are continually opening up and closing over, due to rapid habitat change, especially along the electricity line wayleave.

In addition, I have data from standardised searches for eggs and autumn larvae in Savernake Forest from 2009 to 2019, but this is incredibly laborious work (see Chapter 10). More monitored sites are required, but you may need to experiment in order to find out what works best at your site. My advice is to seek help from your local Butterfly Conservation branch Purple Emperor Champion or County Butterfly Recorder. In effect, monitoring Purple Emperor populations is still in its research and development phase.

It is so difficult to record Purple Emperors that every sighting away from a small number of well-known localities is valuable. It is easy to feed your sightings into the UK butterfly recording (distribution mapping) scheme via the Butterfly Conservation branch websites, details of which are found on the main society website. Many of the relevant (i.e. Purple) Butterfly Conservation branches have a designated Purple Emperor Champion, or lead recorder.

Records of Purple Emperors along the western, northern and eastern (and southern, in the case of the Isle of Wight) borders of the Purple Empire are particularly important. This basic knowledge of where the Purple Emperor occurs is essential to its future in this era of climate change and ecological breakdown. The days when the butterfly was deemed so rare and vulnerable that its locations had to be kept secret are long gone (that thinking never helped the Purple Emperor anyway, rather the reverse).

Above all, write all your sightings of the Purple Emperor down, and describe habitat conditions, especially sallow quantity and quality; otherwise, facts become impressions which will flicker in and out of focus, like the Emperor's wings, and mislead you. This is especially important at sites that you intend to work regularly. Maintaining detailed notes will prime the development of your intuitive feel for this butterfly, and your relationship with the place. It will guide you to where you need to be to see Purple Emperors, and will serve you better than anything else; but it needs to be evidence-based, rather than the product of your dodgy memory. I never cease to be amazed by the number of field naturalists who never write anything down.

At many of the better-known localities one can get ensconced in lengthy conversations, often in the car park. Beware of false prophets, especially those that hang out around parking areas. There are no experts on this butterfly, only people on different stages of experiential pilgrimage, all of whom are regularly bemused by the Purple Emperor. I still have my L-plates on.

Push limits, any limits. That is precisely what the Purple Emperor does. Do not conform to the patterns of this world, the Emperor doesn't. Think well outside the box; in fact, burn the box.

Most Purple Emperor localities are privately owned woods. The Countryside and Rights of Way Act (2000) did not grant open access to woodland, and many woods within the Purple Empire are managed primarily for pheasant shooting. There is a considerable amount that the pheasant-shooting industry can do to assist the conservation of the Purple Emperor. Landowners and gamekeepers tend to have heard of this butterfly, and many are keen to allow sallows to grow in order to encourage it. Don't let's fall out with country sportsmen unnecessarily; so seek permission to wander off-piste (ask at the local pub or garage), or keep to designated rights of way when prospecting for new sites. Many landowners will be delighted to learn that they have Purple Emperors on their land. Liz Goodyear and Andrew Middleton have discovered over a hundred new localities in the East of England region simply by observing from roads, byways, bridleways and footpaths, often from a distance, using binoculars.

CHAPTER EIGHT

Habitats and breeding grounds

A denizen of oak woods? — The clay lands — Plantations and sallow clearances — Traditional wood pasture — Hedges, wood edges and copses — Roadsides and screenings — Riverine woodland — Scrublands — Parks and gardens

Contrary to mythology, and what one reads in the old butterfly textbooks, the Purple Emperor is not a butterfly of ancient oak woodland and almost certainly never was. It's just that this was where people looked for it, and saw it. The Purple Emperor is, in fact, primarily a butterfly of damp clay land, which happens to be where English (or Pedunculate) Oak was grown — extensively — prior to the twentieth-century conifer revolution.

The good news is that Purple Emperor's needs can be variously met. This means it can occur in a surprising diversity of habitats, including some that are normally dismissed as scrub or, worse, wasteland. The Forestry Commission used to have a dismissive term for Purple Emperor breeding habitat: 'Low Grade Broad-leaved', which abbreviated to LGBL on old forest stock maps.

Sallows, and indeed willows more generally, favour clayey soils, or other water-retentive situations such as riverbanks, peaty fens and carr (wet) woodlands. The Purple Emperor's strongholds are on the Weald Clay of West Sussex, the sinuous belts of Gault Clay in Sussex,

Hampshire and Oxfordshire, the mixed and muddled clays of the lower Weald of west Kent and East Sussex, the London Clay that reaches from the London area eastwards into Essex and Suffolk, the Oxford Clay belt that runs from Wiltshire through to Oxford and up into Lincolnshire, and the Boulder Clay which runs from Northamptonshire and the south-east Midlands eastwards into East Anglia. Some of these favoured clays also occur outside the known range of the Purple Emperor, and there are other clays outside the butterfly's current range, many of which support sallow-rich woodland. This begs the questions of is the Purple Emperor there – in clay vales outside the accepted known range – and has anyone actually looked?

Away from these heavy clays, the Purple Empire is more fragmented. On the chalklands, the butterfly is restricted to patches of clay-with-flints (flinty marls) overlying the chalk bedrock and to damp woods with narrow-leaved sallows growing in calcareous peaty valleys in central southern England. Sallows can, though, establish themselves in remarkably dry terrain, such as chalk downland or even limestone pavement. They can be highly tenacious, especially in higher-rainfall regions – I am amazed where they grow in the Lake District, a high-rainfall area. On acidic soils, the butterfly is restricted to small-leaved sallows growing in areas of impeded drainage on wet heathland and in valley mires (Eared Willow and Grey Willow mostly, and their hybrids). In the New Forest, though, it was primarily a butterfly of silvicultural inclosures on the clayey Headon Beds, though it might now also breed in Grey Willow carrs (the status of the Purple Emperor in the New

Forest is unclear). Elsewhere, pockets of alluvium (soil, often clayey, which has been carried and deposited by rivers) that have not been claimed for farming provide suitable conditions for sallows.

For decades, butterfly enthusiasts looked for Purple Emperors over tall oaks close to young plantations choked with sallows, which constituted the butterfly's breeding grounds. In those days our woods abounded with oak, planted to supply timber for the navy and for industry. Then steel replaced timber in ships and industry.

In 1919 the Forestry Commission was established. Its vision was to replace our slow-growing native trees with faster-growing conifers, many of which had not been grown in the UK before (at least, not on any scale). So much for the evidence-based approach, this was a massive experiment. Caught up in a maelstrom of woodland change, the Purple Emperor tried to carry on regardless. However, sallows are quickly outcompeted in conifer plantations. More critically, the Commission was assiduous about clearing young plantations of 'weeds', such as sallows. The butterfly, in consequence, took a massive hit, particularly during the 1940s and 1950s, when sallows were viewed as being Forest Enemy Number One ('FENO'). The nation was still in Dig for Victory mode, which is what prevented the likes of Heslop and BB from raging all-out warfare on a hugely unsympathetic Forestry Commission.

The FENO mentality still persists on some estates in private ownership, for example in the Cotswolds, and, more incredibly, in some enclaves of public-owned forest managed by Forestry England. This is now an old, sad and sorry saga, overtold and hacked out by aggrieved nature conservationists, myself included, and now counterbalanced by some outstanding examples of forest conservation work and Forestry England's laudable Plantations on Ancient Woodland Sites (PAWS) policy. I have merely sketched it out here, but suffice it to say that I lived through much of it – and grieved spiritually as all too many ancient woods succumbed to the onward march of lavatory-brush conifers.

In recent decades, many of the Purple Emperor's breeding grounds have been unweeded thicket-stage conifer plantations, which had been created on ancient woodland sites. Such plantations remain suitable for 10 to 15 years, before the conifers suppress the native sallows; fewer if some bright spark weeds the sallow outs, and longer if the conifer crop is ailing. In contrast, sallows growing in young Beech or oak plantations remain suitable for around 25 years, depending on the vigour of the crop growth and forestry thinning interventions. Indeed, sallows and other so-called scrub species will act as 'nurse crops' for oaks and other valuable timber crops, if retained, while bramble patches offer splendid protection from browsing deer (they are nature's tree shelters).

Where conifer plantations are properly thinned (and thinning programmes are notoriously difficult to maintain, not least due to fluctuating market prices), sallows can reappear as a subcanopy below tall conifers around the time when the crop receives its final thinning. This is precisely what is happening now in many Purple Emperor woods, providing new breeding habitat with suitably shaded sallows for egg laying and the early larval instars.

During the second half of the twentieth century, the Purple Emperor also bred freely in neglected copses, on ageing sallows struggling to maintain themselves through densening Hazel canopies. The first colony I studied, near Southwater in West Sussex, was based on sallows growing in abandoned oak–Hazel copses. Eventually, sallows die out in such neglected woodland, having been outcompeted by taller-growing trees and starved of the opportunity to establish new saplings. That was the fate of the woods where I saw my first Emperors. Eventually, though, the dense canopy will break up, and sallows will regenerate. Ash dieback disease should greatly speed up that process.

Overall, it is likely that the Purple Emperor suffered more from the abandonment of much of our surviving southern lowland broad-leaved woodland than from coniferisation. Most of the young conifer plantations I knew during the 1970s and early 1980s, which supported colonies of Pearl-bordered Fritillary, Small Pearl-bordered Fritillary and Duke of Burgundy, went on to become Purple Emperor breeding grounds, until the sallows were weeded out or outcompeted.

The Purple Emperor can also occur in wood pasture (or pasture-woodlands; that is, grazed woods) on clayey soils. These are almost invariably ancient commons, grazed by local smallholders' livestock (usually cattle). Sallows are highly palatable to cattle, and can therefore be scarce in wood pasture unless grazing pressure has fluctuated over the years, enabling pulses of sallow regeneration. In most wood pastures, including the most renowned of them all, the open New Forest, grazing animal numbers have varied greatly over time; each dip allowing a pulse of tree regeneration, often spearheaded by sallows.

Many of today's best-known Purple Emperor sites were formerly grazed wood pastures. Stock grazing has returned to some of these sites, for example Ashtead Common, the Bookham Commons, and Ranmore Common in Surrey. At others, grazing managed to hang on. Binswood, a Woodland Trust property near Bordon in east Hampshire, is an ancient wood pasture with a long and perhaps unbroken history of grazing. Giant old sallows, of the large narrow-leaved variety, occur in profusion, and the Purple Emperor occurs there in goodly numbers.

Knepp Wildland itself is, in a nutshell, developing (or New Age) wood pasture. The land at Knepp was probably occupied by wood pasture at other points in its history, and was largely scrubbed during the agricultural depression of the 1930s (Tree, 2018).

Hedge and roadside sallows are a key element of the Purple Empire's habitat matrix. They undoubtedly facilitate dispersal and colonisation, though there is as yet precious little proof of that.

Hedgerow sallows were prominent in the West Sussex landscape where I first discovered the Purple Emperor. I saw females fluttering around them. Then, during the 1970s, the tall and outgrown hedges, which were effectively strips of linear woodland, were severely rationalised, to create larger fields suitable for new and bigger machinery as farming intensified. Since then, 7-metre-reach flail-cutters have wreaked further havoc. Many farms in that landscape would now be featureless were it not for the scatter of veteran oaks that spreads the illusion that all is well. The same happened in east Hampshire, where I lived from the mid-1970s into the early 1990s, and elsewhere. Hedges vanished by the mile each winter, and those that were retained were then ravaged by hedge cutting. It was the same everywhere, as farmers worked their socks off to produce more and more food under the EU's Common Agricultural Policy, creating milk lakes, butter mountains and filling huge grain intervention stores. The EU even stipulated that hedges needed to be low and narrow. The farmers were almost as much the victims as the wildlife that many of their farms had supported – and, yes, the Purple Emperor was almost certainly a species of farmed lands, just as it was of woodland, utilising tall, outgrown hedges and farm copses.

There was often a narrow zone of younger trees and scrub along wood edges, growing in a broad corridor between where the wood ended and the field began, as forest fences had capsized, or boundaries had become indeterminate. Sallows often abounded along that borderland. Again, during the 1970s and early 1980s this scrub zone was cleared, to enlarge fields and put the forest back behind its fence. This happened along entire forest edge systems – most acutely, along the fringes of the main blocks of Bernwood Forest, north of Oxford. There, the main victim was not so much the Purple Emperor as the rare Black Hairstreak, whose favoured Blackthorn thickets had already been cleared from inside the forest and for whom the wood-edge scrub zone had become a vital refuge.

Today, a great many of our woods have uniform and abrupt wood edges: rows of densely packed, tall trees that suddenly give way to vast open fields. The woodland-edge shrub zone that supported so much wildlife has gone. That loss has made the structure of rides all the more crucial, but so many woodland rides are narrow, lacking the crucial ride-edge shrub zone. Conservationists have been harping on about this for my entire career, but foresters are inherently loath to fell the two or three rows of crop trees necessary to accommodate broad, wildlife-rich rides.

Copses, too, vanished to create more or larger fields, or were part-felled for new houses for the wealthy, each one nicely screened by a modicum of retained trees, giving the impression of hidden kingdoms. These woodland garden realms are of considerable potential for the Purple Emperor, needing only the odd sallow tree in distant corners. The main hindrances are a lack of awareness of this potential, the fashion for ride-on lawnmowing over sweeps of flowerless, lifeless lawn, and the onward march of bland pony paddocks. It would not take much to turn all this around, as sallows would be at the forefront of any recovery, being great opportunists and early colonisers. There are even garden varieties of sallow and willow, developed for their blossom or pendulous form. All is far from lost, but opportunities need to be recognised and encouraged – perhaps through peer pressure-led fashion.

The lower slopes and bottoms of steep-sided valleys remain important breeding grounds for the Purple Emperor. Here, farming is seldom intensive (though horse keeping is increasingly taking over) and sallows are often now permitted to line streams and to occur in thick hedges. The combe bottoms of the East Hampshire Hangers are, for example, rich in sallows and constitute important breeding grounds for the butterfly. Sallows increased greatly in abundance on the combe slopes there following severe storm damage inflicted during 1987 and 1990.

Road improvements have provided new habitat for sallows, and many a stretch of bypass, or section of road straightening, has alleviated the impoverishment of the hedgerow and copse matrix within the farmed landscape on the clay lands. Now that the importance of sallows for biodiversity is becoming recognised, they are being encouraged along new roads, where appropriate. Unfortunately, it seems that Purple Emperors will not lay eggs on sallow foliage facing busy road corridors, and I have searched hard for eggs and larvae on roadside sallows along the A325 that runs through Alice Holt Forest, and along the A4 and A346 that border Savernake Forest. The buffeting seems to put them off. However, they will lay readily on the sheltered forest side.

In places, sallows have been deliberately planted, as wildlife-friendly screening, and on account of the pace at which they grow. The National Trust and other conservation organisations regularly include sallows in plantings to screen off new car parks and workshop buildings. Sallows can even help form a useful shelter belt between gardens and their hinterland.

Until recently, railway corridors provided much suitable habitat for Purple Emperors, before Network

Rail declared war on trees and shrubs. On many a rail journey I have looked out for trackside sallows, and by doing so have traced the fingers of the Purple Empire that run in and out of London and other southern cities and towns. The utilisation of railway, road, canal and river corridors may explain how the Purple Emperor has become a butterfly of suburbia. Also important here is our habit of allowing developers to 'sit' on land scheduled for development, whilst prices rise. Sallows and their insect fauna can thrive during that period of neglect, before the bulldozers move in. In other European countries, though, urban brownfield habitats scarcely occur, as redevelopment is instant. Pop-up nature reserves, as these transient sites become, are undoubtedly of significant potential for the Purple Emperor in more urban areas, especially where sallows and willows are allowed to grow around water edges and in damp hollows.

The Purple Emperor is now also becoming recognised as a species of riverine woodland in shallow valleys and on floodplains, breeding in sallow carrs and perhaps also on willows growing along riverbanks and in the hedges of riverside meadows. This may be a new development, or us simply playing catch-up on a long-established occurrence. The butterfly might actually be quite well established in shallow river valleys rich in sallows and willows within its range, but we have only just begun to look. Such populations appear to be very small, diffuse and unusually hard to spot – even by Purple Emperor standards.

New localities are steadily being discovered along the shallow chalk streams of Hampshire and Wiltshire, where the Purple Emperor seems to be breeding primarily on Grey Willow and its main hybrid, Rusty Sallow, where it occurs, and possibly on some true willows too. Whether this represents new colonisation or a gross oversight may never be known. I suspect a bit of both.

The butterfly certainly occurs around old gravel pits in central southern and South East England, though probably excluding those dominated by Osier and its close hybrids (which may be too narrow-leaved for the larvae). It may be very under-recorded in such habitats, where sallows and willows abound. I for one deserve a serious black mark for not looking for it in the Cotswold Water Park on the Gloucestershire–Wiltshire border, where I live, until 2019, when I quickly turned it up.

What is hugely impressive is the Purple Emperor's recent colonisation of the Cambridgeshire Fens, including long-established and well-recorded nature reserves such as Woodwalton Fen National Nature Reserve (see county accounts in Appendix). Research is required to determine the extent to which the Purple Emperor breeds on these small-leaved, narrow-leaved sallows.

Our nature conservation movement struggles to recognise scrub as a valid habitat. Scrub is regarded as an incursion, because it ousts more valued old grassland or ancient heathland. At best, it is seen as a transitional habitat towards another derogatory term, secondary woodland. The amount of money, effort and resources

that go into 'controlling scrub' is scarcely justified by the
end product, which is almost invariably the
recommencement of the process of scrub invasion and
development. The war against scrub is everywhere, and
conservationists are losing it, as they lack the technology
to kill it off. Like the Daleks, it keeps coming back. The
stuff is running rings round us, much to the benefit of
the Purple Emperor, which is, essentially, a species of
sallow-rich scrubland. (For more on the war against
scrub, see Chapter 17.) The current desire to establish
more woodland, to address climate change issues, is likely
to rationalise the conservation management of scrub.

Scrub moves in whenever we let go. This is the
message from Knepp Wildland, where vast sallow thickets
quickly developed over fields taken out of cereal and
maize production and allowed to revert to wood pasture.
Within 15 years, what was previously intensive yet
unproductive dairy and arable farmland was hosting the
largest population of the Purple Emperor ever
documented in the UK, and much of continental
Europe.

Knepp is not, though, unique. There is a scatter of
fields and field margins elsewhere on the clay lands that
have come out of arable production, on which cereal
farming proved unprofitable. Nature has been allowed
back in, and, if downwind of sallows, these fields and
margins quickly become colonised, and taken over.
There is a block of 10 hectares of pure sallow jungle in
the south-west sector of Junction 15 of the M4 (Swindon
East), which has developed over an abandoned cereal
field on heavy clay. It is on land sloping down towards,
and in full view of, that busy motorway, and is crowned

by ancient oak woodland. It has been suitable for the Purple Emperor for nearly 20 years. How many butterfly enthusiasts have driven past, not realising that they are passing one of the best tracts of Purple Emperor habitat in the UK? It may soon be lost to development, of course, when the amorphous mass that is Swindon jumps across the M4.

Likewise, in August 2018 I was shown an 8-hectare abandoned wood-edge field on the Weald Clay just west of Lewes in East Sussex, which had been taken out of arable production in 1997. Broad-leaved sallows immediately sowed themselves in, and took over entirely. They were coppiced in 2002 but immediately regrew. This is the best Purple Emperor breeding ground I have ever seen, in terms of sallow quality and quantity, even better than Knepp's, being almost wholly of the preferred Goat Willow-type sallows. Along with the adjoining ancient woodland, which is managed primarily for pheasant shooting, it holds one of the best populations of the Purple Emperor in England – and is in the safe hands of enlightened farmers.

The simple truth is that clay fields taken out of uneconomic cereal farming, or maize production, make excellent Purple Emperor habitat – even fields with a history of being heavily fertilised and sprayed with herbicides such as glyphosate and atrazine. All that's needed is for the fields to be downwind of a sallow stand and to be left bare or, better still, scarified, so that sallow seed can fall down on bare clay – and for them to be within the butterfly's impressive colonisation range.

The Purple Emperor has recently been discovered in a number of historic parks, including several of the outer London parks, where sallows and other willows occur around waterbodies and in damp hollows. There is a now a well-known colony on Hampstead Heath, and the butterfly appears to be resident on both Richmond Park and Wimbledon Common.

The Butterflies for the New Millennium database holds modern era records of Purple Emperors from over 50 gardens in 11 counties (up to and including 2017). This list consists mainly of passing visits to gardens in private ownership, but also includes some of England's most famous gardens, notably Cliveden in Buckinghamshire, Mottisfont and The Vyne in Hampshire, and Nymans and Sheffield Park in Sussex (all of which are owned by the National Trust). One of the most memorable Purple Emperors I ever saw was a pristine male weaving its way through tall delphiniums standing sublimely in a well-maintained herbaceous border in a large private garden near Alton in Hampshire, inspecting each bloom, and flickering its full range of iridescent blues and purples in approval. This butterfly gets around.

Although the Purple Emperor may not be breeding at all frequently in ordinary gardens, due to the absence of sallows, the males certainly establish territories over tall trees along the edges of many privately owned gardens. There are at least five territories in gardens along the eastern edge of Alice Holt Forest, including one of the forest's best – a property I mentioned in *In Pursuit of Butterflies* (2015) and named 'Seven Ways', as it was then the headquarters of a branch of a religious movement.

One could watch Purple Emperors from the kitchen window there, though a better display could be seen from the mezzanine window upstairs. Best of all, in Odiham, Hampshire, males fly up to an old Victorian town garden from sallows along the Basingstoke Canal and nearby bypass, half a mile downslope. Imagine seeing Purple Emperors squabbling while you are doing the washing up, or taking a bath! That option is probably open to dozens of households in central southern and South East England, only no one has realised (at present, I am probably the only person to have observed *Apatura iris* from the bath, which I have managed to achieve on two occasions while in the outdoor bath at Knepp glamping site).

Every wildlife garden of any real size on clayey soil within the Purple Empire needs to have its own small sallow stand. It may not be visited annually, but it will be used by the butterfly from time to time and would form an essential component of the habitat matrix that the Purple Emperor requires, besides supporting much other biodiversity. The bushes could be maintained by periodic coppicing, to prevent them becoming oversized.

A large female Goat Willow tree in the garden of Seven Ways was visited annually by egg-laying females during the early 2000s. I regularly found eggs and young larvae there. It was the perfect tree, precisely the type of tree which the females arduously seek out. Would that such trees – I call them alpha sallows – were common, and easy to describe!

CHAPTER NINE

Sallow identification and preferences: a veritable nightmare

Egg-laying résumé – Sallow taxonomy and identification –
Breeding site selection: a study in Savernake Forest – Leaf
thickness, foliage development and tree age – Some conclusions

One might think that the positioning of eggs by a female butterfly would be a straightforward affair. Wrong, very wrong. A female butterfly will seek to lay her eggs on or close to the right species of plant, which is in the correct physical and biochemical condition, and is growing in a position that offers a suitable microclimate to support the resultant caterpillars. She has to plan ahead.

Worse, with species like the Purple Emperor whose larvae feed during two differing seasons punctuated by winter hibernation (see Chapter 11), the location needs to satisfy larval requirements during two differing vegetation growth phases, and must provide hibernation niches. Egg laying is therefore scientifically complex. Understanding it is fundamental to understanding a butterfly's ecology, though with some species it is very difficult to study, notably with canopy-dwelling species, and especially with the Purple Emperor.

The situation here is complicated by the fact that the identification of the numerous different types of southern lowland sallows is extremely difficult, due to rampant hybridisation, and the Empress favours some types more than others – if she can find them – but 'type' itself is hard to define. I am sorry that all this is both dense and scientifically naive. Treat it with a pinch of salt or, better, a large G and T (see Taxa in Glossary, p. 394).

Nothing is simple with Purple Emperors, including identifying the larval foodplant, the humble sallow, which we learnt as children to call 'pussy willow'. Sallows are indeed a type of willow and belong to the same family, Salicaceae, which also includes poplars and Aspen. Unfortunately, sallows and willows hybridise with each other like mad, with different taxonomic forms dominating from place to place. Trying to identify individual bushes and local forms is generally a nightmare.

Worse still, sallow identification characteristics, as in R D Meikle's *Willows and Poplars of Great Britain and Ireland* (1984) and Stace's *New Flora of the British Isles* (2019), are not strongly relevant to foodplant selection in the Purple Emperor. This is because the Empress usually selects leaves with certain characteristics that are at best loosely relevant to tree identification. In other words, the Purple Emperor is speaking a different language to our botanists, and is functioning rather outside our botanical framework.

I would like to say that I am confident at identifying the southern lowland sallows, willows, Osier, poplars and Aspen that the Purple Emperor might utilise. It may even be that few people have looked at the southern lowland woodland sallows as closely as I have (it is not a fashionable or attractive area of botany – in fact, it's maddening). However, this subject area is a miasma, and the more I look the less confident I am, because hybridisation is rampant and the taxonomy often seems inadequate. My conclusion, having been taught sallow identification by some of the country's top botanists during different eras (including Dr Francis Rose, Dr Oliver Rackham and the original 'tree man', Alan Mitchell) is that the taxonomy of the UK's southern lowland woodland sallows needs serious attention – a life's work for an ace botanist.

Our butterfly books state that the type of sallow most favoured by the Purple Emperor in England is the Goat Willow or Great Sallow (*Salix caprea*). For once, the books are (almost) right, though sallow taxonomy has become more complicated since most of them were written. Goat Willow is a small tree that usually produces orbicular (round) leaves, though leaf shape is not consistent and diverse shapes occur, including obovate (wider near the tip than the base). Often, Goat Willow has leaf-tip spikes that bend to one side. The leaf undersides possess fine grey hairs, though variably. The Purple Emperor seems to use some of these leaf shapes but avoids others, but I have not managed to figure this out.

The difficulty is that Goat Willow readily hybridises, producing narrower-leaved forms. Some of these hybrids are close to true *S. caprea*, while others are close to the Rusty or Common Sallow (*S. cinerea oleifolia*), the main source of hybridisation and the commonest of our sallows. These *S. caprea* x *S. cinerea* hybrids are generally known as *S. x reichardtii* hybrids. I call them 'Reichardtii hybrids'.

From the point of view of Purple Emperor ecology, these 'Reichardtii hybrids' divide three-ways: (1) those

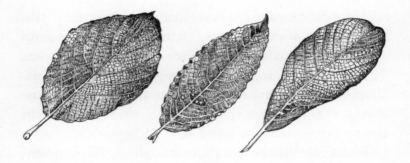

leaning towards true Goat Willow, which can be called 'caprea-type hybrids' or 'Goat Willow types'; (2) 'mainstream Reichardtii hybrids', which are approximately halfway between Goat Willow and Rusty Sallow, and are moderately broad-leaved, though decidedly long-leaved; and (3) 'narrow-leaved hybrids', which veer more towards Rusty Sallow and are narrow-leaved. In winter, buds and bark characteristics assist identification.

Although generally short-lived, Goat Willow trees can live for up to 300 years. Savernake Forest in Wiltshire holds a scattering of veteran Goat Willow-type trees (mostly 'caprea-type hybrids' and 'mainstream Reichardtii hybrids' in my language). These specimen trees have been number tagged, and are included in the Woodland Trust's Ancient Tree Inventory. But few sallows, of any description, live long – because foresters deem them valueless, and hoick them out.

The true Rusty or Common Sallow has leaves that are twice as long as they are wide, and leaf undersides that have a fine silver felt and rusty hairs beneath the veins, supposedly (often these reddish hairs are scarcely visible).

Rusty Sallows and the three main 'Reichardtii hybrids' are the commonest sallows in most Purple Emperor woods. True Goat Willow is quite scarce in many districts. For example, it is all but absent from Fermyn Woods and Rockingham Forest in Northamptonshire. Meikle says that it is often restricted to wood edges, as seems to be the case in Rockingham Forest.

The Grey Willow or Grey Sallow (*S. cinerea cinerea*) grows mainly in peaty fens in southern and, especially, eastern England. Many of these fens have recently been colonised by the Purple Emperor. Similar colonisation has also taken place in Holland. Until the last decade or so, this small-leaved bush (and its close hybrids) appeared to be unused by the butterfly. Perhaps this usage was overlooked, historically, though available evidence suggests that the Purple Emperor started to use it during the 1990s.

Eared Willow (*S. aurita*) is primarily a shrub of northern and western Britain, but it also occurs in acidic marshes in southern and eastern England, where it hybridises with other sallows. It is a known foodplant of the Purple Emperor in Germany and may be utilised here, perhaps especially its hybrids with broader-leaved sallows.

There are also various true willows that may be relevant to the Purple Emperor, plus their hybrids (between the above sallow types and true willows). The extent to which the Purple Emperor breeds on true willows has yet to be clarified. We simply have not looked. I keep an open mind, not least because the butterfly appears not to be as fixed in its ways as butterfly experts thought, and may be locally adaptive.

It is clear that the females will sometimes lay eggs on White Willow (*S. alba*) and that larvae will successfully develop on it. Indeed, some of the people who breed butterflies in captivity use it as the main pabulum (foodplant) for the species. A full-grown larva was found on White Willow at Bookham Common by beetle expert Ian Menzies. At Knepp Wildland, I regularly see males sallow searching over stands of White Willow, and in 2019 I finally observed a female laying an egg on a streamside White Willow tree (and tossed my hat into the air).

The extent to which other types of willow are utilised by the Purple Emperor has yet to be determined. It may be that Crack Willow (*S. fragilis*) and the Cricket Bat Willow (a hybrid between *S. alba* and *S. fragilis*) may be used in some situations.

There is, incidentally, a single record (noted in *The Entomologist's Record*) of a half-grown Purple Emperor larva being found on Aspen, at Black Down near Haslemere, West Sussex, in 1918. In Germany, larvae have occasionally been found on Aspen, Black Poplar (*Populus nigra*) and Balsam Poplar (*P. candicans*). I have looked on Aspen in and around Savernake Forest in high egg-lay years, but without success.

As suggested in the section on egg laying in Chapter 6 (p. 175), the whole subject area of where Purple Emperor females deposit their eggs needs thorough scientific investigation, as it is fundamental to understanding the insect's ecology. I have only carried out some basic work. Nonetheless, I am confident that at least 25 per cent of eggs are laid randomly, perhaps by stressed females, though the vast majority are placed on foliage that appears to have been carefully selected.

In the late summer of 2009, I conducted what is termed an absolute search of all accessible branches of 62 sallow bushes within an area of some 20 hectares in Savernake Forest, using a shepherd's crook to pull biddable branches down (if it did not readily come down, it stayed put). The task took an entire Ashes Test match, which I listened to diligently via a pocket radio.

A sample of 61 eggs and young larvae were found on Goat Willow, Rusty Sallow and their hybrids. This sample indicated that the insect was selecting leaves of a certain texture and colour, which were strongly associated with sallow growth in moderately heavy shade. These findings were then trialled as a survey technique in the rest of the forest, with considerable success – I had cracked how to find Purple Emperor eggs and late summer larvae, big time. I have continued to develop this method, finding a total of nearly a thousand eggs, young larvae and failed breeding sites (where larvae had vanished, but where egg-case bases and/or the distinctive leaf-tip silk pads were present) over a period of 10 years.

Back in 2009, I measured what could be measured on the leaves, and estimated what I could not (estimations were carried out over a short time period, to ensure some consistency). Most of the resultant data proved irrelevant, and does not need to be recorded here (data are often meaningless, including that most easily gathered).

What appeared to prove meaningful was leaf thickness, as measured crudely by a rather inadequate micrometer (better-quality equipment was needed), and percentage of midday and afternoon shade (as guesstimated, I hope consistently) on the selected leaf spray. These crucial characteristics largely determined leaf colour and texture.

I found that Goat Willow and Goat Willow types (caprea-type sallows) were preferentially selected, even when they formed only a small percentage of the available sallow resource, revealing 80 per cent of eggs and larvae. Mainstream Reichardtii and narrow-leaved hybrids produced only 8 per cent of eggs and larvae, even though they constituted the bulk of the sallow resource. Rusty Sallow types held just 12 per cent of eggs and larvae, again suggesting avoidance.

On average, one egg or larva was found every 28 minutes. On Goat Willow-type trees the encounter rate was one every 17 minutes. This compares to one every 45 minutes on Rusty Sallows, and one every 50 minutes on mainstream Reichardtii and narrow-leaved hybrids. Female trees more regularly produced leaves of the preferred colour and texture, and were consequently preferred to male trees.

The ideal foliage is mid-green in colour, of medium thickness (neither thick nor thin), matt or dull on the upper surface (as opposed to glossy) and soft to feel (as opposed to being hard and stiff). The Empress generally avoids laying eggs on leaves with glossy upper surfaces, perhaps because the efficacy of the 'glue' she uses – which adheres the egg to the leaf – is significantly reduced. Favoured leaves are small to medium-sized, as large leaves are generally too thick, hard, glossy and dark.

Here's a bit of rubbish science for you, though a useful field test: if the leaf makes a 'thwacky' sound when vigorously pinched between finger and thumb it's probably unsuitable for young Purple Emperor larvae.

'Thwacky' leaves suggest, as to an extent do thick leaves, that foliage can be too hard for tiny first-instar larvae. There's a lot of subjectivity and (consistent) guesstimation here, but it's the best I could manage. If you're unhappy with it, go and do better. This favoured foliage is a product of moderate to heavy shade, produced either by the sallow tree itself or, more commonly, by taller trees of other types.

Crucially, my study data suggested that only some 25–33 per cent of the total number of sallows in Savernake produced foliage that met the *mid-green medium-thickness soft, matt* category, and then only locally on the trees themselves (mainly on subcanopy sprays). Furthermore, a sample (effectively a stratified random sample) of 100 trees of all sallow taxa within the whole forest found sprays fitting the desired *mid-green medium-thickness soft, matt* profile patchily on only 34 trees.

However, Savernake, as a study site, lacked some of the sallow types that occur frequently in other Purple Emperor localities, notably some of the narrow-leaved varieties that are readily used, for example, in Southwater Forest, where they abound and where Goat Willow is scarce.

Leaf thickness and hardness seem to be strongly influenced by degree of shade and sun exposure, and also by how early in the year the host tree comes into leaf. The latter could well be vital, for I strongly suspect that the butterfly can become out of sync with a crucial phase of foliage development, with the females laying eggs when the leaves are past the optimum phase of suitability for young larvae, having become too thick and too coarse.

This might explain why the Purple Emperor population in a large Pyrenean valley system between Setcases and Camprodon in Catalonia collapsed spectacularly in 2019, during a good summer in that region. In August 2018, all the sallow foliage examined in the valley appeared to be far too thick for larvae, and no larvae were located during extensive searches that autumn. The population collapse was by far the biggest I know of (other than local declines caused by the mass felling of sallows).

Early springs that are followed by lengthy spells of wet weather, which delay larval and pupal development but permit foliage progression, may lead to much of the sallow foliage being less than ideal for the laying females and unsuitable for first-instar larvae. This might explain poor egg lay in early spring years, such as 2017, and good egg lay after late (or old-fashioned) springs, such as those of 2013 and 2018. I will return to this issue in the final chapter.

This is a massive area, and I have not even mentioned the possible (or likely) impact of atmospheric nitrogen deposition on sallow leaf suitability, the issue here being that atmospheric nitrogen has been found to thicken upper leaf surfaces. I am way out of my depth here, and merely hope that these musings stimulate the much-needed scientific research.

Another key factor to consider is the age of the branch or spray selected by laying females, and used by pre-hibernation larvae. My data indicate, clearly for once, that relatively young branches are selected, usually two to four years old, and that the leaf sprays most readily utilised by first-instar larva are on first-year twigs. This means that relatively young sallow trees are often preferred (five to 10 years old, approximately) but that young leader shoots (one to three years old) coming off old-growth trunks and branches are also readily utilised, as is coppice or pollard regrowth – if sufficiently shaded. Tree age itself is rather a red herring, as old trees can produce suitable foliage on young shoots. Thus, in Savernake Forest I regularly find eggs and larvae on genuinely old trees, including centenarians, but only on young growth in shaded situations. Old leaves on old growth are wholly unsuitable for young Purple Emperor larvae, as are young leaves on first-year leaders.

Please treat this entire section as hypothesis, not as proven scientific fact. I am, however, convinced that this subject area holds the key to understanding the ecology of the Purple Emperor, although the crucial factors may be something to do with leaf hardness or density, rather than thickness alone. Degree of exposure and leaf spray age are almost certainly important.

Focusing in on what is known, the Purple Emperor lays the majority of its eggs on foliage with the specific growth characteristics that are desired by first-instar larvae. This ideal foliage is by no means frequent at site level. Indeed, much of the available foliage is at best only marginally suitable. Degree of shade is clearly important, playing a key role in producing and maintaining foliage with the right characteristics. Of course, branches can be too heavily shaded, and consequently unsuitable, offering pale foliage and sprays suffering from dieback.

None of these findings are radically new, and mainly constitute refinements of thinking and knowledge that have been developing for some time. Ken Willmott, in his detailed 1987 report states that some 80 to 90 per cent of eggs are deposited high up, just below the shaded crowns of tall sallows, and that females often disappear from view whilst in the process of laying their eggs. He believes that this is because young larvae are uncomfortable in the bright and hot sunshine that late summer brings, adding – crucially – that the essential requirement appears to be shade, irrespective of aspect.

Available evidence indicates that shade serves two essential purposes: first, to prevent first-instar larvae (and possibly eggs) from desiccating, and secondly, to ensure a supply of foliage of the optimum condition for first-instar (and perhaps second-instar) larvae. This may even be the key aspect of the ecology of the Purple Emperor, but it will take much seriously good science to prove it!

CHAPTER TEN

Eggs and late summer larvae

The egg stage – Vulnerable first-instar larvae – Second-instar larvae – Third-instar larvae – The 'egg lay', and some data

I found my first Purple Emperor egg on 6 July 1976, in Alice Holt Forest. This represented a major breakthrough, as previously I had watched exasperated as females flew high into sallows, presumably laying eggs, but always out of reach – on high-stemmed trees impossible to climb, or high up on coppiced stems too thick to bend down. I had glimpsed an egg momentarily, through binoculars, the previous July, as a female condescended to lay in view, but tantalisingly out of reach, in Dragons Green. That sallow stem was too weak to support my weight, too thick to bend down, too flimsy to support a leaning ladder, and inaccessible for a step ladder. I was owed eggs, big time, and the profuse egg lay of the long hot summer of 1976 provided the payback.

When first laid, a Purple Emperor egg is a dull blueish-green, about half the size of a glass pinhead, maybe 1 millimetre high and of similar width. It is dome-shaped, widest at the base, and has a number of vertical ribs or keels that almost meet at the top – rather like a miniature product of the Edwardian blancmange mould my mother used. Some authorities, including Frohawk, say there are 14 of these finely serrated ridges, others say 15 or 16. The small number I have bothered

to place under a microscope had 13. This represents yet
another piece of trivial science.

After three to five days, depending on the weather,
much of the lower third, above the egg base, turns a
curious purplish-brown, forming a dark band. Later, the
entire egg becomes dull black as the tiny larva develops –
the blackness is caused by the larva's (relatively) huge
black head, and the dullness by the thickness of the egg
case. Until the caterpillar shows through, the egg resembles
the pouch galls induced by gall mites (Arachnida:
Eriophyidae), or even smaller versions of the pepper
pot-shaped galls produced by sawflies (*Symphyta*), a clever
piece of mimicry. These galls are commonly found on
sallow leaves, especially the narrow-leaved varieties.

Different books offer different figures as to how long
the egg stage lasts. Take those figures with a pinch of salt,
or two, for the duration of the egg stage depends entirely
on the weather, particularly the temperature. In heatwave
conditions, Purple Emperor eggs may develop and hatch
within 10 days. The shortest duration I have recorded (in
the wild) is nine days, during the heatwaves of 1976 and
2018. In cool, wet seasons I have recorded eggs taking as
long as 20 days to hatch. The normal range is 13–15 days.

The earliest egg recorded in any year in British
entomological history was the one laid at Knepp
Wildland on 18 June 2017, observed by Neil Hulme.
That record will not last long, given the pace at which
the timing of the Purple Emperor flight season is
advancing. The latest unhatched eggs have been recorded
is mid-September 1965 (see *Notes & Views of the Purple
Emperor*). My own latest unhatched egg date is 30 August
1977, an exceptionally late season.

Above: a pristine male Purple Emperor feeding on fox scat, Fermyn Woods, Northamptonshire, July 2014.

Left: male underside on a ride, also Fermyn Woods, June 2014 (Neil Hulme).

Below: female underside, Knepp Wildland, West Sussex, July 2018.

Left: a pristine female Purple Emperor displaying, Knepp Wildland, June 2018.

Left: female aberration *lugenda* upperside, Fermyn Woods, July 2012.

Below: a middle-aged male on his oak-top territory, Knepp Wildland, June 2018.

Above: a male Purple Emperor feeding on a diseased oak tree, Knepp Wildland, June 2018.

Below: three male Purple Emperors, one female and a Comma feeding on a minor oak sap bleed, Knepp Wildland, June 2018.

Top: two pristine males feeding on fox scat, Knepp Wildland, June 2018.

Above: a male cleaning his tongue after feeding on the track, Knepp Wildland, June 2018.

Right: a mated female sulking on a bramble flower after rejecting an over-amorous male in a 'tumbledown', Knepp Wildland, July 2018.

Above: male Purple Emperors battle for territories based on prominent canopy gaps, like between these tall oaks at Knepp Wildland, July 2017.

Below: Knepp Wildland's Purple Emperor Safari group, July 2017.

Opposite, clockwise from top left: A larva waiting for a sallow twig to flower before coming into leaf, Savernake Forest, Wiltshire, March 2019. A fully-grown female larva, note the silk pad, Savernake Forest, June 2019. A larva colouring up on a yellowing leaf in preparation for hibernation, Savernake Forest, October 2018. A pupating larva, Marlpost Wood, West Sussex, June 2018.

Right: a fully-grown larva wandering up tree to pupate, Savernake Forest, June 2019.

Below: the vacated pupal case of 'Raymond' (see p. 277), Knepp Wildland, August 2016.

Above: mixing the shrimp–paste bait to pour out as puddles along the open rides, in order to encourage Purple Emperors to descend and feed, Fermyn Woods, July 2014.

Right: Neil Hulme reacting to 'a trousering', Fermyn Woods, July 2014.

Below: the author experiencing a visitation from above, Fermyn Woods, July 2012.

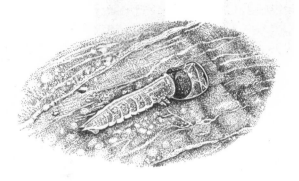

Immediately prior to hatching, the larva's oversized head and yellowish body, curled up, become clearly visible. Eggs hatch, seemingly, at all times of day and night. According to Frohawk, the larva literally eats its way out, nibbling away on the inside until a lid on the top casing splits open. The big-headed larva crawls out and almost immediately begins to consume the walls and roof of the egg case (called the chorion), but almost always leaves the base untouched.

The uneaten egg-case base may persist on the leaf for weeks afterwards, though these shiny bases are readily washed off when August or September are wet. I have found remnant egg-case bases on leaves as late as 5 November (Marlpost Wood, West Sussex, 2011). This last fact indicates the durability of the material of which the egg case is made, and of the biological glue with which it is adhered to the leaf – our technology may be able to learn from this natural superglue. The egg casing is not quite tough enough though, for eggs can be pierced and their contents sucked out by predatory invertebrates with needle-like, piercing mouthparts, such as the Tree Damsel Bug.

Occasionally, infertile (empty) eggs are laid, especially during exceptionally hot weather – maybe by females in need of a second mating. I feel I find every infertile egg the Empress lays, as part of my trials and tribulations with this wanton butterfly.

The entire world seems to be set against the survival of baby caterpillars, known by entomologists as first-instar or L1 larvae. Survival rates are low, with larvae readily succumbing to a variety of predatory invertebrates – various ants, beetles, bugs, hunting spiders, wasps, weevils and earwigs. One Victorian vicar confessed in one of the entomological journals to suffering recurrent nightmares about 'monstrous earwigs' consuming his precious Purple Emperor larvae, kept in a muslin bag (known as a 'sleeve') on a sallow branch in his garden.

Denys Watkins-Pitchford (BB) believed that the Common Flower Bug is a major predator of infant Purple Emperor larvae. Its mouthparts are strong enough to pierce human flesh. He had nightmares about it. However, it is more likely that his problem species was the highly similar *Anthocoris nemoralis* (often called the Common Tree Flower Bug) which occurs commonly on trees.

Expert butterfly breeders Martin White and Colin Wiskin hold that flower bugs are major predators in captivity, and I have also lost captive Purple Emperor larvae to these small heteropteran bugs – by failing to ensure newly sleeved foliage was free of them. In the wild, I have recorded L1 larvae being killed or taken by flower bugs, common social wasps and, in one instance, the Brown Tree Ant, a very local arboreal species. Dennis Dell once watched an L1 larva being carried off by 'a brown ant'. In addition, it is likely that arboreal species of shieldbugs, notably the Red-legged Shieldbug, as well as the Tree Damsel Bug, the larvae of various arboreal lacewings (*Neuroptera*) and the Harlequin Ladybird, are major predators of young Purple Emperor larvae – the problem is catching them in the act. These should all be assumed guilty until proven innocent.

Wasps may well be major predators. However, the two similar-looking species of social wasp that constitute what we call the 'common wasp' (the true Common Wasp and the German Wasp) were relatively scarce during the bulk of the period 2009–19, in which most of my studies took place. The scanty evidence that is available suggests that their populations collapsed during the excessively wet summer of 2012 and only started to recover properly during the hot summer of 2018. The problem here is that wasp populations, unlike those of butterflies, are not yet being closely monitored in the UK.

Infant Purple Emperor larvae, measuring 3 millimetres long when newly hatched, are highly prone to being washed off the leaves by heavy rain during their first few hours of life. Even a short, sharp shower can cause losses of newly hatched larvae, while a heavy thunderstorm can be devastating. After a few hours, as Frohawk discovered, they spin some silk strands, to form a loose pad to which their rear claspers can properly adhere. Once they are a few days old, and have spun a proper pad, they are not easily washed away.

On a leaf, L1 larvae usually rest, when not feeding, on the midrib extremity, always facing inwards towards the stalk, on leaf tips that are often curled and downward-pointing, and which therefore act as funnels for water run-off. Sitting in the rain drip undoubtedly affords protection from some predators, but has its own, very obvious disadvantages in very wet weather. Larvae might be less prone to rain-wash if they lived on the leaf undersides, but would then probably be more vulnerable to invertebrate predators sheltering there. This behaviour suggests that larvae are more concerned about predators than heavy rainfall, and use rain to their advantage.

I have also observed first-instar larvae die due to desiccation during hot weather (in 1976, 2006, 2017 and 2018). Heat desiccation, primarily through exposure to direct sunlight, is almost certainly a major cause of mortality in the highly vulnerable L1 stage, both in captivity and in the wild.

Most of these tiny larva rest on the leaf on which the egg has been laid, moving periodically to feed on the nearby leaf edges. They feed intermittently, when the foliage is dry, retreating to their flimsy leaf-tip silk pad after each feed. They are in a hurry to get through this highly vulnerable instar as quickly as possible, though they must also spend time digesting their food. As the larva feeds, the body gradually expands, to nearly 5 millimetres in length, and changes from yellow-green to mid-green, with oblique paler stripes. It matches the colour of the leaf surface increasingly well. In fact, and crucially, Purple Emperor larvae are masters of the cryptic arts, slowly changing colour to match their substrate as the seasons change.

My (very basic) research found that infant larvae cannot feed on leaves that are too coarse and thick, though I was unable to quantify the limits. When I first suspected that this was an issue, I condemned – in the name of science – a number of larvae to death by trying to force-feed them a range of thick, coarse leaves, in a crude but necessary experiment. In brief, L1 larvae are never found on large, thick leaves on the outer foliage in situations exposed to the sun, especially leaves that are dark green or blue-green in hue and with crinkled edges. Instead, they are found almost exclusively on leaves in the medium size range (3–6 centimetres in length by 2–4 centimetres in width) that are mid-green in colour, have non-glossy (that is, matt) upper surfaces, and are of what can loosely be called medium thickness. Such foliage occurs only in-bush or on shady edges. I will explore this further when describing the second and third instars, in the following pages, and in Chapter 16. As suggested in the previous chapter, the issue may not so much be leaf thickness, as hardness or density.

Most L1 larvae feed on a single leaf, providing it is suitable, but they can change leaf, or feed from a different leaf while maintaining their original 'seat leaf' (where the egg was laid). If highly dissatisfied with the leaves on their egg spray they can travel fair distances to relocate – I have recorded L1 larvae journeying distances of up to 1.5 metres, over foliage and smooth stems. They can be surprisingly mobile.

Frohawk, ever with an eye for detail, records that one (captive-reared) first-instar larva produced 245 excrements – tiny black parcels of caterpillar droppings, called 'frass'. I confess to never having counted. He states that his captive larvae were ready to change their skins, into L2 (the second instar), after nine days. In the wild, I have found that this period can be as short as seven days, in warm dry weather, or as long as 14 days, in cool wet weather. It is probably safe to assume that mortality rates increase with time spent in the L1 state, but I simply do not possess the data to demonstrate this.

Frohawk states that the moulting process from L1 to L2 takes three days to complete, and that larvae then rest for a day afterwards. Much, again, depends on the weather, for in fine weather larvae can go through a skin change with relative ease, but in poor weather the skin changing process can take a week. Ken Willmott timed one larva taking more than 40 hours to change from L1 to L2, and I have recorded the skin change taking around 30 hours in fine weather. Rather wondrously, caterpillars do not merely change skin, but gain a replacement head with each skin change – just imagine that!

Sadly, at best about 40 per cent of L1 larvae seem to make it through to the second instar in the wild. However, rates vary from year to year, and many of my annual samples have been unsatisfactorily small (around four or five larvae).

The earliest I have found second-instar larvae is 20 July 2018, in Marlpost Wood. In addition, larvae were entering this L2 stage in late July in 1976, in Alice Holt Forest, and in 2009 in Savernake Forest.

Once out of the L1 stage, Purple Emperor larvae possess a prominent pair of forward-facing V-shaped horns, covered with miniature tubercles (warts) and fine whitish hairs. I have little idea what purpose these horns serve, but they are handsome, and I have observed Purple Emperor larvae use them to toss small insects, such as aphids, away, and also to wrestle with each other when one larva dares to invade another's seat leaf – a glimpse into the territorial antics of the adult males. Perhaps they are some sensory device, maybe even with a built-in weather station?

The body of an L2 larva is mid-green, granular in texture, with nine oblique pale stripes and with each segment clearly defined, ending with ochreous-brown anal points. The sixth pair of oblique stripes are bright yellow in colour, slightly raised, and join at the top, giving the impression of a bright yellow 'V' just over halfway down the body. In contrast, the head is a dull, deep brown colour, with whitish hairs.

The insect is in less of a hurry to get out of this instar, but progress depends on weather conditions. Some larvae move to a new seat leaf shortly after changing to L2, usually on the same leaf spray as the vacated L1 seat leaf and the egg-case remains. Such moves are probably associated with food quality – primarily leaf thickness or hardness – and climatological factors, notably exposure to heat.

Second-instar larvae, again, feed intermittently, mainly on either side of the leaf, close to the tip, where they sit. These paired and almost symmetric feeding hollows become increasingly prominent. They are quite distinctive, to the practised eye, and are unique to the Purple Emperor (at least in the UK). Searching for this feeding damage is a good way of locating L2 and L3 larvae during the late summer and autumn periods.

Once in the L2 stage, larvae also start to produce considerable amounts of silk, primarily on their leaf-tip silk pad but also along the leaf midrib. The latter acts as a secure highway between the silk pad and the weak point where the leaf petiole joins the main stem, which they assiduously reinforce with silk. Vacated leaf-tip silk pads shine quite prominently in certain light conditions and persist for several weeks in dry autumns.

When disturbed, autumn larvae in both the L2 stage and the highly similar-looking L3 stage, journey up the midrib to deposit more silk, moving their heads from side to side as they spin. For a while I thought they were scything leaf hairs away, but it appears that they are primarily laying more fine silk strands, and bending the leaf hairs down, then using silk to keep them down, while maintaining designated highways. This seems to be similar to what White Admiral larvae do, as documented in a fascinating study by Barry Fox in 2005. From late-L2 stage onwards, Purple Emperor larvae are serial spinners of silk.

Losses during the L2 stage are modest, much lower than in L1. Loss rates do not vary greatly from year to year, presumably because the larvae have become too large for some predatory invertebrates. I suspect that the L2 skin is thicker, and more difficult for small sucking invertebrates to penetrate. More crucially, L2 larvae seem to be much more weatherproof, and do not succumb to wash-off or heat desiccation.

When the larva is ready to change its skin into L3, the area behind the head – the neck, if you like – becomes yellowish and taught. Skin changing again takes two or three days, on average, depending on weather conditions. The earliest I have observed third-instar larvae in the wild is mid-August (2018). During my study period, larvae started to enter the L3 stage at the end of August, but most changed into L3 during early or mid-September. Occasional slow-developers have been recorded, notably in late seasons such as 1977, and after a poor August. It is rare to find L2 larvae after 21 September.

It is, though, difficult to tell the difference between late L2 and early L3 larvae. Both sit on leaf tips, facing inward. The difference is in head size and colour, with the head capsule being small and dark in late L2 larvae and large and mid-brown in L3 (until larvae change colour prior to hibernation). The body is highly similar, a handsome Lincoln green with oblique yellow-green stripes. This combination harmonises perfectly with the colour and texture of the sallow leaf surface.

In the wild, most larvae move to a new feeding and seat leaf after changing skin for the second time, to the L3 stage. This often involves moving to a new leaf spray, sometimes over distances of 2 or 3 metres. A few sedentary larvae remain on the same spray, even the same leaf, until they quit the foliage to enter hibernation on the stems.

Third-instar larvae spend much time in the 'praying mantis' position, in which the front two-thirds of the body is arched: the prolegs (front feet) are tucked in, and the head dips down towards the leaf. All the while the rear legs, or claspers, hold on tightly to the silk pad close to the leaf-tip edge. Larvae readily adopt this position when disturbed, suggesting that it is a

simple anti-predator device – the frequency with
which we see them in this posture suggests they are
often on red alert. If the foliage is moved violently,
though, they will crawl up the stem to add more silk
to where the midrib and the petiole join with the
main stem, fearing a gale.

One major problem for autumn Purple Emperor
larvae is Sallow Mildew. This white, powdery mould
occurs profusely on the upper surface of leaves on *Salix*
bushes (including poplars) growing below or close to
taller trees, especially bushes beneath the drip line of tall
oaks. Almost the entire foliage of sallow bushes can
become covered in the off-white mycelia (the vegetative
part of the fungus), though the mildew can easily be
rubbed off by dexterous use of finger and thumb. It is
often fatal to Purple Emperor larvae, though I know not
why. Fortunately, larvae are adept at finding unaffected
leaves or leaves that are only mildly affected. They may
be able to stomach modest amounts of mildew. This
mildew seems to be most prevalent in wet autumns and,
especially, after rainy Augusts, and likes the same, shadier
sallows as the Purple Emperors.

Once Purple Emperor larvae enter the third instar,
the pressure to grow rapidly is off them, and they slow
right down. Their minds appear to be set on winter.
They feed intermittently, only every few days, from
their feeding leaf, which may be different to their
chosen seat leaf, though it is always close by, if not
adjacent. The feeding leaf seemingly deteriorates in
quality, due to the ageing process, so it appears that
larvae are merely bulking up, rather than taking in more
nutrients – but I may be wrong here. As autumn

advances, their feeding events become more and more spasmodic, and the gaps between sessions lengthens, ceasing altogether by mid-October. They spend hours sitting there, doing precisely nothing, seemingly in some blissful Buddhist state, though it is actually one of watchful wakefulness.

As part of my studies in Savernake Forest, I methodically searched for eggs and, especially, young larvae throughout the forest. I did this religiously, from 2009 to 2019. I also recorded failed breeding sites; that is, vacant larval seat pads on leaves bearing larval feeding damage attributable to this species, plus or minus egg-case bases – places from where larvae had gone missing, presumed killed. I was conducting what is known as a standardised search, using a fixed method. We can call what I was trying to ascertain, and monitor, 'the annual egg lay', though 'autumn larval count' might be more accurate.

Each year, as summer waned and autumn flared, 40 hours of leaf searching took place, from the ground, lowering branches by means of a shepherd's crook. No tree climbing was involved, which would have been against Forestry Commission bylaws, health and safety consciousness for lone workers, and the capabilities of a knee in need of a replacement kneecap.

This sounds like one of the dullest tasks ever undertaken by humankind – staring obsessively at foliage for hours on end, until severe eye strain kicked in. Had I not been accompanied by cricket commentary on the radio I would have gone insane. The main trouble was dog walkers, who for reasons best known to them

sometimes regarded me as a threat (I was once reported
to the police, who presumably identified me from my
car registration, googled me, and determined that I was
looking for Purple Emperor caterpillars and was
completely harmless – top policing, love it, carry on).

I am rather proud of the data, shown in the table
below. This is thoroughly kosher data, which speaks
volumes about Purple Emperor population dynamics.

Year	Number found
2009	141
2010	59
2011	21
2012	22
2013	190
2014	24
2015	20
2016	17
2017	18
2018	76
2019	16
Total	604

The table suggests that the butterfly largely bumbles
around at relatively low population levels, producing 20
or so findable eggs and larvae a year in Savernake, but is
prone to sudden years of plenty, *annus mirabilis* years –
notably 2013 and 2009.

I would have found far more than a rather modest 76
in 2018, which was probably the best Purple Emperor
year of the 11, but for a local idiosyncrasy: the main ride

through the forest, called Grand Avenue, along which vehicles have right of access, had been resurfaced with limestone chippings, as opposed to the usual orange-coloured road hoggin, and the all-too-necessary speed bumps were not reinstated. Vehicles (mostly associated with dog walking) sped along Grand Avenue that hot dry summer, spitting high-speed chippings at any pedestrian foolhardy enough to dare to walk there and generating a dust cloud that must have been visible from space. All tree foliage within a 200-metre- wide corridor along this Capability Brown-designed avenue was coated with a thick film of chalky dust. This almost halved the number of suitable sallows for the Purple Emperor in Savernake that year (and again, more modestly, in 2019). It also severely damaged the lichen flora on the tree trunks.

Additionally, 2010 would have been a bumper 'egg-lay' year, had the adults not been blasted away by a mid-July gale before a proper quota of eggs had been deposited. A poor July can, of course, dramatically reduce the amount of eggs laid.

In summary, within the 11-year sequence I recorded two great years (2009 and 2013), two 'nearly were' years (2010 and 2018) and a lot of bumping around at low levels. It seems, then, that the butterfly periodically erupts out of subsistence-level existence, when weather conditions permit the larvae, pupae and adults to flourish.

What this table does not show, of course, is the number of sallows searched each year. Suffice it that tree numbers remained relatively stable until the 2018/19 dust storm episode, though it is hard to clarify what constituted a 'searched tree' (some trees offered an hour's searching, while others provided only two minutes' worth of reachable boughs).

The whole venture, of course, is based on the (massive) assumption that the females lay the same percentage of their eggs low down each year – for which there is no evidence either way. This has been a monumental piece of work, which I followed up by conducting detailed studies of the fate of Purple Emperor caterpillars during the winter months.

CHAPTER ELEVEN

Hibernation and the winter months

Introduction to hibernation – Colouring up – Journeying into hibernation – Buds, forks, scars and lesions – Predation by tits, and winter survival

Most British butterflies pass the winter as larvae. The Purple Emperor, for once, is content to be one of the pack, with its caterpillars spending five long and arduous months in hibernation. Strictly speaking, they are in diapause (the suspension of an insect's development due to adverse environmental conditions; in this case, winter). During my larval study period, 2009–19, most Purple Emperor larvae entered hibernation between late October and mid-November. Those that survived wakened between late March and mid-April.

Unless the temperature is around or below freezing, when they effectively freeze (though without perishing), larvae do not completely conk out but remain aware, while in a shallow torpor. They seem to know what's going on, but generally choose to ignore it or are unable to respond properly. In most winter weather conditions it is possible to rouse them with care, by breathing on them; they will waver their heads about briefly, before thinking better of it and bedding down again.

I like to think that they are lying there in meditative contemplation, quietly conjuring up spring, somehow, rather than merely dreaming wanly of it. In that respect they may be in harmony with the sleeping trees, which surely dream up and then summon almighty spring?

Hibernation is a very challenging time for Purple Emperor larvae, as they are mercilessly predated, primarily, it seems, by tits. They can also become stressed by extremes of wet, mildness and perhaps wind (which may cause them to desiccate). My studies suggest that mild winters, a major modern phenomenon, are providing significant new stresses for Purple Emperor larvae, by spoiling effective hibernation. It remains to be seen how this and other butterfly species will cope with these new challenges, which are almost certainly associated with climate change.

As sallow trees are deciduous, Purple Emperor larvae have little choice other than to vacate the leaves prior to leaf fall. Their caterpillar silk is not quite strong enough for them to affix their seat leaves to the tree for five wintry months. Although in captivity some larvae certainly hibernate on spun-up leaves, as Frohawk found when he bred the species in 1902/03, and Dennis Dell found more recently through captive-breeding studies in Switzerland, it seems that larvae seldom, if ever, attempt this in the wild – and I have looked, repeatedly. However, in December 2019, Ben Greenaway found two larvae attempting to hibernate on small silked-on leaves in Southwater Woods, West Sussex. One was quickly predated.

To date I have seen over 200 Purple Emperor larvae in hibernation in the wild, mostly in Savernake Forest. That's a sizeable sample by British butterfly standards, and mega by the Emperor's. It took 11 long winters. They are incredibly hard to find, even on trees known to have held larvae in early autumn. I find it hard to stomach, and somewhat difficult to believe, that an entomologist by the name of Dunk managed to find 12 hibernating larvae in three hours of searching in the early 1950s. However, Ben Greenaway managed to find an impressive 38 hibernating larvae in my old stamping ground of Southwater Woods during a marathon search early in the 2019/20 winter. Few others have looked, and then only fleetingly. Heslop and Stockley provide scanty information here. It seems that they, at best, occasionally dabbled. It can be done though, and the record to beat is a staggering 46 hibernating larvae found in a single day near Stuttgart in Germany.

Although hibernation is essentially something undertaken by L3 larvae, I have recorded a lone second-instar larva entering hibernation (during the winter of 2009/10). Unfortunately, it vanished during February, almost certainly succumbing to predation. However, butterfly breeders occasionally report the successful overwintering of second-instar larvae in captivity. Successful overwintering in the late L2 stage has also been recorded in the wild in Switzerland by Guy Padfield, and was reported on the Purple Emperor blog.

In autumn, Purple Emperor larvae become true masters of the cryptic arts (the correct scientific term is 'procrypsis'). They gradually change colour, usually starting in mid-October, from Lincoln green to the drab greys and browns of the coming winter. The paired projections nearly halfway down the dorsum (upper surface) change from yellow to dull orange.

Larvae cease feeding before they lose their green hues. The extent to which they are responding to shortening day length is unclear.

It is highly likely that colouring up occurs when larvae reach a certain size and weight. However, caterpillars are difficult to measure, as they expand or contract with elastic ease; and my studies lacked the sophisticated equipment necessary to weigh larvae of 7–9 millimetres in length, being based primarily on observation and recording. A detailed scientific account of the processes of pigmentation and diapause in *Apatura iris* was published in *The Entomologist's Record* in 1954 by F V L Jarvis. Like so much published science, though, it will appeal only to readers familiar with its specialist sophisticated language.

Colouring up usually takes 10 to 14 days to achieve, sometimes as long as 20 days. It is a gradual process which, curiously, is not linked to changes in leaf colour. Thus, you will find brown larvae on green leaves, and green larvae on yellowing or browning leaves – the latter stand out like sore thumbs. On two occasions I have observed distinctly green larvae go off into hibernation. One green larva successfully survived the winter of 2015/16, as did one found in the wild by H C Dunk.

Before quitting their final seat leaf, Purple Emperor larvae become obsessed with silking up the leaf petiole, to strengthen the join. They add more silk whenever they are disturbed, even by gusts of wind. It is as close as the insect ever gets to displaying signs of paranoia during its entire metamorphosis. Some larvae create prominent silk motorways up the midrib of their leaf, from leaf-tip seat pad up to the petiole join. This petiole silking ensures that withered feeding leaves can remain on the tree far into the winter, though most have fallen by early December.

When they are ready, these autumn larvae go walkabout, in search of a spot in which to hibernate. Beforehand, coloured-up larvae often take short exploratory journeys, usually of up to 30 centimetres, only to return to their seat leaf, realising perhaps that it is not quite time yet. They lay silken trails and are testing, always testing. You might assume that they would undertake their journeys into hibernation in fine weather, when the foliage, stems and branches are dry, but their wanderings seem to be stimulated by temperature rises – seemingly when the temperature reaches 7 degrees Celsius or more – rather than by dryness. I have seen larvae wandering off to hibernate in steady rain, and when the branches are running wet – but always on a temperature rise.

I carefully measured the (assumed minimal) distance travelled from seat leaf to hibernation position by over a hundred Purple Emperor larvae. The shortest distance was a mere 1 centimetre, and the longest a staggering 3.5 metres – not bad for an animal less than 1 centimetre long, about the size of a slim woodlouse. Of course, they are unlikely to travel directly, in simple straight lines, so their true journeys may be significantly greater than my measurements suggest (Purple Emperors do not make science easy, and I have observed particularly annoying larvae return to their starting points after making quite long journeys).

My data indicate that 52 per cent of larvae travel less than 0.5 metres, with 25 per cent venturing less than

25 centimetres. Around 80 per cent travel at most a metre, but then there are the itinerant few to whom, stimulated by mild late autumn weather, distance is no real object. Of course, the further they go before they settle, the harder it is to find them, and on more than a dozen occasions I have refound 'lost' larvae in spring, having failed to locate them in hibernation – usually because they had journeyed unusually far. Hardened travellers tend to go down-stem to a junction, then back up towards the tip of a new branch.

Each autumn some fully coloured-up larvae vanish without trace, apparently while journeying off to hibernation. I suspect, then, that there is a fairly high mortality rate, with maybe 25–30 per cent of larvae succumbing to predation while crawling on stems, but I am unable to present any real evidence. Certainly, they are much safer when resting on the leaves than when crawling on stems, for very few larvae disappear (to assumed predation) during October while colouring up on their seat leaves.

The earliest I have found a hibernating larva is 17 October (2010), followed by 21 October (2016) and 23 October (2009). Those dates are exceptions, and may result from larvae that had developed unusually rapidly. Interestingly, all three larvae were on trees from which the leaves fell early. The bulk of Purple Emperor larvae enter hibernation during the final days of October and the first seven days of November, but of course there are early and late years. Cold weather and persistent rain and gales can push larvae into hibernation early, while in mild autumns larvae will linger on the foliage long into November, especially on sallows that retain their leaves for a long time.

The latest I have recorded Purple Emperor larvae not yet in hibernation is 24 November (2013), when one was still on his seat leaf and two others were observed crawling around on stems, seeking out hibernation spots. That record was pipped by one found crawling off to hibernate in Southwater Woods by Ben Greenaway on 26 November 2019. These are exceptionally late dates, though I also observed larvae still on leaves on 18 November 2011 and 16 November 2010, in mild autumn weather.

My data indicate that larvae travel further in mild weather than in cool weather. In one cool, damp early November the average (apparent) distance travelled was 40 centimetres; in another, milder season the mean distance was 70 centimetres – assuming larvae had not undertaken longer there-and-back journeys. Larvae that stay on the leaf late, into mid-November, seldom venture far before hibernating.

Every autumn I pray, in earnest, for cold, wet, miserable weather at the end of October and during early November, so that larvae will venture only a few centimetres before conking out – so I can find them easily. It can take an hour to find one that has travelled more than 1.5 metres, and the chances of finding a hibernating larva diminish with distance. However, the years 2009–18, were bedevilled by mild weather during that crucial period. At times one feels like poor Job. My prayers were answered by the wet (and thoroughly miserable) autumn of 2019, when larval mobility was severely restricted, and survival rates on foliage were unprecedentedly high (at 100 per cent). The average measured distance travelled to hibernation then was 63 centimetres, because the data was skewed by one vagrant who journeyed 2.2 metres just to thwart me! The others had travelled less than 40 centimetres.

Some Purple Emperor larvae go through a pre-hibernation phase, lasting perhaps a day or two, in which they move off their seat leaf and rest on the adjoining leaf petiole or stalk, or take up a temporary position on the nearby stem. These larvae are in an insecure situation, having not spun a silk pad on which to cling. I am not sure why they do this, for it is an unsatisfactory halfway house and a high-risk strategy. Maybe they're being brainless, but it's more likely that they were caught out by sudden temperature drops.

When they select a final hibernation spot, larvae spend several minutes spinning a longitudinal silk pad, then turn around and sit on it – religiously, for some five months. The first larva I watched doing this (one named 'Joshua Son of Nun', on 17 October 2010) spent eight minutes spinning a silk pad on which his feet could adhere. Later, I discovered that larvae will often add more silk to their pad during the first week or so of hibernation. (You may be relieved to learn than 'Joshua' made it through the winter, and all the way to pupation, and proved to be male, fortunately.)

As previously noted, their vacated seat leaves, carefully fixed to the main stem, may dangle on silk strands quite far into the winter, withering, until detached by wind, rain or snow. I have found these old leaves still attached as late as mid-February in sheltered spots, which indicates how strong Purple Emperor caterpillar silk can be.

Just over half the Purple Emperor larvae I have found in hibernation had aligned themselves on stems next to or close to a live bud, facing outwards. The terminal bud is seldom selected. The third or fourth buds down from the stem tip are favoured, some 3–6 centimetres down, and it is rare to find a larva further away than the seventh or eighth bud. Strangely, large buds are rarely selected, either because branches with huge buds produce leaves that are too coarse and thick for young (L1) larvae, and are seldom selected by egg-laying females, or because large buds produce flowers before leaves, thus prolonging the period before larvae may commence feeding. Likewise, tiny buds are also not selected, as they provide inadequate cover (larvae utilise forks, leaf scars and bark lesions on small-budded sallows). The caterpillars almost invariably line themselves up against medium-sized buds, preferring leaf buds over flower buds, when available.

These bud-dwelling larvae mimic either the colours of the bud or the section of stem on which they are aligned, changing from the drab brown or grey colour in which they entered hibernation to a prettier yellow-green, yellow-brown or even yellow-pink, somehow consciously changing colour to blend in with their background. They look well camouflaged, to us.

Nearly a third of larvae curl themselves into, or line up alongside or below, stem forks – the junctions of minor branches less than a centimetre thick, where the bark is smooth. They resemble callouses that occur naturally in the branch forks. Such larvae normally remain brown or grey, especially those that curl themselves up within a fork, although some attain a pretty mosaic of mottled greens and greys, and others become covered in algal growth and are very well disguised. Forks (or technically, nodes) were oddly favoured during the winter of 2019–20, as if the larvae knew that the winter would be mild and that they needed to tuck themselves into shady nooks, or they knew tit numbers were high, and that hibernating next to buds would be unduly risky.

A smaller number of larvae, around 16 per cent, select fissures or lesions in tree bark, or scars where twigs or leaf stems snapped off a while back. These larvae have to journey more than a metre to find such positions. They are usually grey, or mottled grey-green, in colour. They prove to be wise, for reasons that will be explained in the next section.

I have also recorded four larvae hibernating on dead twigs, two of which were lined up against dead buds. These were all beautifully camouflaged, appearing grey upon grey. However, although perhaps safer from predatory birds they were not in tune with living tissue and swelling buds, which proved disadvantageous in spring.

There is also a lovely blackish colour form, in which the front half is heavily mottled with black and the rear half is grey or dark green. This form occurs on dark stems of some narrow-leaved sallows. There should be a strongly red form, associated with red-stemmed sallows (such as Eared Willow and its close hybrids).

All this experience contrasts, sharply, with what Heslop believed – that larvae hibernate deep in bark crevices on major branches or main trunks. Under Heslop's spell, I searched assiduously for larvae hibernating among crevices in bark, and located precisely one. That was in Hampshire, back in the mid-1980s, in

the fork where a major branch joined the trunk of a large sallow, some 5 metres above the ground.

The well-known and highly experienced butterfly breeder Harold Short found that in captivity grey-coloured larvae often hibernate on the trunk. He also suggests that some may overwinter on or even in the ground, perhaps among leaf litter. The latter might explain how on occasions I have refound 'lost' larvae on small sallow bushes in spring, having carefully searched the entire bush more than once.

Do not think that hibernation is a safe venture for these caterpillars. In all the years of my study, just over half (55 per cent) of monitored larvae vanished without trace. These were almost certainly predated by birds, most likely by tits. Most losses occur during the second half of winter. All that remains is the vacated silk pad, shining wanly in the winter light. In time, it soon fades, and is washed away and forgotten, but not by me.

Originally, I checked hibernating larvae fortnightly, but I found it too stressful, as all one effectively does is record losses. I now check them monthly, except in high-volume years – that is as much as my nervous system can cope with. All one can do is pray for them, and I do. I love each one of them too dearly. Eventually I learnt not to give them names, especially of characters one likes, but to give them bland numbers, as proper scientists do.

My sample sizes have varied greatly from year to year. In lean years I have found and followed as few as two (2014/15), three (2011/12) or four (2017/18) hibernating larvae. I think four is the minimum required to get a realistic reading on survival rates. In contrast, in 2009/10 I followed 38, and after the miraculous egg lay of 2013 I found no fewer than 63 larvae in hibernation, which proved to be too large a sample to study.

In both the *annus mirabilis* years (2009/10 and 2013/14), nearly two-thirds of all hibernating larvae vanished without trace, almost certainly to avian predators. The exact percentages were 58 per cent in 2009/10 and 60 per cent in 2013/14. The loss rate was even higher during the 2010/11 winter, when 10 out of 15 larvae perished (67 per cent). Losses commence in late November in winters when predation rates are high. Our friend Mr Dunk states, in a paper from 1954, that only one out of 12 hibernating larvae found in the wild in early December was still present in early February.

You need some proof that birds are the guilty party. Here it is. Firstly, larvae do not fall off. I have deliberately beaten branches bearing hibernating larvae, using a beating sheet and a heavy stick (the standard piece of entomological equipment for dislodging invertebrates from tree foliage): none fell. I have hung collecting sieves under hibernating larvae: none fell. Best of all, during the 2013/14 winter the Forestry Commission felled and bulldozed a tall sallow containing two hibernating Purple Emperor larvae, both some 3 metres up, while renovating a pond in Savernake Forest. The two larvae survived the felling and subsequent transportation (and were rescued). Furthermore, during that same winter, which was gale-strewn, several tall sallows were blown down in Savernake. I diligently searched the upper branches of these prostrated sallows for hibernating larvae and for vacated silk pads, concentrating around buds and minor forks. I found three larvae (which had been between 8 and 18 metres up the tree) and no vacated pads, suggesting that larvae did not come adrift when those sizeable trees crashed down. Lastly, in January 2020 I managed to locate and rescue two larvae that I was following from sallows felled and stashed away during forestry thinning works in the northern part of Savernake Forest. Both were still in situ, despite their tribulations.

Secondly, one might surmise that many larvae wake up on mild winter days and simply move, and are not refound. The answer here is that they should not move once they have entered hibernation, and I searched hard for movement with each larva that vanished. In captivity, very few of the 150 or so larvae I have reared over the years woke up and moved. In the wild, one somewhat errant Savernake larva woke and moved twice during the winter of 2009/10, in late November and again in December. During the absurdly mild, wet and stormy winter of 2013/14, six larvae moved position during December, mostly around 20 centimetres. One moved in early January; two moved short distances during the second half of January; and another in early February. Then, in early March, long before the sallows had begun to bud up, let alone come into leaf, 11 more larvae moved distances of more than half a metre. All bar two of these 22 winter wanderers shrivelled up and perished before the sallows came into leaf in what degenerated into a late spring. Seemingly, then, waking up and wandering during the winter leaves larvae with little fuel in the tank. This could well be a major problem for the species if climate change continues to deliver mild winters, especially when spring does not follow quickly on.

Incidentally, I suspect that the trigger temperature for rousing Purple Emperor larvae from hibernation is at least 14 degrees Celsius, though it must be accompanied by mild nights. February 2019 was the warmest February on record, producing a new UK record high temperature of 21.2 degrees Celsius at Kew Gardens in west London on the 26th. Throughout that week-long February heatwave, the 10 Purple Emperor larvae I was following in Savernake Forest stayed in hibernation, as did the five captive ones in my garden. However, each night was cold, with frosts in the -1 to -3 degrees Celsius range at Marlborough, on the edge of Savernake.

Thirdly, predation by invertebrates is highly unlikely during the winter months, as invertebrate predators of sufficient size to remove caterpillars of 7–9 millimetres in length will either be in hibernation themselves or active only among leaf litter on the ground. Few are in the adult stage. I have tested this by putting 1-centimetre-mesh wire cages around 20 hibernating larvae, which allowed invertebrate access but excluded birds and small mammals: all those larvae survived. However, during very mild weather at the start of February 2020, I found the Common Tree Flower Bug active on sallow branches in West Sussex, when they were supposed to be hibernating in bark crevices.

Fourthly, mammal predation is unlikely in leafless sallow tops during the winter months, with the possible exception of occasional forays by the Yellow-necked Mouse, which has been recorded 20 metres up in treetops.

Trail cameras can provide ready answers. Unfortunately, Savernake Forest is too heavily visited by the Great British public for the extensive use of contemporary trail cameras – the gadgets soon vanish, not just the caterpillars. A new generation of smaller, twig-size trail cameras is awaited. Luckily, the use of this technology in more secretive places produced highly incriminating evidence against the Great Tit and the Blue Tit. Worse, I actually caught a flock of Long-tailed Tits in the act: they swooped in minutes after I'd checked the presence of a slumbering larva, and my caterpillar (called 'Sir Cloudesley Shovell', after an ill-fated British admiral) vanished. At that moment the Long-tailed Tit was removed from the list of eight species of British birds I would take with me to a desert island in lieu of gramophone records.

Finally, while checking hibernating larvae in January and February 2019 I encountered a flock of tits (four species), at least 50 strong, working an area of the forest where four larvae were marked out. Within days, three larvae had vanished. In previous winters I had determined that caterpillar loss was highest in areas patrolled by wintering tit flocks.

We know from the UK bird monitoring programmes that tit populations fluctuate greatly from year to year, largely on account of winter weather and conditions during the breeding season. Even the citizen science data from the RSPB's annual Big Garden Birdwatch show these fluctuations. I attempted to conduct tit counts in Savernake Forest during the winters of 2010/11, 2011/12 and 2012/13, before giving up in the belief that I was gathering rubbish data. I ended up developing the hypothesis that tits get driven out of the forest by severe cold, particularly frost and ice, and migrate to bird feeders in gardens in nearby Marlborough and Burbage.

In a fascinating but all too brief book, translated from the German and entitled *Searching for Butterflies in Winter* (2007), Gabriel Hermann also blames tits for the disappearance of hibernating Purple Emperor larvae. He states that larval survival is higher during winters when Purple Emperor larvae are present in low numbers, because tits quickly home in on hibernating larvae after high egg-lay years, when larvae are numerous, and massacre them. My findings suggest that Hermann is absolutely right.

Hermann also states that large emergences of adults are likely after winters when populations were at a low ebb because the survival rate is so much higher. Something like this may well have occurred in Savernake Forest during the winter of 2012/13. I was following only eight larvae then, when the period January to March was very cold. Only two larvae were predated that winter: one during a mild and wet December, and another during mild weather in mid-January, before the big freeze commenced. The summer of 2013 then saw a massive emergence of the Purple Emperor – and after a meagre egg lay in 2012. Something very similar happened during the 2017/18 winter, when only one of four Savernake larvae was predated, and one of four more in other woods. The sample of eight larvae suggests a 25 per cent winter predation rate that winter. Then, 2018 went on to be the best Purple Emperor season I have experienced. Perhaps, high egg-lay years need to be followed by cold winters in order for populations of this butterfly to increase dramatically.

The Savernake Forest data suggests that it is possible to place winter predation rates into three general categories: high, moderate and low. Of course, my sample size was too small in some winters for judgement, but I did openly predict (on the Purple Emperor blog) that 2018 was going to see a large adult emergence, based on the low winter predation rate (albeit from a small sample).

For the record, my data suggest that larval mortality is highest in minor forks and on buds on thicker twigs (I call the section of stem between the fourth to sixth buds 'Suicide Alley'). Survival is best among larvae who tuck themselves well into scars, lesions and crevices in bark, or hibernate by buds near the end of thin, flimsy sprays which would not take the weight of a Blue or Great Tit (though tits will use their wings to hover when feeding at spray tips). The best survivors seem to be the fortunate few larvae who choose to hibernate in forks or fissures and which become coated in algal growth. These lucky fellows have a 100 per cent survival rate, albeit from a small sample.

There must be a PhD opportunity for someone here – studying hibernating larvae, each with an attendant trail camera, in comparison with tit numbers during different winters, and analysing larval survival rates in comparison to winter weather and tit densities. Such a study should reveal that woodland tits, spend significant amounts of time in sallow stands. It may well conclude that 'when tits are down, Emperors go up'.

However, it cannot be that simple a matter, for a scientific study would also have to look at winter food sources available to tits in Purple Emperor habitats, and their food preferences, for it may be that tits (and other passerine birds) ignore Purple Emperor larvae when other, perhaps more preferable food sources are available to them, but are forced to predate Purple Emperor larvae at times when other food supplies are short. In any case, as the classic study of British tits by Chris Perrins (*British Tits*, 1979) indicates, the birds can concentrate so heavily on a particular food source that they eat it out.

Clearly, the five-month hibernation period is a very difficult time for Purple Emperor larvae. It may be in the process of becoming even more challenging, due to mild winters that interrupt diapause (hibernation) and exacerbating predation by increasing predator survival. However, because Purple Emperor larvae are (supposedly) immobile during the winter, this stage of the insect's life cycle is relatively easy to study. That cannot be said of post-hibernation larvae, which become increasingly mobile and increasingly difficult to follow and study.

CHAPTER TWELVE

Spring larvae and the pupal stage

Caterpillar ambition — The departure lounge — Fourth-instar larvae — The glory of final-instar larvae — The mysteries of pupation

Those Purple Emperor larvae that survive winter wake slowly in spring, one by one. Those in the sun wake first; those in heavy shade, last. They change colour gradually, to vernal green; begin to feed, fitfully at first, then steadily; change skin, feed voraciously; and then change skin again, to feed and grow rapidly to reach a length of 35–40 millimetres. The larvae become increasingly sun-loving, in contrast to their behaviour prior to hibernation, when they are habitués of dappled shade. They also become remarkably mobile and agile. When full to bursting point, larvae have to journey through the startling process of pupation, processing themselves through the biological equivalent of a kitchen blender. Please don't underestimate the will of these ever-expanding grow-bags to fly. The phrase 'as ambitious as a caterpillar' needs to enter common English usage.

Purple Emperor larvae normally wake between mid-March and late April, depending on the winter's duration and severity, and the timing of spring's arrival — and when spring comes, of course, it is a matter of stops and starts. They need a temperature in the region of 14 degrees Celsius to waken, coupled with the absence of cold nights. Day length may be a further cue. Larvae that have not hibernated next to live buds have to journey to align themselves next to swelling buds. Most of them start to change colour back to green before they waken; others reposition themselves while still wearing their winter colours, and change later. A few sit for a short while on the undersides of unfurling leaves, transferring to the uppersides as soon as possible.

It is likely that Purple Emperor larvae are awakening earlier nowadays than of yore, due to the precocious springs of modern times, which are almost certainly a product of a changing climate. In 2014, spring arrived prematurely, such that 11 out of 23 larvae inspected in Savernake Forest on 16 March had already woken up and repositioned themselves. That is by far the earliest I have recorded Emperor larvae out of hibernation, though I suspect that it will not last long as a record due to the gathering pace of climate change, and the burgeoning trend towards over-early springs. The latest I have recorded larvae exiting hibernation is 11 April 2010 and 20 April 2013, during cold springs after winters that deigned to offer some bite. Some time ago, in captivity, after the genuinely bitter winters at the start of the 1980s, I recorded larvae waking from hibernation at the very end of April and, once, at the beginning of May. Times have changed, and are set to change further.

After awakening from hibernation, Purple Emperor caterpillars have to sit out a difficult period, as mature sallows flower before coming into leaf. In effect, larvae become like airport passengers stuck in the departure lounge, waiting to be called for their flights — there is nothing for them to eat yet, as the trees are putting their efforts into flowering, before leafing. In slow springs, sallows may take two or three weeks to flower and start to come into leaf. Moreover, in some springs sallows flower prodigiously, such as 2010, 2015 and, most notably, 2019, when in response to the drought of 2018 stressed sallows put all their efforts into flowering, and consequently came into leaf surprisingly late. In other springs, such as 2013, sallows flower only weakly. There are also individual trees that flower strongly, moderately, weakly or not at all, and those that come into leaf early, in the mainstream, or late. I found that Purple Emperor larvae utilise all such trees, without any obvious preference.

Larvae often become visibly stressed during this long, cruel wait, having become dangerously short of energy reserves. Such larvae are desperate to commence feeding, as they can wither up while waiting in the departure lounge, having run out of fuel, especially when spring is late or slow. In Savernake Forest, in 2010, the departure lounge duration period lasted from 8 to 24 April. Predation can also be high during this period, as was the case in 2014, when tit predation carried on relentlessly into April.

Some desperate adventurers jump the starter's gun and bite into the tip of softening buds that have not yet begun to unfurl, but most larvae do not commence feeding until the leaf buds have started to open properly. Some take tentative meals from the pale green sepals that grow below the flowers. Larvae on non–flowering trees are at some advantage here. This cancels out the disadvantage their first- and second–instar counterparts faced on such trees in July and August, when non-flowering trees offered a preponderance of coarser, thicker leaves, as a result of early leafing and subsequent advanced development.

The earliest I have recorded larvae beginning to feed in the wild are 20 March 2019 in Savernake Forest, 30 March 2017 at Knepp Wildland, and 1 April 2014 in Savernake Forest. In contrast, two larvae had yet to commence feeding in Savernake Forest by 2 May 2010 (both subsequently perished; they had left it too late and had been running on empty).

More normally, feeding commences during the third week of April, around St George's Day. A couple of hours of temperatures in the region of 15 degrees Celsius seems to be necessary. Once larvae recommence feeding properly, they move back on to the leaf tips (upperside only), where they spin silk seat pads and construct silken highways along the midribs.

In early spring, most larvae are a grubby green, with smudges of drab winter colours; they green up with the spring, though they do not regain full Lincoln green colouration before they change into the fourth instar. These post-hibernation larvae are disinclined to be mobile, and can be extremely difficult to spot, hidden among clusters of developing leaves, distended flowers and swelling seed capsules. Their feeding marks give their presence away, for I have yet to find any other lepidopteran feeding on sallow foliage that early in spring.

Fully fed third-instar larvae are not pretty, appearing rather like discoloured and distended vegetables well past their sell-by date. They change skin while ensconced on their leaf-tip silk pads. The process often takes several days, due to the vagaries of spring weather. This is not an easy skin change, and fatalities occur, particularly during poor weather.

The earliest I have recorded fourth-instar larvae is mid-April, at Knepp Wildland in 2017; the latest is staggeringly late, on 25 May, at Savernake Forest in 2010. More generally, the early spring skin change occurs at the end of April and during early May, and is completed by mid-May. The discarded skin is left on the leaf, but is quickly washed off by dew or rain (previous instars tend to eat their cast skins).

The newly emerged fourth-instar larva has a prominent head with huge pale horns, which indicate how large the larva will become before it needs to change skin again. Larvae quickly become too large to sit simply on leaf tips, and tend to occupy the whole rear half of a leaf, resting on the silked-up midrib, often with their front portion raised up, in the hunched 'praying mantis' position adopted by third-instar larvae during the autumn, with the prolegs tucked in.

Unless the weather is poor, this instar does not last long, for fourth-instar larvae eat regularly and steadily on the unfurling, lengthening leaves, especially during warm afternoons and evenings. Their feeding marks are salient for a while, especially during early May, but are then lost within the laceration of foliage generated by developing moth larvae and other foliage-feeding invertebrates. Early May, then, provides a reasonable window of opportunity for finding Purple Emperor larvae in the wild, as any feeding marks are likely to be of this species. They favour both ordinary leaf sprays and large, developing leaves on strong leaders, but feed only when the foliage is dry. Wet weather slows them right down.

After changing into the fourth instar, Purple Emperor larvae want to be in sunny positions. Almost invariably they change spray, and often branch, moving upwards or around to south- or west-facing aspects, unless already there. I have recorded early fourth-instar larvae wandering as much as 5 metres in the wild, from dappled shade into sunlight. Many journey up the tree, to sunlit realms in the canopy, and are lost to study. The assumption here is that the sun's warmth enables them to digest their food rapidly and speeds up their development, as has been proven with other British butterflies (such as the Marsh Fritillary).

Spring Purple Emperor larvae maintain silken seat pads on which they rest between bouts of feeding and wandering, and silk runways along the midribs of their chosen leaves and up adjacent stems. They seem, though, to be less bothered about strengthening the petiole of their seat or feeding leaves than they were during the late summer and autumn, presumably because the join is naturally stronger, though they may silk up the petiole join in very windy weather or when disturbed, to ensure their interpretation of what we call biosecurity.

The fourth and final skin change takes place on the seat leaf, which is by then often well nibbled down at the sides. The change normally takes two or three days; longer in cool or wet weather, and less in anticyclonic conditions. As with previous skin changes, Purple Emperor larvae like to be immobile while changing skin, though early on they will wander if disturbed.

The earliest I have recorded fifth-instar larvae in the wild is 1 May 2011. Normally this skin change occurs

between the 10 and 21 May. The latest I have observed
larvae changing into the fifth and final instar in the wild
is 30 May 2010.

Purple Emperor larvae now become horned gods that
rule the sallow trees. They bask in hot afternoon sunshine,
glorifying themselves. At rest, while digesting their feeds,
they stretch themselves out lazily along the whole length
of a well silked-up seat leaf, and much of the width too.
They soon become so heavy that the leaves they occupy
hang down, almost perpendicularly. Yet they are
incredibly hard to dislodge from their silked-up seat leaf.

Purple Emperor larvae feed intermittently during
May and early June, voraciously devouring leaves,
primarily in late morning and again during the evening,
and sometimes on warm nights, favouring the upper
third of the leaf. They feed only when the foliage is dry.
At this stage they take to young leader growths with
large leaves, which were avoided in late summer and
autumn. They will range far and wide to feed, returning
after feasts to their chosen seat leaf by means of their
silken highways, which function rather like the ball of
string Ariadne gave to Theseus to help him find his way
through the Minotaur's labyrinth. One Emperorphile of
the Heslop era remarked that the early summer larva
uses its seat leaf as 'a kind of sitting room'. Larvae can
devour several neighbouring leaves, leaving the basal part
of the midrib and, sometimes, bare stalks. These feeding
marks are fairly salient and indicative of this species,
being matched only by the feeding of some larger moths
(notably the Poplar Hawkmoth, Eyed Hawkmoth and

Puss Moth). The silk pads and highways are so extensive and dense that they persist well into the autumn, long after their makers have flown the midsummer skies.

Purple Emperor larvae are so mobile at this stage that it is impossible to determine rates of predation, and wider mortality. Many simply vanish, either because they have been crunched by a large predator (bird or mammal) or because they have moved up the tree. Indeed, of the 63 larvae I followed in hibernation during the winter of 2013/14, only three definitely became full-grown larvae, though my hope and belief is that others did make it that far, but out of sight and mind.

Despite reaching the size of a small person's little finger, these full-grown larvae are also incredibly hard to spot, as their colours and texture blend perfectly in with the foliage. They almost make themselves invisible, such is their mastery of colour, shape, shadow and tone.

The fully-grown Purple Emperor larva is a handsome caterpillar, unique among British butterflies in its shape, colour and pose. The head is pale green, and appears eyeless, but from it spouts two forward-facing horns, some 6 millimetres long, which are tipped dark pink and have purple warts, and an almost luminescent blueish tinge. I have little idea what they are for, but I have followed a larva in the wild which lost (presumably to attack by a predatory invertebrate) the bulk of one of these horns in October. It survived until late April, then died while skin changing. Two yellowy stripes run backwards along the dorsum (top), from the base of each horn. The body is almost a uniform mid-green, finely granulated, and with small yellowish hairs called setae. Each abdominal segment is bordered by a slanting pale-yellow stripe, the second pair of which meet on top of the dorsum. The legs and hind legs (claspers) are paler. The body tapers towards the rear, so that the anal segments are sharply pointed.

At this stage it is often possible to tell whether a larva is going to develop into an Emperor or an Empress. Larvae destined to become males possess a pair of pale patches on the top (dorsal surface) of their eighth segment. These vague yellowish blobs are destined to develop into the male testes. They are best seen by looking from tail to head, with the larva in a near-horizontal position. However, these patches are not always visible and I have wrongly sexed larvae as a result. It may be that some larvae are too thick-skinned for these patches to show well, but the light and angle of view are also crucial. In addition, final-instar larvae destined to produce males appear to have longer horns. This was first noticed by one of Heslop's contemporaries, H Symes. The pupae are easier to sex, as explained in the passage on the pupal stage, on p. 270.

The earliest I have recorded full-grown larvae in the wild is 23 May, at the end of the remarkably early spring of 2011, in Savernake Forest. My latest ever was one spotted high up on a sallow bush in Alice Holt Forest on 24 June, late on during the excessively wet June of 1977. It was still in full Lincoln green, a few days off pupating. In the modern era, most larvae become fully grown in early June, with a few lingering on into mid-June.

When they are full, almost to bursting point, Purple Emperor larvae turn pale, assuming all over the wishy-washy grey-green colour of the final-instar larva's hind legs, or claspers. They are ready to pupate, and to venture on to the hitherto avoided sallow leaf undersides.

The larvae of many British butterflies wander far and wide prior to pupation, in part to find somewhere suitable to pupate, but perhaps mainly in order to get themselves into a state in which pupation is possible – to kick-start the process of mass chemical and biological change. I have found Peacock larvae wandering over 100 metres from the nettle patch where they had fed, and most of us will have noticed Large White larvae – and pupae – well away from any of their cabbage family foodplants. I once found a Large White pupa inside my attic light switch! Better still, I tracked a full-grown Marsh Fritillary larva wandering through dense, rough grassland, covering 150 metres during the course of an April morning. Purple Emperor larvae may at times be equally adventurous (see Chapter 13).

This means that Purple Emperor pupae are excessively hard to locate in the wild, even on relatively small trees where fully fed larvae have been closely observed. There are precious few records of pupae being found, and then mainly by accident (including one by lamplight while out moth hunting). It has been achieved, though: Symes (1954) describes finding a pupa on a 12-foot-tall bush near Oxford, after spotting the tell-tale feeding signs of a large larva. It was, he states, 'in the middle of the bush'.

Many fully fed larvae appear to go on very long journeys, which may be hazardous. For a while, my data suggested that larvae destined to produce females remain relatively sedentary, journeying less than 5 metres, while those destined to produce males ascend high into the canopy. I was misled, but such are the dangers afforded by small samples. Experimentation proved unhelpful. I have placed out 10 full-grown larvae on to relatively small individual bushes in the wild, in order to find the resultant pupae. All bar one disappeared. The insect, or nature itself, was not cooperating. I have put in the hard hours, scanning high branches through binoculars and climbing trees, but to little avail. I am confident that most larvae undertake journeys of many metres. I strongly suspect that some even change trees – either that, or wandering larvae are heavily predated, or both.

One technique I have employed to some effect, at least after autumns lacking serious gales, has been to search for vacated pupal cases in early winter. This is because Purple Emperor larvae adhere the petiole of their pupal leaf (the leaf bearing the pupal case) on to its twig with copious amounts of silk, such that the withered leaf can stay attached for weeks or even months, fluttering vacantly in the breeze; and also, because the pupal case is formed of chitin, a particularly enduring material. Indeed, the stub of a pupal case I discovered in Savernake Forest early in the winter of 2011/12 lasted *in situ* until the mid-autumn of 2013, having persisted for a monumental 18 months! I have even managed to discover new Purple Emperor localities in early or midwinter by spotting the remains of pupal cases on incongruously attached leaves high on sallow bushes; for example, at Toys Hill in north-west Kent on 14 February 2013.

In all the hundreds of hours I have spent searching for eggs and pre-hibernation larvae, I have found vacated pupal cases only on three occasions: once in Bernwood Forest, on the Buckinghamshire–Oxfordshire border, and twice in Savernake Forest – and I have spent some 500 hours looking in Savernake during the late summer and autumn periods. One of these had produced a female and one a male, but the other was too battered a remnant to tell. All were in sunny positions, close to evidence of larval activity. I know of no other instance of a pupal case being found in the wild by someone searching for eggs or autumn larvae. All this suggests that Purple Emperors rarely pupate low down, where we look, and that they pupate in different locations to where eggs and autumn larvae are found.

In the early summer of 2018, I had a wondrous breakthrough, first in Marlpost Wood, where I had sought the Emperor as a schoolboy, and then close by at Knepp Wildland: I managed to find four pupae, having earlier located fully grown larvae. Two of those larvae had been feeding in full sun positions, and had pupated close by; the other two had been feeding in shadier situations, and had wandered several metres up to the sunlit treetops before pupating. So, at present, my evidence – from a sample of nine wild pupae – suggests that larvae that feed in sunny places do not travel far before pupating, but those in cooler, shadier situations travel long distances. This is more of a hypothesis that merits further investigation, rather than anything firm, as it is based on a small sample, but it would make sense for larvae to be in warm microclimate situations in order to shorten the process of pupation and the duration of the pupal period.

Purple Emperors (seem to) pupate exclusively on leaf undersides, attaching their anal claspers to the basal section of the heavily silked-up midrib of a leaf which needs to be at least as long as the larva itself. They take rather a long time selecting the right leaf, wandering around, testing and rejecting many leaves before finding one that meets their requirements – or before they tire, or feel ready to pupate, in which case actual leaf selection may be quite random.

The larva then spins an elongated silk pad over much of the leaf underside, concentrating on the midrib area and the leaf petiole join, before resting along this pad for several hours, head towards the petiole, then turning around and, after some time, suddenly dropping its head end clear of the leaf. For a nanosecond the larva seems to be unsuspended, but then the rear claspers grip the silk pad hard, by means of a claw device called the cremaster, and the distended larva hangs down, perpendicularly, and periodically wriggles. Suddenly, the larval skin splits, head casing and all, and the amorphous pupa emerges and within about 10 minutes assumes its proper shape. In captivity, the entire process of pupation normally takes around 50 hours, but it can be extended considerably by poor weather, and shortened to around 40 hours during hot, dry weather (during the cool, wet June of 1977, captive larvae were taking more than a week to pupate).

Two pupae and three pupating larvae that I followed in the wild mysteriously disappeared. The leaf remained intact, plus a fraction of peripheral silk. This may suggest predation, most likely by mammals such as the Grey Squirrel or even the Hazel Dormouse or

Yellow-necked Mouse, but possibly birds. It may well be that predation is relatively high among wandering and pupating larvae, and also in pupae – but as yet there is precious little evidence either way. One larva vanished during the latter stages of pupation in mid-June 2019 in Savernake Forest. Again, the leaf was left fully intact (see account in the next chapter).

Like all the other immature stages of this most remarkable insect, the pupa is highly cryptic. It matches the underside of the sallow leaf perfectly, in both colour (grey-green) and texture. You can stare at a known pupa for several minutes from less than a metre away before you spot it. It is not just the clever manner in which they use colour, tone, texture and shape, but also their use of light, which they absorb rather than reflect. When viewed broadside on, Purple Emperor pupae are triangular in shape, but a triangle on which you struggle to focus. The overall impression is of a nebulous leaf, a trivial piece of foliage which matters not in the least. It is designed to deflect the hunting eye, the very opposite of being eye-catching.

I have already hinted that it is quite possible to tell the sex of Purple Emperor pupae, though it is only obvious when you see male and female pupae together (in captivity). When viewed side-on, at eye level, the upper portion of the female pupa, just below the narrow isthmus attaching the pupa to the leaf, is much broader and higher than in the male. Size alone is only a rough guide, though female pupae are generally larger.

The duration of the pupal stage is influenced greatly by weather conditions. Data from larvae and pupae reared in nylon sleeves in my garden, and developing in synchrony with their wild cousins, suggests that pupae take 16 to 33 days to hatch into butterflies, depending on the weather (from a sample of 120). Dennis Dell found that in outdoor captivity in lowland Switzerland the average time spent as a pupa was 19 days for females and 21 days for males. It is surprising that the males spend longer in the pupal state than the larger females. Dennis also found that in hot summer weather, pupae could take as little as 14 days to hatch, but in cool, wet summers as long as 31 days (for females) and 28 days (for males) — with the females now taking longer.

More work is required before the mysteries of pupation in *Apatura iris* are finally understood. Where

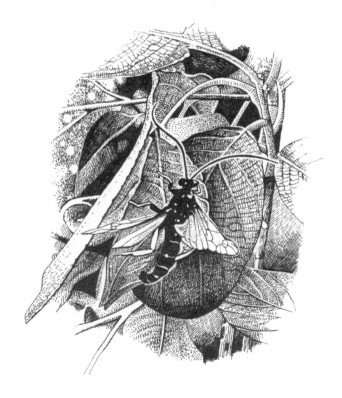

exactly do the wild larvae pupate? What dangers do they face? What is predating them? Does, as I strongly suspect, a prolonged pupal period lead to reduced adult numbers, and if so, precisely why? How many Purple Emperors perish while emerging in poor weather conditions?

Studying the pupal stage has driven me to the brink of mental derangement. Someone else can crack it. It may take a lifetime. I wish them well. I've had enough.

CHAPTER THIRTEEN
Adventures with remarkable caterpillars

The soul of Adonais — Number 198 — The tale of Raymond
— Alastair Cook — The other side of the coin

The following tales are offered as case studies of the weird and wonderful lives lived and endured by Purple Emperor caterpillars in the wild.

The soul of Adonais

The first caterpillar I fell in love with (yes, you did read that correctly, for caterpillars are deeply endearing characters) was found in mid-August 2009 on a leaning Goat Willow-type tree (female) towards the west end of Three Oak Hill Drive, a straight ride at the southern end of Savernake Forest. I was naming caterpillars after Romantic poets at the time, so this late second-instar larva was named 'Keats'. With such a name this caterpillar, all 7 millimetres of him, had to be destined for greatness. In late August he changed skin, into his third instar, and moved to a new leaf spray, some 30 centimetres away.

'Keats' gave me a hard time, as he was somewhat peripatetic and was forever getting lost, in danger of becoming mixed up with other larvae on the same branch, most notably with 'Leigh Hunt' and 'Shelley'. He had a particularly difficult relationship with the latter: they kept invading each other's seat leaves during late

August and early September, and squabbling; at one point they locked horns and tried to shake each other off. Sadly, 'Shelley' did not survive the winter, and 'Leigh Hunt' wandered far up the tree in early May, after changing skin, and was lost to my studies. I am reasonably confident that 'Keats' and 'Leigh Hunt' managed to maintain their respective identities.

'Keats' entered hibernation in early November, after a journey of around half a metre, on the scar where a twiglet had become detached the previous autumn. It proved to be a sound choice, for he made it through to the spring, returned to the spray tip in early April 2010, and lined himself up against a swelling bud.

But he then had to wait, and wait, for the bud to open and flower, before any palatable leaves appeared. This sojourn lasted over two weeks, yet all the time 'Keats' was greening up, matching the changing colour of the bud. At last, around St George's Day, he began to feed.

After changing into the fourth instar, sometime around 7 May, he moved to the sunny side of the bush, a journey of at least 3 metres – at least, I think it was him. Well horned, he fed avidly, notably during the heat of the afternoon and in evening sunshine. Sometime around 25 May he changed skin for the last time – and became downright impossible to follow. From then on he was a veritable nomad, regularly wandering 4 metres from his seat leaf to feed on some far-flung Elysian spray before returning, to bask in dappled sunshine. At one staged he travelled 9 metres to feed, or to bamboozle me.

He was last seen, almost full to bursting point and ghostly pale, ascending from his seat bough, some 2.5

metres above ground level, to the top of the 10-metre sallow that had been his home for the last 10 months. The journey took a mere seven minutes, during which time I recited lines from Shelley's poetic tribute to John Keats, whom he called 'Adonais', and which ends (as recorded in my book *In Pursuit of Butterflies*):

> The soul of Adonais, like a star
> Beacons from the abode where the Eternal are.

My travails to find 'Keats' as a pupa were monumentally unsuccessful. I even spent 45 minutes lying on my back on the forest ride, scanning every spray through binoculars. A woman with two Irish setters wandered past while I was so prostrated. We chose to ignore each other.

Number 198

'Savernake 13/198' was a most remarkable caterpillar. He was first found on 10 November 2013, late in the caterpillar-searching season and quite by accident; and long after I had run out of silly names for that year's huge batch of larvae, so he was merely numbered. He was about to leave his seat leaf.

Nine days later he was found hibernating in a small fork 0.6 metres from his feeding spray, but he quickly moved further up the branch and was refound on 30 November, hibernating in heavy shade on the underside of a fork in relatively thick branches (3 centimetres and 1.5 centimetres in width, respectively) about 3 metres into the bush, a mottled grey caterpillar on mottled grey bark. That proved to be a great place to hibernate.

This caterpillar emerged from hibernation late, having wintered away from the sun's reach. He was not seen when searched for on 4 April 2014 but was found some 4.5 metres away on 21 April, changing his skin. He then had a difficult time as the old gnarled sallow tree he was on came into leaf very late indeed (in an otherwise early leafing year). But he grew sedately and successfully.

My visit on 3 June 2014 coincided with his decision to crawl off his final resting leaf and embark on the great adventure towards pupation – and his size, horn shape and the presence of developing testes indicated that he was indeed going to be male. He went on walkabout along the branch system, covering 11 metres in 40 minutes, pausing to freeze for a minute when disturbed. This journey included U-turns back down dead branches. Throughout his wanderings he kept waving his head from side to side, leaving a silken trail behind. After 40 minutes he encountered his first leaf, the underside, from below. He crawled over its basal third, continuing to wave his head from side to side, and attempted to line himself up along the midrib. This was surely his first ever venture on to the underside of a leaf, as apart from occasional sorties at budbreak time, Purple Emperor larvae live exclusively on leaf uppersides prior to pupation. Here we go, I thought, pupation!

But he changed his mind and moved on, and quickly rejected the undersides of two other large leaves, again approached from below, and returned to the main branch network. This routeway effectively led him horizontally rather than upwards, though he was definitely trying to ascend. He travelled some 13 metres in exactly one hour, including freezes, U-turns and leaf rejections. All told, he rejected six leaf undersides, all approached from below, after expressing keen interest in the basal third of the midrib, and with much side-to-side head movement.

The seventh leaf he seemed to like. It was on a moderately dense spray – almost within a little tent well within the tree canopy some 4 metres up, in a warm, sunny nook – though this leaf was the same size as the previous six (fairly large, some 6–8 centimetres long). He quickly aligned himself along the midrib on the underside, head up towards the stem, and conked out. He had not silked it up, or silked up the petiole. I left him to it at 2.25 pm to check on another larva elsewhere. He was still there, unmoved, when I returned at 4 pm. He had stopped wandering because the temperature had dropped as a shower passed by to the north.

Six days later I returned, confident of finding him as a pupa. I searched high and low, even spending an hour up the relevant branch – but to no avail. I surmised that what I had witnessed that awesome Tuesday may have been the first leg of a much longer journey, and that he stopped where he did simply because the temperature and light level had dropped.

Perhaps I saw him gracing the treetops that July, for some brazen male Emperor launched himself at a passing flock of Crossbills upslope of where that caterpillar had lived.

The tale of Raymond

On 1 September 2015 a second-instar Purple Emperor caterpillar was discovered 2 metres up on the inner, shady part of a Goat Willow-hybrid bush in the region of Knepp Wildland known as Woggs Bottom, an old field name. He was named 'Raymond', a regularly used male name in the Burrell family which owns Knepp Castle Estate. He entered the third instar in mid-September, but remained on the same leaf spray, close to where he had hatched out of an egg. As the year aged he gradually changed colour, from Lincoln green to autumnal brown. In mild weather on Remembrance Sunday, 8 November, he crawled off his ready-to-fall, yellowed leaf, pottered 10 centimetres down-stem, and spent some 30 minutes spinning a silk pad on which to hibernate, next to the fourth bud down from the stem tip – in the hibernation region where losses to predation are heaviest. His withered feeding leaves dangled from the stem past midwinter, when the silk finally broke.

Somehow, 'Raymond' survived. Spring arrived late and this caterpillar, now vernal green, recommenced feeding at the end of April, behind schedule. He grew rapidly during May, receiving late afternoon and evening sun, but did not become full-grown until mid-June. Curiously, he spent his entire feeding life on the same branch, a remarkably sedentary existence for a Purple Emperor caterpillar. Then, when full-grown, on 18 June, he was found in the act of pupating, having crawled 4.5 metres up the tree, a pale ghostly green. It had taken me only an hour to locate him.

At that point the folly of naming a caterpillar became clear: as I had suspected for some time, 'Raymond' was going to be female – no male testes were visible, the horns appeared small, and the size of the caterpillar alone suggested femininity.

'Raymonda', as she then became known, pupated on a carefully spun silk pad on the underside of a leaf she matched perfectly in colour. She remained as a pupa there for 25 days, a week longer than is the norm for her gender, due to cool weather and the fact that she had stayed on the shadier side of the tree.

Over the months 'Raymond(a)' had been visited by about 400 people, participants in Knepp's Wildland safaris. She became a cult figure, at least on Twitter and on the Purple Emperor blog. Never mind P G Wodehouse's porcine Empress of Blandings, she was the Empress of Knepp.

She emerged from her pupa, an unusually large and dark female, at 5 pm on 14 July, attended by Sir Charles Raymond Burrell, 10th baronet, as well as a wildlife cameraman, the estate's ecologist, a wildlife artist, a poet and a columnist from *The Times*. Her emergence went viral on Twitter. She was later eulogised in *The Times* Nature Notebook (27 August 2016).

The following late morning, 'Raymonda' was wedded and bedded high up in an oak, for four heady hours. Thereafter, she was glimpsed flying over sallow bushes in the Woggs Bottom area on several occasions, feeding on sap running from a wound in an oak, and finally, on 1 August, staring aloofly down at me from a lofty treetop. Her pupal case remained attached to its leaf long into the autumn, and still received visitors. In that manner she must have been visited by around 500 people.

Her final tally of admirers must have been in seven figures, for in mid-March 2018 'Raymonda' took to the airwaves, appearing briefly in a TV programme about British wildlife on Channel 5, having been filmed while emerging. The programme was repeated in February 2019, increasing her tally of admirers further.

Alastair Cook

On Monday 10 September 2018, Alastair Cook was batting at The Oval in his last of his 161 Test matches for England. He scored 147 runs, to secure a Test average of 45.35 runs. The Purple Emperor caterpillar I found on the south-west edge of Savernake Forest that morning was duly named after him, though it was also given a number, No. 64. He was found 1.7 metres above ground on a young sucker coming off the main trunk of a veteran female Goat Willow on the edge of a small glade, with September's sun slanting down through a cathedral of tall Beech trees. He fed slowly but surely on his chosen leaf spray, in dappled sun, and began colouring up for the autumn in mid-October. By the end of that month he was almost fully coloured up, ready to hibernate.

On 13 November 'Alastair Cook' was found hibernating beside a bud 5 centimetres below the spray tip, having travelled a mere 1 centimetre from his feeding leaf – the shortest distance I've ever recorded a larva journey to hibernate (although he might have wandered long and far, before returning to his departure point; there's no way of telling). He was then checked monthly.

He survived the winter, a yellow-green larva closely matching the colour of the bud he was lined up against. In mid-March he began to green up, serenaded by Chiffchaffs calling high above. He was, though, on a weakling branch that was struggling to come into leaf, probably due to the previous summer's drought, and on 1 April he appeared to be starting to shrivel up. On 21 April his branch still hadn't come into leaf, and was dying back ominously. 'Alastair Cook' had become a runt, in serious danger of starvation, and was facing a journey of many metres up the tree's main trunk to healthy foliage.

It was time for action: I pet-rescued him, translocating him to a nearby branch which was well in leaf. Within a week he was feeding well. He changed into the fourth instar in early May, fed up further and commenced changing into the final instar on 22 May. No longer a runt, he fed steadily on a well-leafed leader spray. In early June I had doubts about his gender: his shape, size and the absence of male testes patches suggested femininity, strongly.

On Sunday 16 June he was found pupating, having travelled 4.5 metres up the main trunk of the old sallow, before reaching a patch of dense moss, which acted as a buffer, and turning on to a small branch – only he was now clearly a she. Spotting her took the best part of an hour, but there she was, pupating on the underside of a large leaf close to the tree trunk. I tied a string marker close by.

Ian Shale, a tried and trusted friend of intensely Purple Persuasion, then called in to visit her, but failed to find her, though the marked leaf was still present. She was declared missing, presumed dead. Indeed, 'Alastair Cook' had edged the second new ball, angled cunningly across her, to second slip, and was out, in the mid-80s. She had been predated, by bird or beast.

Sir Alastair Cook opens the innings in my lifetime's England cricket XI, alongside Sir Geoffrey Boycott.

The other side of the coin

There is a reverse side of every coin. Indeed, the fates often conspire against Purple Emperor caterpillars. In addition to the rampant destruction imposed on them by an assortment of predators, which is all normal for caterpillarhood, the following Unmitigated Disasters must be recorded.

Pride of place goes to an early fourth-instar larva which was eaten by a longhorn cow at Knepp Wildland in early May. I witnessed, and indeed videoed, this accidental mishap. Knepp's longhorn cattle avidly browse sallow buds and leaves in spring, so this event is unlikely to have been unique. Then, in early May 2019, one of the larvae I was following in Savernake Forest was inadvertently consumed by a browsing deer (probably a Fallow Deer). Earlier in Savernake Forest, a few early-instar larvae perished when young host trees died after Fallow Deer frayed the soft bark of the trunks, causing the foliage to wilt. More significantly, I have lost at least 25 larvae on trees that had been killed by bark-stripping Grey Squirrels.

The hand of man is not unbloodied here. One larva, in Savernake Forest, perished when a small boy randomly cut off the branch it was feeding on with a penknife. That is remarkable, because small boys are scarcely permitted penknives in this era of health and safety consciousness, and this particular boy had a plethora of branches from which to choose. Larvae have also been lost in Savernake when mountain bikers pruned back overhanging sallow branches prior to staging an (unofficial) event. Another Savernake larva died, by frazzling, when a barbeque was lit beneath its bough, and I once lost a good breeding tree containing two or three larvae to a bonfire of pheasant carcasses and plastic fertiliser bags casually sited by a Hampshire gamekeeper.

I have also recorded the loss of a caterpillar in a road traffic accident, when a speeding vehicle left the road and plunged down a bank, flattening a young sallow on the edge of Alice Holt Forest. In Savernake, sallows used for breeding, hosting larvae, have also been lost when the trees were felled for pond restoration – the recreation of a Capability Brown-designed vista and timber harvesting. The number of larvae I have lost during 'scrub bashes' on nature reserves is best not mentioned here, but does include a reserve managed by Butterfly Conservation.

Foresters, and in particular a leading timber harvesting and marketing specialist, find diverse ways of disposing of sallows hosting Purple Emperor larvae. Forestry contractors do not just randomly fell sallows: in September 2018 I witnessed a giant forest harvester deliberately ram and flatten a lone sallow in the Straits Inclosure of Alice Holt Forest – at 9.30 am on a Sunday morning, just after I had found a caterpillar there – for no reason other than spite.

Purple Emperor larvae clearly have to contend with rather a lot, but whatever mistakes you make in life, please do not underestimate a caterpillar. They have more determination than any other living creature. The strength of their will to live, grow, and fly the golden sky is a salutary lesson to us all.

CHAPTER FOURTEEN

Looking for Purple Emperor eggs and larvae

Eggs and late summer and autumn larvae – Feeding marks and foliage diagnostics – Spring and early summer larvae – Ad absurdum

Many of the old collectors were surprisingly skilled at looking for the immature stages of butterflies, as breeding in captivity was the best way to obtain perfect specimens for the cabinet. Searching for eggs, larvae and pupae drifted out of fashion during the late twentieth century, with the advent of butterfly photography. Now, the development of macro photography and the growing thirst for ecological knowledge have reinvigorated our fascination with these life stages. A new dawn has risen, championed by Pete Eeles's superbly illustrated *Life Cycles of British & Irish Butterflies* (2019). But, make no mistake: this is not for the fainthearted.

Technically, British butterflies are at their most numerous during the egg stage, as each female may lay something in the region of 50 to 500 eggs (it varies between species and individuals, with the Purple Emperor probably performing towards the lower end of the productivity spectrum). Likewise, they can be relatively numerous in the larval stage, but you need to know how, when and where to look. The insect is actually at its scarcest in the adult stage, which perhaps suggests that too much emphasis has been placed on looking at the showy adults. The more I study Purple Emperor larvae, the more fascinating and wonderful they become, so much so that I periodically declare them to be more interesting than the adults. Indeed, for sheer tenacity, and ambition, caterpillars can scarcely be bettered.

Unfortunately, Purple Emperor eggs and larvae are not easy to find, unlike the eggs and larvae of, for example, the Orange-tip, and the overwintering eggs of the Brown Hairstreak. In fact, in many places it is almost impossible, including many of our top sites – unless you climb the sallow trees, if you can. This is because at most localities the Purple Emperor breeds high up in the treetops, with the majority of eggs being deposited on leaf sprays situated beneath the main canopy. Eggs and young larvae are, for example, almost impossible to find in Fermyn Woods and Knepp Wildland, where sallows are abundant, but so much of a muchness that one is effectively looking for a needle in a very large haystack. The difficulties at Knepp are compounded by the high browse line created by cattle and deer.

Searching for Purple Emperor eggs and larvae requires stolid dedication, if not immeasurable patience, as well as considerable powers of visual observation and concentration. I struggle to do it without the background stimulation of *Test Match Special* commentary. Anyone who has not spent time float or fly fishing, bird nesting, grovelling around looking for beetles or digging for hawk moth pupae will struggle. You've either got it in you or you haven't. Many haven't. You have to lose yourself in the task, become absorbed by it. Get yourself a good shepherd's crook (ideally a neck crook, rather than a leg crook), and if you're young and agile then climb as many sallows as is humanly possible, and search the high sub-canopy sprays in late summer and early autumn.

Some Purple Emperor enthusiasts prefer to look for eggs, which are more numerous. I used to, but with advancing years my eyesight is less strained by looking for larvae, especially second- and third-instar larvae which can be searched for during August, September and October. The time to look for eggs is during the latter stages of the flight season, finishing at the end of the first week in August at the latest – something to do while waiting for a long, slow cloud to clear or on late season mornings before the Purple Emperors become active.

The disadvantage of egg hunting is that you have to look over entire leaf surfaces, while with late summer and autumn larvae your eyes need focus only on the leaf tips – and primarily on curled leaf tips at that, with salient larval feeding marks close by. With both eggs and larvae, just the leaf upper surfaces need to be scanned, and only leaf surfaces with certain characteristics. Much of the leafage can be ignored, notably the large, coarse leaves of the outer foliage.

The secret is twofold. First, look for leaf sprays with the right characteristics, or trees in suitable situations, and bear in mind that most leaves are irrelevant to the Purple Emperor in late summer and autumn. Secondly, look out for the distinctive feeding marks produced by all but the youngest of larvae – sections of missing leaf edge either side of the midrib towards the leaf tip, which in time leave the caterpillar's seat pad purposefully stranded at the end of a narrow isthmus along the end of the midrib. No other caterpillar produces these tell-tale feeding marks; they are fully diagnostic.

Look earnestly for sprays that are mid-green in colour, matt-surfaced, soft in feel and of medium thickness. It's rather like dry fly fishing for specimen Brown Trout on a southern chalk stream: you spend most of your time studying the water, seeking out big fish – the last thing you do is cast. While prospecting, I walk past bush after bush, seeking out the round-leaved Goat Willow-type or larger-leaved and narrow-leaved bushes with mid-green foliage which the Purple Emperor prefers. I probably walk past a few eggs and larvae, as the odd one can be found just about anywhere, but I waste little time. BB did the same, homing in on what he called 'apple leaves'. His protégé Ray 'Badger' Walker showed me the trick, but I had already discovered it.

These favoured sprays occur in shady situations, mainly in the subcanopy but also on the north or east side of sallows and on bushes, young and old, growing along shaded ride edges. You may find eggs and larvae along south-facing wood edges or rides, but only where tall trees to the south provide shelter from the hot afternoon sun. Sallows growing in the open will only be suitable if they are large enough to provide their own shade, notably along their north-facing edges where the foliage may be less coarse. Sallows growing in cool, moist situations are often selected, including in hollows and along ditch and minor stream margins.

Highly favoured sallows can be called 'alpha trees'. They may produce larvae almost annually for a number of years, and are also liked by the moth larvae one regularly finds on sallows in late summer and autumn – Pebble Prominent, Buff-tip, and the small larvae of the

Grey Pug and the Common Pug. I discovered a dozen alpha trees over a 10-year period in Savernake Forest, though they only remained suitable for six to eight years. Heslop, who developed the practice of looking for early autumn larvae, swore by 'the old gnarled female *caprea* [Goat Willow]'. He was right, but look for the shaded growth that produces mid-green soft, matt leaves. Exposed foliage, even on trees that are racing certainties, will produce few if any larvae, at least in late summer and autumn.

For reasons beyond my comprehension, female trees tend to produce better-quality foliage – the mid-green medium-thickness soft, matt leaves. Most of my alpha trees have been female. In late summer, sallow trees can only be sexed by looking for the remains of flowers on twigs and on the ground. The swollen female carpels last far longer than the male flowers. In wet summers, though, the flower remains quickly rot away.

Once you have found your first egg or larva you will quickly find others. On a good day at a good site you may find an egg or young larva every 20 minutes, but one an hour is more realistic – and you will have many fruitless forays and blank days.

I would not advise searching for hibernating larvae, except on bushes that regularly support autumn larvae. That is next level stuff. Useful guidance is provided by Gabriel Hermann in his book *Searching for Butterflies in Winter* (2007). He recommends searching for silked-on feeding leaves dangling from bare branches in early winter, on young sallows along shady rides, and in other cool, moist locations, identifying Goat Willows by their blackish fallen foliage. These are cues to finding major breeding grounds, where they exist – though in

many locations, they don't. A useful alternative strategy is
to search isolated sallows along rides away from major
sallow stands, which may be found by dispersing females
– in which case they can support several larvae.

It is possible to find larvae in spring and early summer,
but in far fewer numbers. They are particularly hard to
find when they first come out of hibernation and
recommence feeding, as they are then hidden in
unfurling sprays, sometimes resting briefly on leaf
undersides. However, it is possible, even for beginners. In
a delightful and inspiring essay in Patrick Matthews's
The Pursuit of Moths and Butterflies (1957), N Wykes relates
finding five post-hibernation larvae on an old, gnarled
sallow bush one early spring, his first Purple Emperor
larvae. He was lucky – he had struck gold – though by
the following year his alpha tree had been felled.

There is a narrow window of opportunity to find
fourth-instar larvae in the early to mid-May period, as
any feeding marks on sallow leaves at that time of year
will almost certainly prove to be of *iris*. Moth larvae
commence feeding in mid-May.

Searching for final-instar larvae, in late May or early
June, is proving to be surprisingly effective, at least when
populations are (relatively) high. This is because Purple
Emperor larval damage can be salient then on long,
straight leaders, and because the large and heavy larvae
cause their seat leaves to hang near-vertically at a time of
year when most leaves are in more horizontal positions.
The drawback is that all undamaged foliage looks (and
indeed is) suitable for larvae at this time of year, so it is

virtually impossible to spot trees which would have been selected by the females. Another drawback is that most larvae are high up, out of reach; finding them necessitates scanning high foliage through binoculars. This is worth doing on dull days in late spring or early summer when few butterflies are flying. The technique is still in the research and development phase, but has the potential to develop into a useful survey method.

The record to beat, in terms of ludicrous situations in which larvae have been found, is, first and foremost, the larva I found on sallows growing over the boardwalk above the leopard enclosure in Marwell Zoo, south Hampshire, on 10 October 2015. Heslop would have been proud of me (especially as I later found that males also assemble on oaks on the crest of the hill on which the zoo is based). Second, my September 2009 record of a larva on the northern (anticlockwise) side of the Clacket Lane Services on the M25, by the Surrey–Kent border, made in full view of uniformed police officers enjoying a hard-earned cup of coffee in their patrol car. I followed this discovery up four years later by finding a spring larva on the south (clockwise) side.

Whenever you find an egg or a larva, please give vent to BB's hunting cry, which he shouted every time he found an egg or caterpillar: 'Ai! Ai!' We need to keep that tradition going, to keep his torch alight. We owe it to him, and he would love to share in our joy.

CHAPTER FIFTEEN

The Purple land that England gained

Scene setting – The beginning of greatness – Peak season
– Safari time – Mid-season switch – Season ending

This is an account of the sublime and awesome Purple Emperor season of 2018, at the living miracle that is Knepp Wildland. It shows that once in a Purple moon (which is much more special than a blue moon), everything comes right. It is a tale of wonder, which offers immense hope and demonstrates, strongly, that the Purple Emperor need not be a scarce butterfly; it can truly abound, when habitat and weather conditions are right. My title is derived from *The Purple Land that England Lost*, a novel by W H Hudson (1885).

Hibernating larvae at Knepp had survived the 2017/18 winter well, with low levels of predation. They were then able to grow rapidly during a fine May, and pupate during benign weather in early June. Everything, then, depended on flight season weather. After an indifferent start, from 22 June the 2018 flight season was blessed by a long spell of hot, dry, though sometimes windy weather. The summer months of June, July and August were hotter in England than those of the long hot summer of 1976. No rain was recorded at Knepp Castle between 31 May and 28 July. Heathrow Airport recorded 39 rainless days during that period.

Nationally, the first Purple Emperor of 2018 was recorded on 13 June, at Castor Hanglands in the East Midlands. At Knepp, the first was seen on the afternoon of 15 June, by a member of the Burrell family – a fresh male feeding on the track by Hammer Pond. From 17 June onwards, the butterfly was seen at Knepp every day, until the last was sighted, by Neil Hulme, on 26 July.

The weather at Knepp during the weekend of 16 and 17 June was poor, but Neil managed to see two males sparring at the north end of Green Lane on Sunday the 17th. I arrived at Knepp on the following day, and saw 14 freshly emerged wandering males before 3 pm, when conditions became too windy. I went on to see 2,500 day-individuals at Knepp during a 28 consecutive day marathon. To place that in context, most competent butterfliers can expect to see 250 Purple Emperors here during their lives. They are being sold woefully short.

The weather glimmered and glowered for three days. I saw 29 males, including two pristine males feeding together on a fresh fox scat, and the year's first female (nationally) on 19 June. The following day, after a cloudy morning, I counted 61 males, including a giant which must have equated to ab. *maximinus* of Heslop. The Green Lane Purple Emperor transect count that day totalled an impressive 22.

Things wobbled worryingly on 21 June. The night had been cool and the day took a long while to warm up. I saw only 56 Purple Emperors, including one female, and fretted that the previous day's tally might have been the main pulse of emergence of the year – in which case, the *annus mirabilis* I had predicted on the Purple Emperor blog was not going to occur. Numbers should have increased, at that stage of the season. The day was redeemed by the vision of a male launching itself at a feral White Stork that spiralled over Honeypools Barn field.

I need not have worried, the emergence had just been stalled by a couple of cool nights. The following day saw the start of a long hot spell which lasted until 8 August. In cloudless and calm conditions, with the temperature reaching 26 degrees Celsius, I counted 121 Purple Emperor males that day. Most were busily searching the sallow thickets for females, exploring, and establishing territories on the oaks during the afternoon. The day's only female was, rather predictably, being mated, at 4.50 pm in the top of a classic oak 'master tree' down Green Lane. The mating pair had been flushed out of the oak crown by amoral males trying to muscle in on the act, and was struggling to regain height and resettle.

Saturday 23 June was calm and bright. A tally of 178 Purple Emperors was seen, including a tussle of six squabbling males. This established a new all-time record day count for the Purple Emperor in Britain. This 'record' lasted less than 24 hours. The day's only two females were both being ardently courted, with one performing the classic 'tumbledown' rejection display of a mated female. An impressive 61 males were counted sallow searching in an hour in Rainbow field, which contains around 6 hectares of sallow-rich scrub, from 11.20 am to 12.20 pm – the highest number counted in an hour, ever, anywhere; a tally almost beyond the wildest

of Emperoring dreams. A count along the Green Lane transect route that afternoon totalled 60. Purple Emperors were seen feeding on oak sap for the first time in that season. By now I was suffering from heat stroke, blisters on two toes, a strained medial collateral ligament, and from the bites of innumerable mosquitoes and clegs, spawned by two wet days at May's end.

In such situations one does not merely carry on regardless, but ups one's effort considerably, as a point of principle. So, the following day, Midsummer Day, Neil and I broke the 300 barrier, for the first time in entomological history. In blisteringly hot weather, Neil managed to count 300 Emperors in an 11-hour day and I managed, I think, 311. The situation became farcical, with me trying to nudge Neil over the 300 mark at 7.15 pm near a wooded hillock called Tory Copse, not realising that I was already there, having miscounted my own tally (I passed O level maths at the third attempt). Our marathon included counts of 27 Purple Emperors in 27 minutes in 27 Acres field and 50 in 50 minutes in Rainbow field, all sallow-searching males. We saw only six females all day, including one being pursued by three overamorous males and another laying the first eggs of the year, at 12.25 pm. The paucity of females suggested a mighty hatch of them yet to come. Our Green Lane Purple Emperor transect reached a record 66, all males. Back in early July 1975 I had got plastered in the nearby George & Dragon after seeing 30 Purple Emperors in a day in the local woods. Now, a mile further south and with an extra nought on the Emperor tally, Neil and I were too exhausted to celebrate anything, donating my celebratory bottle of top-quality Prosecco to a young couple in the Knepp camp site. We also thought better of joining the Purple Emperors partying on fermenting oak sap at the southern end of Oak Field.

The first sizeable hatch of females took place the following day, Monday 25 June. It was cloudless, calm and what is ungratefully referred to as 'stinking hot' in the English language. Dennis Dell, the elder statesman of the People of Purple Persuasion, was visiting. An octogenarian, Dennis is only able to venture out for three hours at a time. That afternoon, in three precise hours, we managed to see 90 Purple Emperors – almost as many as Dennis had seen in England in his lifetime. Males were active over most oak trees. Many of them were seeking the shade along north-facing oak edges. Older males were quiescent in the afternoon heat, becoming active again as the temperature cooled from 5.30 pm, putting on an impressive evening flight. At 3.45 pm, the distinctive flight of a virgin female was spotted along the oaks at the southern edge of Oak Field. In a journey of 130 metres she attracted no fewer than nine males, who pursued her with an intent that made Dennis and I hang our masculine heads in shame.

The butterfly was now at peak season, with females becoming relatively prominent, and weather conditions perfect. Males were active by 8 am, and were flying for at least 12 hours each day. Some nocturnal activity was also observed, primarily on the hot moonlit night of Tuesday 26th, but my efforts at watching it then were thwarted by the arrival of a large herd of longhorn cattle.

On 27 June I counted 156 Purple Emperors, including 10 definite females. The males were so numerous that they were overspilling out of the oak canopies, and setting up territories 3–5 metres up along lengths of outgrown hedgerow offering shade from the glare of the sun. One 150-metre-long section of tall hedge was occupied by nine territorial males, squabbling freely with male Commas and Red Admirals in residence there. One of those males was so belligerent, fighting spectacularly with a testosterone-fuelled male Comma, that he will fly on in my memory forever. Normally, Emperors fly at far higher elevations than Commas, so one never sees them fight. Certainly, I had never seen *Apatura iris* versus *Polygonia c-album* and *Vanessa atalanta* before.

I was unable to conduct any thorough counts for a couple of days as I had a stream of friends visiting, coming to see the Purple Emperor in true abundance. Had I been able to do so, I would probably have exceeded the 400 mark, and ascended heavenward on a fluffy white cloud. Two of those friends were John Clark and Dr Pete Merrett, who had worked the great 1976 Purple Emperor season with me, back in Alice Holt Forest. They departed having seen a far greater flight of Purple Emperors.

The Knepp Wildland Purple Emperor Safari season opened on 28 June. That first group of 20 people spotted 29 Purple Emperors, including three females, but the weather had entered a windy phase, which limited activity. Indeed, on several days a north-east wind sprung up, reaching 'moderate' strength at lunchtime and becoming 'fresh' by teatime. Purple Emperors, of both sexes, were drifting downwind and gathering along sheltered, leeward west-facing edges. I attempted a mass count on 29 June but was disappointed to see only 218, including 10 females. The wind prevented more. The following day was less windy and Knepp Wildland naturalist Paul Fosterjohn managed to record 320 Purple Emperors, before retiring, physically hurt and mentally deranged, around 4.30 pm – vowing never to look for another Purple Emperor in his life. That Saturday, the 30th, a daylong Purple Emperor Safari group was treated to 87 Purple Emperors, including a rejection drop, or tumbledown, which took place among the delighted onlookers.

As it was the end of June, some males were already looking worn and torn. They were so numerous that for over a week it had been difficult to go more than five minutes without seeing a Purple Emperor anywhere in the Wildland. Such abundance is surely unparalleled in entomological history, at least since the Victorian heyday of Great Chattenden Wood.

July arrived in searing heat. I began by searching the undersurveyed south-western quarter of the 458-hectare Wildland, where I saw 35 Purple Emperors, including males searching White Willow for emerging females – which suggested that the butterfly breeds on that tree at Knepp. The Purple Emperor Safari group that afternoon, Sunday 1 July, was treated to 54 Purple Emperors, including seven females, four of which were accosted by males and forced to perform tumbledown rejection flights. Safari-goers were entranced by male Emperors shimmering around them, seeking the favours of uncooperative Empresses.

The following day I had to return home, briefly, though I managed to see a few Purple Emperors in wind-tossed Savernake Forest on my way back to Knepp in the late afternoon. I had missed out that day, badly: the wind had been light at Knepp and Neil had recorded a staggering 388 Purple Emperors in a 10-hour marathon, including a knot of 13 males pursuing one unfortunate female. It was enough to convert him to feminism.

The north-east wind returned the following day, but that afternoon's Purple Emperor Safari group still managed to see 34 Purple Emperors, mainly along the sheltered oak edge of Bentons Gorse copse, an ancient woodland relic in the centre of the Wildland, where mated females were again being unduly pestered by males.

Only 4 July the wind veered around to the south, and died down. But the Emperors were by now quietening down. The males were ceasing to search the sallow stands for freshly emerged females, as the female emergence was nearly complete. Also, the males were beginning to age (or were hungover following England's football World Cup victory over Columbia the previous evening). I counted only 147 in a full-day count in ideal weather conditions. Moreover, the Green Lane transect count was down to 56.

Another hugely successful Purple Emperor Safari took place the following afternoon, when 60 Purple Emperors were seen, including 10 females, a posse of six males in flight together, and three tumbledown rejection flights around the safari group. The message to wildlife tourism and nature engagement in Britain is simple: beat that, if you can!

The weather then heated up further. The males were becoming inactive during the morning, though increasingly territorial during the afternoon. I saw 69 on the afternoon of 6 July. Some more night flying was then observed, in bright moonlight around Bentons Gorse, only this time I was joined and distracted by the free-ranging Tamworth pigs, who relieved me of my midnight snack (their need was greater than mine).

Quality was starting to make up for a decline in quantity. The afternoon safari group on Saturday 7 July saw only 34 Purple Emperors, though that included three females seen egg laying simultaneously in sallows near Bentons Gorse. The full-day Purple Emperor Safari on 8 July totalled only 37 Purple Emperors, including an aged male seen feeding low down on an oak trunk before flying off low and falteringly, into the blistering sun, to die. The switch had been flicked: the female emergence was complete and the males were now taking the mornings off. The oldest males were becoming heat-suppressed, and were quiescent between 3 pm and 5 pm.

The surviving Emperors were becoming afternoon butterflies, increasingly dependent on oak sap. Purple Emperors were no longer everywhere; instead, they were aggregating around feeder trees out of the wind. On 9 July I managed to count only 24 on the Green Lane transect route.

As mid-July approached it was still possible to see 30 or 40 Purple Emperors in a day, or rather, in an afternoon and an evening. There was even a little dead time, produced by periods of dense cloud. The males were becoming restricted to the Green Lane oaks and the oaks along the edge of Bentons Gorse.

The final Purple Emperor Safari group, on the 12th, was pleased to see 27 Purple Emperors, including a freshly emerged female – the last of the great emergence of 2018. In all, Neil and I had shown Purple Emperors to some 250 visitors to the Wildland. All had returned home having experienced something deeply memorable, though keeping them hydrated and focused had been challenging. One flagging group had been revived by an enforced chant of, 'Up yours, January!'

A thunderstorm started to brew on the evening of 13 July, but it issued only a single crack of thunder at Knepp, and not a single drop of rain. Horsham, to the north, got a welcome soaking. That afternoon, Neil and I saw our final Emperors of the year as a duo: a male flushed a female out of a sallow bush in 27 Acres Field, and then triggered another pair into action – so our final experience together was of back-to-back tumbledowns. Rumour has it that we walked out together with our trousers on our heads: Neil was going off to save the Grayling butterfly from becoming extinct on the South Downs, and I was going to visit somewhere called Home, then return to Knepp for the finale of the 2018 Purple Emperor season – before travelling to the Pyrenees where the Purple Emperor was approaching peak season. Between the two of us we managed to cover the ending of the 2018 Wildland season.

Drought was now affecting many of the young sallow thickets, where the trees were less than 20 years old. The older sallows in the laggs and around the lakes and streams were untroubled, but many of the younger sallow stands in the ex-arable fields were steadily dropping the subcanopy leaves on which Purple Emperor females lay most of their eggs, especially the narrow-leaved varieties. There was some local variation: stands of young sallows in the south-west corner of Woggs Bottom and at the west end of Brookhouse 8 fields remained relatively healthy, but those in Crabtree, 27 Acres and Rainbow fields were dropping leaves steadily, with a russet carpet of fallen leaves lying on the ground. The broad-leaved sallows, which the Purple Emperor favours, proved more resilient, though some had been dropping the all-important subcanopy leaves on which young larvae feed – the larger, thicker and coarser outer canopy leaves were fine, but those are unsuitable for young Purple Emperor larvae. Incidentally, the 2019 emergence was about half that of 2018, partly because of the impact of the July 2018 drought and partly because of three wet weeks during June 2019. By butterfly standards this is only a modest population collapse, only a blip; and I knew it was coming.

Rain was desperately needed. It was supposed to arrive at Knepp on Saturday 21 July, but went elsewhere instead. By then, I had already found second-instar Purple Emperor larvae, suggesting that the insect was fighting back against developing drought conditions by accelerating through its growth phases.

I worked hard to see 20 Purple Emperors on 21 July, including 15 along the Green Lane transect route. That took the 2018 Green Lane transect annual tally to 201, and the season into its fifth week. The following day I

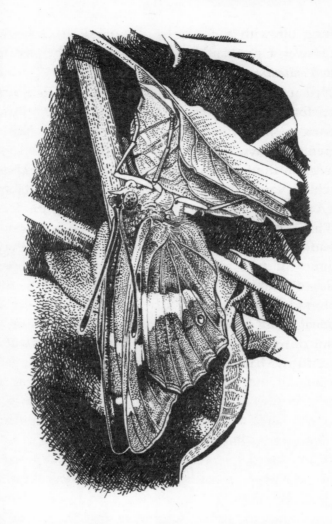

struggled to see 13 Purple Emperors, all OAPs, including five females. The first did not appear until 1.44 pm. Late in the day three females were seen feeding together on oak sap bleeds. They were exhausted, and may have run out of eggs to lay. I saw my last Emperors of the Great 2018 Purple Emperor Season the following afternoon, signing off with a couple of venerable males battling away over a popular Green Lane territory called *The State Penitentiary*.

Neil returned to see a worn and ragged male and a lone female along Green Lane on 26 July. Purple Emperors had flown at Knepp Wildland for 37 stupendous days. Two days later the long-awaited rains arrived, in the form of thunderstorms which clobbered much of South East and eastern England, and blotted out a full lunar eclipse.

This is the account of my 49th Purple Emperor season. It had surpassed all its predecessors, including the great summer of 1976 and the stupendous Purple Emperor season of 1983, Ken Willmott's favourite. It was the most profound temporal experience of my life. Some of the residual lumps from insect bites were present still on the palms of my hands the following July, as stigmata. Even now, if I rub hard, they rise again.

CHAPTER SIXTEEN

Conservation issues

Questionings – A wind through the willows – The sallow's fall from grace – Conservation evidence base – Conservation systems – Habitat management: pollarding, coppicing and propagating sallows – Deer and squirrels – Scientific research priorities

Readers will expect a thorough chapter on the conservation of the Purple Emperor from an author who worked in the nature conservation industry for four decades, not least because the butterfly is categorised as being a Species of Conservation Concern under the UK Biodiversity Framework. Be careful: I am not convinced that the insect needs some of the thinking and practices of contemporary nature conservation, and fear we have devised too many systems.

Above all, the Purple Emperor simply needs understanding, and appreciating better. The former is hugely challenging to us, the latter should come naturally.

I have stated before, and will reiterate here, that the butterfly does not come before the egg, or vice versa: the larval foodplant comes first, in suitable situations, and the butterfly attempts to track the development of new breeding grounds. Sallows and willows are early colonisers of bare damp ground, favouring clays and alluviums, respectively.

Sallows and willows were among the first trees to colonise the postglacial tundra. In his classic book *Ancient Woodland* (2003), the tree historian Oliver Rackham suggests that the first sallows arrived here between 12,000 and 10,000 BC, and that *Salix caprea* and *S. cinerea* types probably arrived before the Atlantic period, some 6,200 BC. That would have given humans plenty of time to use or eliminate them.

It is clear from Rackham's work that sallows used to be valued, greatly. He emphasises that sallow stems were commonly used for rods in medieval wattle and daub houses, and quotes from Holinshed's Chronicle of 1577: 'In times past men were contented to dwell in houses, builded of sallow, willow, plumtree, hardbeme (hornbeam) and elme ...'. He also points out that tenants were often obliged to plant fast-growing sallows in worked coppices; for example, at Cawston in Norfolk, in 1612, 'The lessee shall fell two acres of underwood a year ... He shall yearely and everie yere of the 14 yeres put a good number of Sallows in the vacant and emptye places ...'. It is likely that sallows were not merely planted for wood fuel; they had multiple uses, including hurdles.

Most important of all, though this is understated in Rackham's work, sallows and willows were valued as a source of early spring browse, notably in pasture-woodlands on clay lands where winter stocking, and resultant poaching, held back the growth of spring grass. This is evident today in the New Age pasture-woodland of Knepp Wildland, where cattle browse avidly on unfurling sallow foliage at the critical time before the grass begins to grow well. Isabella Tree and her husband Charlie Burrell believe that Knepp's longhorn cattle extract some kind of natural fly repellent from sallow foliage and/or sap, as well as pain relief from salicylic acid, a type of aspirin. This is hardly surprising, as sallows were a common constituent of the old-fashioned 'medicine fields' where ailing cattle were depastured in order to self-medicate.

Sallow also had, and still has, much cultural significance. Rackham found that 15.5 per cent of English villages and hamlets were named after sallows or willows, from a sample of 812. In another book (*Woodlands*, 2006), he also points out that sallow is one of the trees most frequently listed in Anglo-Saxon charters, after thorn(s), oaks and, interestingly, Crab Apple. This suggests that sallows and willows were far commoner of yore.

It is hard to say when sallows went out of vogue. Rackham casts no light on this. My guess is that they were gradually rendered redundant, and fell into negative equity when conifer forestry came strongly into fashion with the formation of the Forestry Commission in 1919. Actually, the history of coniferisation goes back further than that, to late Victorian times, suggesting perhaps a gradual decline in favour. The Forestry Commission's roots lie in the 1909 *Royal Commission on Coast Erosion and Afforestation*, a report which set the new body's vision.

Whenever it began, sallows were regarded as pernicious weeds during and after the Second World War, because of their potential to outcompete newly planted trees. They got caught up in the Dig for Victory mindset, and in the post-war recovery and food security ethos. Money and manpower were readily available for managing woodland plantations, and sallows are easy to fell by axe — and felling became even easier with the development of light chainsaws during the second half of the twentieth century. As explained in my chapter on the New Forest in *In Pursuit of Butterflies*, the ride-side shrub zone in this forest was steadily eliminated during the 1950s. The same happened in many other forests. There was a budget for it. Also, sallows probably got caught up in the mindset engendered by the (ridiculous) Weeds Act of 1959, which listed a range of 'injurious' farmland plants that had to be eliminated.

This is when the Purple Emperor spiralled into decline, and when most county extinctions occurred. However, it was surely not so much the butterfly that was in decline, but rather its foodplant, at a time when a great many woods were either blackening into dark forests of firs, pines and spruces, being neglected so that sallows dwindled, or being cleared for agriculture, housing, industry or roads.

Today, sallows are still regarded as weeds on many of the more 'traditional' forest estates (though 'traditional' here at best goes back only about a century). However, attitudes are now changing quite strongly, not least because of the recognition of the importance of sallows for biodiversity and because of their potential in wood biofuel production. Dr Mark Young's *The Natural History of Moths* (1997) states that sallow is our third most important tree for moths, supporting 108 species, after birches (121 species) and oaks (119). Sallow blossom is also a major spring nectar and pollen source for a wide range of insects, notably for bees (including the European Honey Bee) and hoverflies. In 1999 there was even a sympathetic piece in the Royal Forestry Society's *Quarterly Journal of Forestry* entitled 'In defence of sallow', by enlightened forester Simon Leatherdale. The Forestry Commission's felling of several hundred ride-side sallows, which destroyed a prime Purple Emperor breeding ground in the Straits Inclosure of Alice Holt Forest early in 2010, generated such a mighty rumpus that they will think twice, or thrice, before acting similarly in future.

It may well be that the current expansion of the Purple Emperor population is due primarily to the permitted return of the humble sallow, in an age of incipient ecological enlightenment.

Evidence-based conservation is not as easy as it sounds, as hard facts are often lacking. With the Purple Emperor, there was until very recently precious little ecological information, and much of what did exist was qualitative or anecdotal. Much of the basic evidence in UK butterfly ecology emanates from the UK Butterfly Monitoring Scheme, which commenced in 1976 and uses a methodology inappropriate for this and other canopy-dwelling species, which are seldom encountered within the prescribed 5-metre recording box – the box is too narrow. Butterfly distribution recording (dot map recording) provides another crucial layer of information, but we have already seen that the Purple Emperor has been significantly under-recorded, at least until very recently.

Our butterfly scientists determine how individual species are performing by analysing both the monitoring data and the distribution data. Butterfly Conservation and the Centre for Ecology & Hydrology conduct (usually) five-yearly reviews of the status of British butterflies, using all this data. The latest review, conducted in 2015, shows that the Purple Emperor increased in distribution by a massive 135 per cent during the period 2005–14, albeit after having suffered a significant decline (in the region of 50 per cent) between 1970 and 1995. The species with the next strongest expansion rate during this period was the Silver-washed Fritillary, which increased by a mere 55 per cent. This makes the Purple Emperor a massive success story, at a time of catastrophic biodiversity decline.

Until very recently there was no baseline for the Purple Emperor, just assumption, mythology, rumour and at times deliberate obfuscation. The baseline that is now being established is being set during a period of unprecedented recording which is almost certainly coinciding with an era of expansion by the Purple Emperor. Never mind shifting baseline syndrome, in which each human generation accepts less wildlife than its predecessor; this butterfly is threatening to give us rising baseline syndrome! It is not just bucking trends, it's smashing them to smithereens. The next *State of the UK's Butterflies*, due out late in 2020, could be most revealing, and may feature the image of a Purple Emperor on its front cover. Conservation needs every success story it can gain, and this spectacular and highly non-conformist butterfly is poised to deliver a mighty success story.

We should be concerned, however, that such success might remove the butterfly from being a Species of Conservation Concern. That would render it a second-class or third-class citizen in conservation thinking.

Our problem, of course, is that despite my efforts here, and those of Ken Willmott before me, our understanding of the ecology of the Purple Emperor is still inadequate. We remain woefully short of understanding what makes the Purple Emperor really tick. Thorough scientific investigations into the detailed ecology of this butterfly are urgently required, so that the current positive trend can be consolidated. I hope my work inspires that research. Sadly, single species ecological studies are distinctly out of vogue in the world of scientific funding.

Butterfly scientists divide British butterflies into habitat specialists and habitat generalists. These are media-friendly terms, and their usage assists the understanding of the role of butterflies as governmental Biodiversity Indicators. Habitat specialists have a limited range of larval foodplants and are associated with habitats that tend to be confined to sites with nature conservation designations. Many are generally sedentary in habit. The generalists are mobile opportunists, whose needs may be variously met, and which are not dependent on foodplants or habitat conditions restricted largely to nature reserves and designated wildlife sites.

The Purple Emperor has been included in the habitat specialist camp, but should in all honesty be moved in with the generalists. Therein could lie problems for it, especially if it continues to show positive distribution trends, as conservation effort is prioritised towards the rarer species – to species in need – especially those whose ecological requirements are well understood. Conservation funding and resources are directed towards reversing species declines. There are targets, monitoring and reporting systems for all this, as part of government commitment to reversing biodiversity decline. The Purple Emperor is coming increasingly outside that box, and its needs may even clash with those of scarcer species, the true habitat specialists. It is not an indicator species, or – as previously thought – an ancient woodland specialist, or one restricted to a narrow niche of valued semi-natural vegetation communities. The Purple Emperor could become the victim of its own success and allowed to slip through the nature conservation net.

Consequently, it could sink low on the list of conservation priorities, and miss out on funding opportunities. As a hopefully hypothetical example, its populations in some of the Northamptonshire woods could be significantly reduced by management targeting two much scarcer butterfly species, the Wood White and the Chequered Skipper (which is currently being reintroduced there).

The fact that the Purple Emperor is a generalist rather than a specialist, almost equally at home in ancient forest, conifer woodland with sallow-lined rides, scrub developing over a reverting ex-arable field, or suburban country parks, could make the UK nature conservation movement somewhat prejudiced against it, or at best neutral, or even confused. If so, its future may lie more off designated sites than on them, where it risks getting overruled by the needs of rarer species and rare habitat features. In contemporary nature conservation, rarity trumps the beautiful and readily sustainable for resources.

Furthermore, the Purple Emperor is an opportunist species and a powerful symbol of new nature land. This is one of the main messages from Knepp Wildland and from smaller rewilding sites within the Purple Empire.

This butterfly is quite at home on over-enriched and ecologically degraded soils, where sallows may abound.

However, nature conservationists are going to find themselves pressurised by people who want to see this butterfly in numbers, and who value it deeply – and cultural significance is everything. Make no mistake, this is one of the most deeply iconic and treasured features of our flora and fauna, a must-see species. It is truly loved. That is what will ensure its future. Wake up, nature conservation: the whole show is about love, beauty and wonder, and with the future – as opposed to what might have been in the past.

So how then should we manage habitats with the Purple Emperor in mind? What are the dos and don'ts? That should be simple. It isn't, not least because the butterfly's needs (as far as they are known) can be variously met.

First and foremost, it must be pointed out that open rides and glades may not be essential to the Purple Emperor. A great many of the woods it has been recorded from, recently and in the past, are dense – Liz Goodyear and Andrew Middleton mainly record from outside woods, working the wood edge. However, open rides and glades – Heslop's 'fissures in the Emperor's world' – are fairly essential to our experience of the Purple Emperor, and probably also to effective monitoring and recording, and open spaces containing bare ground are periodically essential for sallow regeneration.

The essential requirement of the Purple Emperor today is for bushes of the broader-leaved sallows, especially those veering towards the true Goat Willow, which offer the shaded subcanopy foliage required by vulnerable first-instar larvae (medium-sized leaves that are mid-green in colour, of medium thickness, soft, and with matt surfaces, beneath the canopy umbrella, or on the shady side of the bush). The smaller-leaved and narrow-leaved types of sallow are less favoured, as are those in exposed situations, with coarse or glossy foliage.

This means that a great many of the sallows in any wooded place may almost be irrelevant to the butterfly. It will scarcely breed on the small-leaved and very narrow-leaved varieties; they can be cleared away, if needs must, but save the Goat Willow types, especially bushes along shady east- or north-facing edges.

Where sallow quality is low, sallow quantity must be high – as is the case at Knepp Wildland. This is to ensure that the females have a fair chance of finding foliage suitable for the vulnerable first-instar larvae. Consequently, until our understanding of the Purple Emperor's breeding requirements improves further, the emphasis must be on maintaining sallow quantity, to ensure quality.

Sallows become suitable for Purple Emperors after their fifth year, in general, though coppice or pollard regrowth may become suitable after three. So, if there is a need to eliminate sallows, hit them when they are small, not after the Purple Emperor has begun to use them – unless you want complaints and a rumpus in the local media.

There is no 'safe' period in the butterfly's life to fell offending sallows (e.g. those leaning out into woodland rides). The closest would be the first two weeks of the Purple Emperors flight season, before too many eggs have been laid, or perhaps the end of May when the highly mobile final-instar larvae are present.

In many woods, sallows occur primarily along ride edges, having colonised the bare clay of the ditch margins and adjoining verges. Here they can grow thick, fast and straight, battling for supremacy against each other. When cramped, they begin to lean out into the ride, or forest road, where they can obstruct vehicles, horse riders, cyclists, pedestrians, and so on, and pose health and safety issues. The challenge here is to reset the sallow line further back, well behind the ditch line, so that there is a proper graded ride edge, from tall timber trees, through sallow and thorn scrub, through dense bramble patches, to the ditch, and out on to grassy ride edges. Forestry England has recently started to do this in the Fermyn Woods complex. Doubtless their colleagues in other districts will follow suit. That is how to get the Purple Emperor off your back – only do it gradually, not all in one go.

Likewise, Forestry England's management of the sallow resource in Savernake Forest is highly laudable. There are also other exemplar sites on Forestry England land: Bernwood Forest north of Oxford and Eartham Woods north of Chichester in West Sussex, to name but two. Outside the Forestry England sector, I would highlight Bentley Wood as the best-managed wood in the country for butterflies in general, and a model site for all large woods managed with nature conservation and forestry equally in mind. It is owned and managed by a small charitable trust.

By and large, on sites managed for nature conservation the preferred management options for open-grown (non-ride-side) sallows are, first and foremost, non-intervention; second, do nothing; third, leave the bloody things alone; fourth, do something that actually needs doing instead. Open-grown sallows are quite capable of looking after themselves, and living for a surprisingly long time – there are many centenarian sallow trees in Savernake Forest, which established themselves as open-grown trees. When sallows collapse they can resprout again, given glade space, from root plates or from along the trunk. They can even become 'walking trees', with the ends of branches embedding into the ground and rooting to produce new trees. This habit can be encouraged by ensuring that sallows occur within small glades, so that they are neither too shaded nor too exposed. So, leave the sallows alone, but do some limited glade work around them, to prevent them becoming overshaded.

A problem area for Purple Emperor management is where there are myriad drawn-up spindly young sallow trees, which have grown up together as whips, en masse, and are competing with each other for space. The sallow fields at Knepp Wildland are of this habit. There, they will probably sort themselves out: the strong will outcompete the weak, though whole blocks will be vulnerable to wind blow. But along ride, bridleway or road edges, rotational coppicing or pollarding could be a management solution, with pollarding being necessary where deer populations are high, as coppiced sallow regrowth is highly palatable to deer. Coppiced stools or pollarded trunks can produce prodigious regrowth, of 3 metres a year.

Sallows are easy to cut, and coppicing or pollarding them is popular with volunteer labour forces. This can lead to unnecessary work being done – the volunteers like doing it, so it is done. The Purple Emperor can survive in coppiced plots, though not at high population levels, except in extensive coppice woodland systems where there are numerous coppice coups or panels. But, once you start coppicing or pollarding sallows, you will need to continue – as you may well find that Grey Squirrels attack the resultant young bark, and kill the regrowth (see the next section).You may end up thinking, 'Why didn't we just leave the bloody things alone, like it said in the book, and concentrate instead on generating sallow regeneration?'

Volunteers can, however, have a fantastic time planting in new sallows. Given that sallows are, in the main, fairly short-lived trees, there will be a need for periodic sallow recruitment. There is a useful leaflet, produced by the Forestry Commission's Research Station in Alice Holt Forest in 1990 and available online, entitled *Propagation of Lowland Willows by Winter Cuttings*. It states that Goat Willow is hard to grow from cuttings and is best propagated from its seed, which is very short-lived. However, other sallows, including Goat Willow hybrids, can be propagated in numbers by taking winter cuttings from ripe wood leader growths, 20 centimetres long and 12–25 millimetres thick, with a single healthy bud 1 centimetre below the tip. These should be grown on 30 centimetres apart in nursery rows, and planted out a year or so later.

Goat Willow-types are, in fact, best propagated by cutting rods of 1 metre long by 2–4 centimetres thick in late autumn or early winter, and slotting them well into bare clay (getting at least a third of the rod into the ground).Holes can be made with a crowbar.A 50 per cent take can easily be achieved, or exceeded. This technique was developed in Pamber Forest Local Nature Reserve, Hampshire, back in the mid-1980s. Many of the resultant trees are thriving today, many as pollards.

The prime objective of sallow management for the Purple Emperor is to ensure continuity of supply of suitable (mainly broad-leaved) sallows at – wait for it – landscape level. This is difficult and confusing, as it is hard to determine what constitutes a landscape. Suffice it to say that several geographic layers are involved, which all need taking into account. The rational approach is to concentrate on localities where sallow management can be influenced, under the principle of where we can best make a difference.

The Purple Emperor is one species that could benefit well from the current vogue for biodiversity offsetting (conservation actions that are designed to give biodiversity benefits, to compensate for losses on a quid pro quo basis), as sallow thickets can be easily and quickly established. A danger here is that females may readily disperse from small areas of suitable sallows, on a nature reserve, into vast expanses of hostile terrain – which is why a landscape approach is necessary.

Whatever the boundaries of influence are, pulses of sallow regeneration will be needed periodically. In effect, breeding grounds can be pop-up features, which flare Purple for a while before fading, though this is difficult to plan, and cannot be left to serendipity.

One crucial issue is the number of sallow trees necessary to sustain a Purple Emperor colony. This is difficult to determine due to the butterfly's mobility, its habit of occurring diffusely within large areas of landscape, its ability to occur at low population levels, and the fact that many of the sallows present at a site may be unsuitable.

For years I sought out isolated sites which could hold the jigsaw puzzle piece I so desperately needed. Eventually, I found it high on the Lambourn Downs, in the extreme south-west corner of Oxfordshire, up against the borders of Berkshire and Wiltshire. There, the National Trust owns 125 hectares of ancient wood pasture, plantation woodland and parkland around Ashdown House, a seventeenth-century Dutch-style mansion tenanted out to a rock star. Ashdown Woods are surrounded by oceans of arable farmland and open downland escarpments, and are seriously isolated – the nearest woodland, and Purple Emperor colony, is at least 8 kilometres away. The Emperor has probably been at Ashdown for decades, if not centuries – although it was only 'discovered' there around 2015. A thorough search for sallows in the three near-contiguous woodland blocks at Ashdown, during September 2019, produced a tally of 66 sallows, of which about 50 appear to be suitable. Nearly all these trees are, though, genuine veterans – only three are young, as a large population of Fallow Deer hinders sallow regeneration. Many of these veterans are among the oldest sallows I have ever seen. So, there you have it: 50 good sallows in 125 hectares will support a sizeable, sustainable Purple Emperor population in isolation, in perpetuity – as long as the sallows last.

The extent to which the butterfly utilises the true willows is simply not known. I am just starting to work on this subject area now. This is difficult for me as the foliage scarcely meets my mid-green soft, matt criteria – it's highly glossy. Willow usage is outside my box, but

one of the glories of the Purple Emperor is that it takes
you outside of every knowledge box you ever construct,
as a matter of principle – and then pulverises the box. I
have, though, searched assiduously for larvae on Aspen in
and around Savernake Forest after high egg-lay seasons,
and found precisely none. The butterfly is reputed to
utilise Aspen abroad, and there is at least one UK record.
However, the females will encounter severe problems
depositing eggs on its highly mobile foliage – the tree is
not called *Populus tremula* for nothing.

High deer populations pose a major threat to Purple
Emperor habitat, by hindering sallow regeneration and
killing young sallows by fraying the bark. Muntjac Deer,
or more precisely Reeves' Muntjac, are notorious low
browsers, capable of preventing sallow regeneration.
Fallow Deer kill about 15 per cent of young sallows that
appear in Savernake Forest, by stripping or fraying the
soft bark around the trunks of young sallows. At Knepp
Wildland, Fallow and Red Deer avidly strip young
sallow bark during the winter. Luckily, the latter were
introduced to the rewilding scheme as sallow trees were
maturing, and starting to produce fissured, tougher bark.
Had the Reds arrived 10 years earlier, the Wildland
would be supporting a much smaller Purple Emperor
population, and far fewer sallows.

The Grey Squirrel has recently developed the habit
of stripping bark from sallows during the high-summer
months, quickly killing the trees. I first noticed this in
2009, at Selborne Common in Hampshire. Since then,
I have studied it in some detail and can reveal that

Grey Squirrels strongly favour the types of sallows preferred by the Purple Emperor – the broader-leaved sallows, particularly true Goat Willow, and especially the female trees. They largely avoid the narrow-leaved types. I do not know why. I have seen newly developed Purple Emperor breeding grounds destroyed by squirrel damage and am adamant that this mammal poses a major threat to the butterfly, in both town and country. Sallow recruitment rates dropped alarmingly in Savernake Forest when squirrel control ceased around 2012. Interestingly, squirrel damage to sallows is low in the far north of the forest where a pheasant shoot is still in operation, and where squirrels are periodically controlled.

Where squirrel control is deemed necessary, natural control by the Northern Goshawk and the European Pine Marten offer alternative solutions to shooting or trapping. Breeding pairs of Northern Goshawks have been recorded feeding their young almost exclusively on Grey Squirrel carcasses, with squirrel-kill rates of 95 per cent, 90 per cent and 68 per cent being recorded at closely monitored nests on Forestry England land in the Midlands, Derbyshire and Devon, respectively (Raptor Politics website, 2019). The only caveat I would add here is that these three study sites were primarily coniferous woodland, which would have influenced prey choice and availability (the fact that the last Goshawk I saw was being pursued by an irate male Purple Emperor is secondary).

The case for Grey Squirrel control by Pine Martens is even more compelling, and is supported by much first-rate science. The theory is simple: Grey Squirrels

do not recognise Pine Martens as predators, having evolved separately (in North America) – so they are easy prey. The Red Squirrel, on the other hand, knows about the Pine Marten, as they co-evolved, and knows how to avoid being caught. However, do not be surprised if Grey Squirrels learn to avoid Pine Martens in time, for they are canny creatures.

Finally, nature reserve managers and committees will have to ask themselves whether they want Purple Emperor populations or large populations of tits (in winter), as the two are mutually exclusive. There is a strong argument against erecting and maintaining tit nesting boxes in and around Purple Emperor sites.

To date, very little rigorous, peer-reviewed scientific work has been conducted into the ecology of the Purple Emperor, and most what has been published is not particularly elucidating. Much of the necessary technology is not quite there, yet. As already suggested, trail camera technology needs to improve, in the form of smaller, more discrete cameras that mimic twigs, and technology is needed for radio tracking canopy-dwelling butterflies.

In summary, the priorities for proper scientific fieldwork on the Purple Emperor are as follows. Firstly, to test the 'Oates hypothesis': that Purple Emperor females mainly select leaves with particular characteristics, which are necessary for the vulnerable first-instar larvae. This work would quantify what (if anything) is meant by my 'mid-green medium-thickness soft, matt' foliage (and BB's 'apple leaves'). Obviously, it can be broadened out to look at coarseness, hardness, leaf hairiness and wider *Salix* preferences, including the use of true willows (*Salix alba*, etc.), and the biochemistry of selected foliage (including nitrogen levels). In effect, this is work to determine larval niche ecology in *Apatura iris*.

Secondly, mark-and-recapture work, or tracking work, to determine adult longevity, dispersal and landscape utilisation, and to provide indications of population size. This will happen when new, better technology arrives.

Thirdly, biochemistry work to determine the extent of pheromone usage in this species. This could suggest how the species manages to subsist at low population density.

Fourthly, work to clarify the issue of whether climate change will cause invertebrate herbivory to increase on sallows, so that Purple Emperor larvae are outcompeted. This issue is discussed in the next chapter.

Finally, further modelling to suggest where the Purple Emperor's true range in the UK should be, under various different climate change scenarios, and with close reference to the likely impacts of climate change on the butterfly's foodplants and the larval niche. In particular, will climate change cause the young larvae to jump out of synchrony with a crucial stage of leaf suitability? This is also discussed in the next chapter, and will develop from work set out in the *Climatic Risk Atlas of European Butterflies* (2008).

The message to scientists is simple: the door is open; get in there, you're needed, you'll love it!

CHAPTER SEVENTEEN

The future

Mobility and new dynamics – Town and country – Climate
change and the move north – War against scrub – Parasites, pests,
poxes and diseases – Purple haze

Heslop's essay on the future of the Purple Emperor, first circulated in 1953 and included in *Notes & Views of the Purple Emperor*, is a polite and restrained lament against the ravages of mass coniferisation. He writes: 'the fair woods that our grandfathers planted or replanted are disappearing like corn before the reaper, and being replaced in general by alien trees which are not really suited to our soil or our climate but which will yield quick cash.' He predicted that 'by 1975 it seems certain that, at the best, the Purple Emperor will be confined to not very numerous, and wholly isolated communities.' He saw nature reserves, managed with the Purple Emperor in mind, as the solution, augmented by breeding and releasing to help the butterfly jump across unsuitable landscapes to colonise suitable habitat at or outside range edges. Such was the threat posed to woodland wildlife by mass coniferisation, which remained rampant until 1970 when the Secretary of State stopped the near-total coniferisation of the New Forest inclosures, and started the process of turning things around. The difficulty, of course, is that woodland planning is a long-term business, given the slow nature of trees.

Heslop had underestimated the Purple Emperor's mobility and powers of colonisation, though he would not have done so had today's distribution and population monitoring databases been available. Also, today's insights into the problems of habitat isolation and fragmentation, and breaks in continuity of supply of habitat patches at landscape level, show that nature reserves alone will not suffice – unless they are legion, and well connected. Mercifully, the Purple Emperor is clearly a highly mobile insect, capable of crossing hostile terrain to colonise new habitat patches. Therein lies its future. It should take full advantage of the 'bigger, better and more joined up' ethos championed for the government by Sir John Lawton's *Making Space for Nature* review (2010). It could also benefit hugely from biodiversity offsetting, the practice of creating new areas of habitat for those lost to development, and – most important, and usefully – the mass creation of new woods to capture carbon under climate change mitigation planning.

However, it is likely that this butterfly, and many others, will get knocked into new dynamics by a cocktail of environmental changes, positive and negative, linked to climate change and 'bioglobalisation' (the increased movement of species around the globe due to human activity – the inadvertent hitch-hikers).

So, please don't expect more of the same, let alone stability. Expect something radical, like the Purple Emperor being discovered in South Lakeland (and current climate change modelling may well suggest that the species should be there, in which case we may need to establish it there – if it's not already present). And don't be complacent: just because this particular species is on a roll today doesn't mean that it won't plummet tomorrow, for change is the norm with insect populations.

The key to the butterfly's success, and to its future, is its mobility. It can traverse and penetrate landscapes. The fact that it has turned up in isolated places surrounded by urbanisation or oceans of intensive agriculture – toxic wastelands to insects – speaks volumes. There is serious hope for this species, at least for the present. Also, as Heslop cleverly espoused, and Liz Goodyear and Andrew Middleton have demonstrated, it can exist well below our radar, at low population levels, and then resurge unexpectedly.

Certainly, expect the Purple Emperor to become acknowledged as *the* butterfly of Greater London, where sallows can put themselves about wherever periodic disturbance or urban greening occurs. In 2019, Greater London contained three National Nature Reserves, 144 Local Nature Reserves plus 77 other sizeable nature reserves (including 49 county wildlife trust reserves), and no fewer than 968 Sites of Interest for Nature Conservation. Most of the latter are small sites, such as lawns and minor cemeteries, and many more will be transitory, pop-up sites. But as a living matrix, this is impressive – and greater in mass than any amount of semi-natural habitat remaining in heavily-farmed landscapes. Many of these wild places can support clumps of sallows. Birmingham is similarly placed to offer this butterfly a home, not least in the Tame Valley. The potential offered by green belt land to the Purple Emperor is nothing short of enormous.

Suburban environments may well be able to offer the Purple Emperor more than intensively farmed landscapes.

Urban nature reserves and pop-up nature parks on land
awaiting redevelopment offer much scope for sallow
establishment. In addition, sallows can be used for
screening, shelter belts and instant shrubberies, because
they grow fast, flower pleasantly in early spring and offer
considerable benefits to wider biodiversity – and they
are easy to prune or fell, and their relatively soft wood
feeds easily into woodchip machines. They are also at
home, and are appropriate, along roads and canals, and
also in gardens and parks. All this adds up to metahabitat,
which can support a butterfly that wants to occur within
metapopulation structures.

Many country sportsmen responsible for pheasant
preserve woods will have a fondness for this butterfly.
They have heard of it, and want it present in and around
their woods, if only because it provides an interesting
topic of conversation to raise during social sessions on
shooting days. The response I have received from
shooting estates has been most welcoming, and it may be
that more can be done for the conservation of the Purple
Emperor on these estates than on many designated
wildlife sites. This may even help to resolve the war that
is developing between elements of the nature
conservation movement and the country sports
movement. Here I must confess that shooting is
abhorrent to me, being of Quaker and Franciscan
persuasion and having an aversion to explosive noise, but
I recognise that it is central to many people's relationship
with nature and that all country lovers have more in
common than they may have out of common – and the
Purple Emperor simply doesn't care (in my darkest
moods, I wonder whether a new winter country sport

could develop – blasting tit flocks out of the woods with dust shot, or at least their infernal nest boxes). Heslop and Watkins-Pitchford were country sportsmen naturalists (the latter shot only for the pot, and often nearly poisoned himself in the process).

Climate change is arguably the major issue facing this planet, outscaling even human population growth and ambition. Its impact on all our butterflies and their habitats will be legion, and what affects an insect today will affect humankind's tomorrow. It will bring new interconnectivities into play, which are currently lying latent. You might think that the Purple Emperor's current range expansion indicates that the butterfly is benefitting from climate change. Think again, and examine the evidence.

Early springs, following on from mild winters, cause sallows to come into leaf early. That benefits post-hibernation larvae, enabling them to commence feeding early, rather than being stuck in the airport departure lounge and risking desiccation (see p. 228). This, I am sure, helps to explain the Purple Emperor's current expansion.

However, this benefit is countered by the increased loss of hibernating larvae when the midwinter period is frost-free. Mild winters – and in particular spells of winter weather containing warm, sunny days which are not punctuated by frosty nights – are disastrous for the hibernating larvae, interrupting diapause and causing them to wander around and run out of fuel, unable to replenish themselves. Hibernating Purple Emperor larvae require frost, especially after mild days. Mild winters also

exacerbate predation by tits, as bird mortality rates are low and the tits may stay in the forests and not migrate into gardens. Furthermore, mild winters appear to lead to infestations of small geometrid moth larvae on sallows, notably the Winter Moth and Mottled Umber. These larvae feed primarily during May and can defoliate entire stands of sallows, homing in on the broad-leaved varieties and ignoring the narrow-leaved types. They outcompete the larger, slower-feeding Purple Emperor larvae and then render sallow foliage unsuitable for the Empress to lay her eggs in high summer, so forcing the Purple Emperor to breed on these less-favoured sallows.

One crucial issue for the Purple Emperor is whether climate change will cause it to jump out of synchrony with its foodplant. When the jet stream moves south after an early spring, slowing larval and pupal development down – without also slowing foliage development – then the situation arrives in which the egg-laying females are forced to deposit eggs on foliage that has gone through the phase of being suitable for the vulnerable first-instar larvae, having become coarse and thick. I am adamant that this happens, increasingly (e.g. in 2016 and 2017). It may well have been happening on occasions throughout history, but it is now occurring in more years than not. Part of the problem here is that the weather almost invariably collapses after an early spring – the jet stream moves south and the UK experiences six to eight weeks of cool, wet weather. This slows insect development down, but not foliage development. Early springs would not pose a problem if the fine weather continued, and the butterfly appeared in synchrony with the crucial mid-green medium-thickness soft, matt leaf stage, albeit in early June (as suggested earlier, a May Purple Emperor will be reported sooner rather than later, I'm sure).

All this could force the Purple Emperor to move north, into higher-rainfall areas, which may impact adversely on adult longevity and egg lay (as appears be the case in the Pyrenees). The best-looking sallows I have seen in recent late summers and autumns have been in the southern Lake District and, incredibly, in the Tay Valley, upstream of Perth. Most of the foliage on the Tayside trees was suitable for young larvae. Down south, it is now rare to find more than 25 per cent of a bush's foliage suitable for late summer larvae, yet my diaries suggest that suitable foliage occurred far more frequently during the late 1970s (as measured by the frequency of suitable-looking trees).

Linked in here is the actual or potential impact of atmospheric pollutant deposition on sallow (and willow) leaf suitability – including sulphur, reactive nitrogen, chlorine, base cations and heavy metals. Levels of these tend to be high within the Purple Empire, with the welcome exception of deposited nitrogen. All this is supposition, but it does merit scientific investigation.

I suspect that the main reason the Purple Emperor is expanding so dramatically at present is simply the ending of the war against sallows, in which the butterfly was an unscheduled victim. Foresters will remain wary of them, so these fast-growing trees are unlikely to take over entire commercial woods or forests – unless a new use is found for them, such as biofuel production. Likewise, most farmers will not be interested in sallows, though some will be interested in iconic wildlife. However, sallows are no longer vilified within our culture.

So, this petty war is, in theory, over. It ran out of steam. Nobody won. It was pointless. Incredibly, though, sallows are still being victimised on land managed for nature, particularly on Special Areas of Conservation and Sites of Special Scientific Interest where grassland and heathland communities are being restored, and work is being conducted to get these sites back into 'favourable condition'.

In the previous chapter I wrote that I expressed concern that the Purple Emperor, in its modern boom era, will lose conservation significance and be effectively outcompeted for prioritisation, funding and resources by other, rarer species and habitat features. The nature conservation movement's (understandable) obsession with habitat restoration – as opposed to allowing new nature to develop – is likely to restrict this butterfly.

Moreover, throughout the land the battle against sallow has now been replaced by a general and escalating campaign against scrub. The very word is vilified in our language. A young antihero in C S Lewis' *The Voyage of the Dawn Treader* (1952) is called Eustace Clarence Scrubb. He starts out as a nasty piece of work but by the book's end has become a jolly decent chap. The choice of surname here speaks volumes about our cultural attitude to this habitat. Indeed, the word 'scrub' is a derogatory term in forestry, farming and, especially – and incredibly – in nature conservation, because it invades and supplants other, more valued habitats such as downland and heathland. It is seen as needing radical transformation, like poor Eustace. It is, of course, a transitional habitat, into woodland, and the world desperately needs more trees; it's just a matter of how, what and where.

The challenge is how we get scrub back into our agricultural landscapes, where it truly belongs, and to manage it better than the flail-maddened, wildlife-depauperate hedges that characterise many of today's rural landscapes. At the very least, our hedge matrix should be assisting dispersal and colonisation by our more mobile wildlife, including the Purple Emperor. There are a great many butterflies that our mainstream farmers cannot assist, but they can easily help the Purple Emperor, by simply allowing more sallows into the landscape, in hedges, field corners and pheasant covers in patches of sticky clay. Foresters can act similarly.

The seemingly inevitable and catastrophic loss of the most widespread tree in the British Isles, the Ash, to Ash dieback disease should enable other trees to pullulate, in both rural and urban environments. Sallows will be one

of the main replacement trees on damper soils, and along
many roadsides. In an odd – and unwelcome – way, the
Purple Emperor is likely to be a beneficiary of this
human-induced disaster.

My studies and investigations suggest, strongly, that
parasitism is extremely rare in all larval stages of the
Purple Emperor, at least in England. In a useful 1954
paper in *The Entomologist's Record*, H Symes reports the
absence of parasites emerging from an impressive sample
of 26 final-instar larvae collected from the Oxford woods
and reared through in captivity. My friend Dennis Dell
reared Purple Emperors in Switzerland for many years,
after harvesting 274 eggs and 476 young larvae from
woods outside Basle. During the period 1993–2002

individuals of the large and distinctive ichneumonid wasp *Psilomastax pyramidalis* emerged from 18 of his pupae. This handsome black wasp with flame-orange hind legs appears to be a parasite of *Apatura* butterflies in Europe and Asia. The wasp has been recorded from the UK, but it is not known whether it is specific to the Purple Emperor here and we have no idea how widespread it is, as few entomologists study this challenging insect group.

In the wild, and perhaps especially in captivity, larvae are occasionally affected by a fungal disease which blackens first the rear end and then the entire body length. It is nearly always fatal, though in 2017 Dennis Dell managed to nurse one badly affected (captive) larva back to sound health, by spraying it regularly with clean water. In the wild, I have encountered this disease twice in early May and twice in October. On each occasion it proved fatal.

Parasitism at present appears to be insignificant to Purple Emperor larvae. The same applies to viral infection. However, at this time of massive global environmental change, there is potential for new invertebrates to arrive in Britain and become pests on sallows and willows, or to become serious parasites of tree-feeding lepidopteran larvae.

Bioglobilisation (the accidental spread of species around the globe on the back of human activity) could pose threats to the Purple Emperor, and in particular to the suitability of sallow trees. A rampant phytophthora disease (a fungus–like plant pathogen) affecting *Salix* taxa could radically reduce or wipe out much of the associated biodiversity (and force me to emigrate to Australia and support them at cricket).

There is also the possibility of climate change tipping 'harmless' indigenous species into becoming pests. There are several species of weevil and leaf beetle that feed fairly harmlessly on sallow (and especially willow) foliage at low population density at present. I have never encountered any of them in profusion here, and I have spent innumerable hours poking about in sallow bushes.

In September 2018 I encountered severe decimation of sallow foliage in the Catalan Pyrenees, caused by a small weevil-type thing that had peppered the foliage with its adult feeding damage (the adult weevil, if that's what it was, had vanished). Every leaf held multiple pockets of damaged leaf cuticle. Then, the following month I found the weevil *Byctiscus betulae* in abundance at a Purple Emperor locality in Holland. Most sallow leaves there had been heavily damaged by the feeding marks of the adult weevils, rendering them unsuitable for Purple Emperor larvae. This weevil is a very local leaf-roller species in the UK, associated mainly with Hazel. Invertebrate pests have the habit of suddenly erupting, in population explosions. Perhaps something could tip this current rarity out of kilter here – as had seemingly happened at the Dutch site? It might not take much to make one or more of these currently harmless resident species abundant, and drastically reduce the amount of suitable sallow foliage for the Purple Emperor. They are, after all, warmth-loving insects, whose population dynamics are strongly influenced by weather changes.

The larvae of the Winter Moth and Mottled Umber periodically infest sallow foliage, favouring precisely the types of sallow preferred by the Purple Emperor and avoiding those that the Emperor avoids. The larvae of some other small geometrid moths, similar in looks and behaviour, may also occur in profusion at times, such as the Dotted Border and Scarce Umber. Virtually every leaf is severely lacerated when and where infestations occur. Laceration happens, primarily and rapidly, during the second half of May, and sometimes into early June. It causes *iris* larvae to be short of food during their main growing period. These local infestations then also render individual sallow trees, and often entire breeding grounds, unsuitable for egg-laying Purple Emperor females that year, as the trees seldom produce new leaves by the time the butterfly is on the wing. These infestations tend to follow mild winters, which are a strong feature of contemporary climate change in the UK, and may well constitute a massive and growing problem for the Purple Emperor. Conversely, the three species of sawfly (*Symphyta*) that feed on *Salix* do not appear to have any adverse impact on the butterfly, yet.

I have also recorded periodic localised infestations of spittlebugs (the nymphs of various froghoppers, treehoppers and leafhoppers) on sallows. These outbreaks have at times impeded feeding Purple Emperor larvae, causing larval development to slow down, and probably exacerbating loss rates. The real problem they pose, however, is that they are potentially carriers of the bacterium *Xylella fastidiosa*, which attacks xylem vessels in the trees. *Xylella* has the potential to kill off a wide range of trees, shrubs and herbaceous plants if it arrives in Britain (and I'm sure it will, given that our plant biosecurity protocols are far too slack – as demonstrated by our abject failure to prevent Ash dieback from arriving).

Tied into all this is the possibility of the aerial spraying of wooded landscapes to kill off new agricultural or forestry pests that might erupt under climate warming scenarios, or after arriving here as accidental hitch-hikers. For example, during 2012 and 2013 the Forestry Commission sprayed Pangbourne Woods, near Reading in Berkshire, with a variety of the *Bacillus thuringiensis* bacterium designed to kill off Lepidoptera larvae, in an effort to eliminate a colony of the invasive Oak Processionary Moth. The Purple Emperor almost certainly occurred in those woods.

Finally, Sallow Mildew can be fatal to Purple Emperor larvae. It occurs locally in late summer and autumn, especially on sallow foliage close to or below taller-growing trees. It appears to flourish in warm, wet seasons and might be on the increase with climate change (I never noticed it while searching for Purple Emperor larvae during autumns in the late 1970s, yet it is now commonplace).

But all of the above is mere biology. Cultural significance has more clout. If this butterfly becomes genuinely valued within our society, and understood, then it should have a rosy, or even a Purple, future here – and in many other European countries, where it is also an iconic species.

Love is the key. It provides hope, energises action and offers a way forward, especially when it gathers critical mass. I am not obsessed with this butterfly: I love it. So did Heslop, and Watkins-Pitchford – and so do Mick and Wendy Campbell, Dennis Dell, Liz Goodyear, Ben

Greenaway, Neil Hulme, Andrew Middleton, Mark Tutton, Ashley Whitlock and Ken Willmott, and all the others who have put in the hard hours in the field. We are legion, and we are just the beginning. That does not render any of us worthless eccentrics, or naive beings, who at best provide transitory entertainment to the bored masses. Love knows no boundaries and readily jumps the species barrier – ask any pet owner. Don't underestimate it, for it makes all things possible. Get that right, and the rest will follow, including in this case the much-needed scientific research, policy inclusion and development of better habitat management practices.

Despite a catalogue of serious character defects, of which extreme levels of aloofness and vanity (for the females) and arrogance and misogyny (for males) spring instantly to mind, the Purple Emperor is highly endearing to us, on account of its strength of personality, love of life, and infinite capability to surprise, entertain and enthral. All this means that there is something unique about Emperoring, which goes way beyond the insect's glorious unpredictability and eccentricities.

This butterfly flies at summer's zenith, I think because it epitomises and personifies that pinnacle in nature's cycle. Perhaps, even, the Purple Emperor is the one of whom the Nightingale sings, and for whom summer's birds fly several thousand miles (only to be violently attacked by an insect with a humungous ego). The Purple Emperor has a major role to play in instilling deep magic back into our wooded landscapes, now that numbers of Nightingales and songbirds generally are so sadly depleted.

Human beings spend much of their lives seeking situations which set them free of all the man-made stuff and nonsense that binds them to the human, corporate frame. The Emperor does just that, with a single flick of its wings. Towards the end of *In Pursuit of Butterflies* I alluded to the Sukebind – the plant of Stella Gibbons's glorious parody *Cold Comfort Farm* (1932), the heady aroma of which sends people into mild insanity (it is also an aphrodisiac, but never mind that). Sadly, no such plant exists, but the Purple Emperor does exist, and performs much of what Miss Gibbons mused. Sadly, to the best of my knowledge no one has yet drunk, smoked, snorted or injected extract of *Apatura iris* – not even Neil Hulme (and I would strongly advise against it, as I dread to think what might happen). There should be a spontaneous national holiday at the peak of the Purple Emperor season, whatever. This would not just be a silly season, but a time of glorious celebration, of G and T walks in our summery land, a time of great libation and liberation. Knepp Wildland's Purple Emperor safaris are moving in that direction. The Purple Emperor flag should fly brazenly at the entrance to every one of its localities during the butterfly's flight season, to let the world know it's Emperor Time.

Now is the moment to enhance our relationship with the Purple Emperor, for we are on the brink of cracking the butterfly's mysteries, and of finally understanding this most elusive and enigmatic of creatures. This book is (hopefully) the launching pad for reaching that understanding. The Purple Emperor is not a rare butterfly, and probably never was, but one inadvertently suppressed by human activity, and terribly misunderstood.

The main challenge for us as nature lovers and conservationists is to determine how we, as individuals, can make a lasting difference. I can best do that by championing the Purple Emperor, but only alongside others of similar persuasion – as tributaries of some mighty river flowing into one ineffable ocean. This may sound obsessional to some people, or off-message to many nature conservation professionals, but maybe that's their problem (and they need to consider how they can best make a difference). I cannot save the world, or arrest devastating 3 degrees Celsius global warming and the sixth (Anthropocene) mass extinction, but I can help to give this truly wonderful butterfly some semblance of a future, and by God's grace I will. We are all in this world for a purpose, I believe.

Our problem with the Purple Emperor is simple: we are down here and it is up there, and that is where we need to be. Oh, for a tree canopy walkway, or two, in every good Emperor wood, right up there in the tops of the male-infested oaks – or at least a few good observation towers! Then, and only then, can we start to experience, understand and appreciate this butterfly fully. We are in the gutter, though some of us are gazing at the stars.

It is time to up our ambition with this animal. It doesn't need to be rare. In fact, it should be widespread and locally common throughout southern Britain, in town and country – and heading steadily north. This is doable, because the Purple Emperor can quickly colonise, and abound in, new nature land. That is the main message from Knepp Wildland, which was intensively managed farmland just 20 years ago. We need more wildlands, large and small, long term and pop-up, rural and suburban – more purple lands.

The world desperately needs more trees, and forests too. Here it is significant to point out that the developing population of Purple Emperors in the new Heart of England Forest, in Warwickshire, will soon rival, and probably eclipse, the population at Knepp. The truth is that the Purple Emperor is a new nature icon, whose (relatively simple) needs can be variously met. For decades the butterfly was imprisoned in forests, where it was manacled by forestry. Rewilding, the creation of new multi-objective woodland, and large-scale investment in new woods under climate change and flood mitigation can set it free.

To help, we need to establish 'Purple Emperors UK', a loose affiliation of informed and inspired champions prepared to help landowners and site managers paint the land Purple, in their own individual ways and without the need for trustees, councils, steering groups and chief executives, and associated interminable meetings, or resorting to overcomplicated grant aid systems – the butterfly will guide and coordinate them. That can spring from this book.

Nature needs spokespeople; its human voices, echoing and translating its messages into our languages. Our love of wilder places and of our more iconic species, both of which can offer life-altering experiences aplenty, will ensure that this happens. The history of our engagement with the Purple Emperor, the manner in which it impassions us, its lofty position within our art, poetry and literature, and its tropical habits and appearance, which can transport us to sunnier lands, indicate that this is England's national butterfly – only being English, we haven't realised it yet. Let's recognise that, and give this stupendous butterfly the future it deserves.

The history and current status of the Purple Emperor, by region and county

My main sources of information for these county accounts are the butterfly books which exist for nearly all Purple counties, most of which are of fairly recent origin (see the list of county butterfly books and reports, p. 398), and the annual butterfly reports that many branches of Butterfly Conservation publish (the Hampshire and Isle of Wight Branch, for example, have been producing these annually since 1985). There is also a considerable amount of information in the public domain on the Butterfly Conservation branch websites and on the Purple Empire blog. Much of the more recent information came through to me via the Purple Empire WhatsApp group.

In addition, I am privileged to have been granted access to the Butterflies for the New Millennium (BNM) database (formerly the Biological Records Centre butterfly database), up to and including 2017, which I have used to fill in gaps and for updates. I do, though, believe strongly that the butterfly remains seriously under-recorded in most if not all regions, counties and districts, and that recording effort is very much still in catch-up phase. There also appear to be older records in literature, from the Victorian era to the late twentieth century, which have yet to get into the BNM database.

The following accounts, county by county within administrative regions, from South West to North East, aim to summarise the history of the butterfly in each county, its current known status and its future prospects. They are succinct summaries, and will rapidly become out of date given the current pace of change. They are not offered as definitive accounts.

Some butterfly enthusiasts devote much of their annual leave allocation to looking for Purple Emperors. Their dedication and skill levels are impressive, as are the rewards for their efforts. The following paragraphs reflect their work, and that of the diligent County Butterfly Recorders within the branches of Butterfly Conservation.

I have had to be careful about naming sites here, not in order to deter butterfly collectors (which pose no threat to the Purple Emperor), but because of the extent of woodland in private ownership. Many landowners kindly granted permission for specialist butterfly surveys but would not be so keen on open access or inadvertent promotion. The public have rights of access to a mere 10 per cent of England overall; the right to roam in privately owned woodland was excluded from the Countryside and Rights of Way Act of 2000. Also, many landowners do not seek publicity for their good works.

South West England

Cornwall

The two books on the butterflies of Cornwall suggest that the few Cornish records of Purple Emperors emanate from casual releases, escapees from captive breeding or from accidental importations (inadvertent hitch-hiking). *A Cornwall Butterfly Atlas* (2003) treats the records of three specimens seen near Lands End in 1988 as individuals released by a local butterfly breeder (though why anyone would release Purple Emperors on West Penwith beggars belief). The record of a male on a car bonnet at Feock, between Falmouth and Truro, in 1998 is similarly treated, though it might possibly have been a wanderer from Brittany. *The Butterflies of Cornwall and the Scilly Isles* by Roger Penhallurick (1996) argues that the records of larvae feeding on heather in 1933 should – rightly – be dismissed as those of the Emperor Moth, which regularly breeds on heathers. He also mentions a record made by a reliable early collector, in the Polperro area, in 1826, and a specimen captured by a railway worker near Bodmin during the late Victorian era. The latter may have accidentally hitched a lift on a train.

Interestingly, Penhallurick is optimistic that genuine colonies could become established in the south-east of the county, via natural spread from Devon. There is suitable-looking habitat in wooded valleys just west of the Tamar, in south-east Cornwall; notably, on the National Trust's Lanhydrock estate just south of Bodmin, and in forested valleys around Liskeard. It is certainly possible that Cornwall may yet declare itself to be Purple, and may also receive occasional migrant Purple Emperors from Britanny or Normandy.

Devon

The most bona fide of the south-westerly records come from the Plymouth area and from the eastern edge of the Hartland Peninsula, near Clovelly. The Plymouth records are of particular interest, as a male was captured in Plymbridge Woods, Plympton, in early July 1976 (I recently met the then young collector and fully accept this record), while another was seen in Plymouth in 2002. These are preceded by one back in 1906, suggesting, perhaps, low or intermittent population status in the Plym Valley.

The 1993 book *Devon Butterflies* states that a colony was known from the Hartland area, towards Clovelly, during the 1940s and 1950s, which persisted up until at least 1973 when a Purple Emperor was seen there by a thoroughly reliable recorder, Tony Archer-Lock. Certainly, there was much suitable-looking habitat during the 1990s on the National Trust's Brownsham estate nearby, where broad-leaved hybrid sallows had invaded abandoned Culm grassland meadows. I must confess that I was part of the team of Trust staff that worked to restore open meadowland there, at the expense of myriad sallows, and never checked for Purple Emperors.

Devon Butterflies questions some of the old Devonian records, including those from the Barnstaple area in 1862 and from Mortehoe, near Woolacombe in north Devon, in 1903. I have known the Mortehoe area since the late 1950s and doubt that there was ever a colony there. King's Nympton in the Taw Valley produced a sighting in 1988.

The scatter of records from the 1980s in the south Dartmoor river valleys – the Teign, Dart and Avon – are thoroughly plausible, and back up records in those valleys from the 1930s into the 1950s. Most are from the Teign Valley, where records date back to 1878 (at Dunsford). The last record is from the Avon Valley in 1992. I know those valleys well, having searched hard for High Brown Fritillaries in them. There are pockets of suitable-looking sallows along the valley bottoms. Lastly, one was seen in the small town of Ashburton, outside these main river valleys, in 2000.

One problem is that we do not yet know how to look for Purple Emperors in steep-sided valley systems. In these south Dartmoor valleys, sallows grow mainly in narrow corridors of abandoned riverside grazing meadow along the valley bottoms, suggesting that it would be possible to see sallow-searching males and egging females there. The males may well be holding court on territories at the top of the slopes, along wood edges where the dense woodland breaks into moorland or pastureland, but how to find their assembly areas in such terrain is beyond current knowledge. They may even be hill-topping, outside woodland.

One of the best-known sites in Devon is Ashclyst Forest, on the National Trust's Killerton estate just east of Exeter, but it is unclear as to whether the Purple Emperor currently occurs there. Ashclyst is one of my favourite haunts. I worked hard with National Trust staff to maintain the Pearl-bordered Fritillary population there for many years, but never had the time to look for Purple Emperors, until I looked unsuccessfully for larvae in May 2019. The butterfly was known from this small mixed forest during the 1980s and into the 1990s, with the last definite record coming from 1998. Since then, a small number of bred adults were released there c. 2006 and sightings of two 'probables' were made in 2017, and of 'several probables' in 2019. In theory, territorial males must battle away gloriously around specimen conifers towering above the picnic site on the forest's highest point each afternoon, but people have looked there recently without success. Also in that area, colonies were known from the Forestry Commission's Stoke Park Wood, just north of Exeter, up to about 1950, and from a wood near Cullompton into the early 1980s. In 2019, I was told that Emperors had been seen in Stoke Park Wood in 2018.

The other well-known site in Devon is Venn Ottery, a Devon Wildlife Trust reserve of wet and dry heathland and damp woodland on the eastern edge of the East Devon Pebblebed Heaths, in the Otter Valley, south of Ottery St Mary. Purple Emperors were recorded there during the 1980s and into the mid-1990s. The butterfly may well still be present on the reserve, or elsewhere in the secondary woodland parts of this extensive wet and dry heathland system. The last possible record is of diagnostic autumn larval feeding marks in the early 2000s.

Somerset
Heslop, despite his Scottish connections, was essentially a man of Somerset, being brought up in Bristol and then running a family home at Burnham-on-Sea after returning from Nigeria. *Notes & Views of the Purple Emperor* begins with a short paper on two rare butterflies in Somerset, the Large Blue and the Purple Emperor. Later in the book is an essay entitled 'Somerset in its Relation to Some of the Problems of Entomology'. This concentrates on the mysteries of the Purple Emperor's status in the county. Those mysteries still pervade today.

At present, it appears that the eastern edge of Somerset, around Frome, constitutes the western fringes of the Purple Empire, at least in terms of actual records. However, there are a couple of mid-1990s records from the Blackdown Hills, just south of Taunton, in south-west Somerset. The woods and scrublands on heavy clays there appear eminently suitable, with goodly amounts of broad-leaved sallow growth. However, *Butterflies in Somerset and Bristol* (2010) states that the butterfly is believed to be extinct in those hills.

Also of interest is a mid-1990s record from the Shapwick nature reserves complex, on the Somerset Levels. Heslop was instrumental in establishing this reserve, and would dearly love his butterfly to be resident there. It may be present, but in need of being looked for. The plantation woods on the eastern side of the nearby Polden Hills also appear suitable.

There are a couple of late 1990s records from the north edge of the Mendips, in the vicinity of the Chew Valley lakes. Again, that area may well merit proper investigation, as would the dampish woodland on the Tickenham Ridge, immediately south of Bristol, and Somerset's historic Purple Emperor stronghold, the wooded hill land of Brockley Combe near Congresbury. The latter, though, is heavily coniferised and maintained as private land for pheasant shooting. *Butterflies in Somerset and Bristol* suggests that the two individuals seen in Lords Wood, south of Bristol, in 2010 could have been bred-and-released individuals, though the site is close to the locality of the late-1990s records and is well within the butterfly's former Mendip range.

It may be that, to use one of Heslop's idiosyncratic phrases, the butterfly still maintains 'an exiguous existence' within Somerset.

Dorset

This is another county which is having problems determining the extent of its Purple credentials. There are few historical records, perhaps because the small number of collectors that lived there exited to the New Forest in search of the July forest species. Today, though, a great many experienced butterfly enthusiasts live in Dorset. Roger Smith led a posse of activists on a countywide search for the Purple Emperor during the years 2005–10, which culminated in its rediscovery on Dorset's eastern fringes. In 2010, a modest population was discovered in the Dorset sector of Cranborne Chase around New Town, right up against the Wiltshire border, south-east of Shaftesbury. This almost certainly represents a rediscovery, rather than natural recolonisation, though it is some distance to the east of the site documented by Jeremy Thomas and Nigel Webb in their *The Butterflies of Dorset* (1984) during the late 1970s and early 1980s.

The 2018 record of the wing remains of a predated male in Duncliffe Wood, just west of Shaftesbury, may represent spread from Cranborne Chase. Additionally, the butterfly appears to be established a little to the south-east in woods between Wimborne St Giles and Verwood, from where there have been a number of records since the mid-1970s.

Dorset is not without its Purple mysteries, and broad-leaved sallows of the Goat Willow type are distinctly scarce in the county.

There are recent records from the clay commons of Rooksmoor and Deadmoor, south-west of Sturminster Newton; recent sightings from the gardens at Minterne, between Dorchester and Sherborne; some older records from around Powerstock; an intriguing 1998 record from Langton West Wood on the north slope of the Purbeck Ridge; and, less surprisingly, recent records and rumours from the extreme south-east of the county around Ringwood. The Dorset records give the impression of a wandering minstrel butterfly.

Wiltshire
Wiltshire is soundly Purple, and proud of it. Woodland tends to occur in large, often isolated blocks. As elsewhere, public access can be poor, due to shooting interests and military use. In addition, there are linear sallow and willow carr habitats in the chalk-stream river valleys which are virtually unexplored.

A full account of the history of the Purple Emperor in Wiltshire is provided by Mike Fuller in his definitive work on the county's butterflies, published in 1995. Since then the butterfly has been discovered in several new areas and the *Wiltshire Butterfly Report* (2018) states that it is now considered to be 'widespread' in the county, though rare in the open lands of Salisbury Plain and the Marlborough Downs, and in the north-west corner between Chippenham and Malmesbury.

Heslop conducted most of his activities in Bentley Wood, just east of Salisbury, and at Whiteparish Common, a little further south. Bentley Wood was purchased from the Forestry Commission in the early 1980s by a small charitable trust, the Bentley Wood Trust. A superbly run nature reserve, it is a major honeypot site for the Purple Emperor, attracting hordes of visitors at weekends during the Emperor season. The car park overflows. Heslop would loathe it. Few people manage to see more than a dozen Purple Emperors there in a day, suggesting that the population is not actually that strong, or that Bentley Wood's Purple Emperors are unusually recalcitrant. The truth, though, is that there are no known visible 'master trees', or male assembly areas, which means that the males simply vanish in the afternoons. Whiteparish Common holds few sallows today, and the butterfly has only a weak presence there.

The butterfly ranges throughout the wooded landscape to the east of Salisbury, occurring even in the plantations on Ministry of Defence land at Porton Down. It must surely occur in the nearby Avon and Bourne river valleys too.

West of Salisbury, the Purple Emperor occurs in modest numbers in Grovely Wood and, more sparingly, in Great Ridge Wood, two large forestry woods on clay-with-flints overlying the chalk. Recently, it has been discovered in woods on the slopes of the Vale of Wardour near the two Donhead villages, and right up against the Dorset border in Cranborne Chase. It is not known whether the butterfly occurs in the Longleat estate woods a little to the north, where sallows are scarcely tolerated, or in Great Bradley Wood close by.

There is another known outpost along the border with Somerset, between Warminster and Frome, in Black Dog Woods, and the butterfly is occasionally seen in woods either side of the A350 just to the north of Westbury. There is also an interesting modern record from Bradford-on-Avon, in north-west Wiltshire, which might indicate that the butterfly has a presence in the Avon Valley, where sallows abound locally.

In north Wiltshire, there are a few records from the south and north of Swindon, including from Braydon Forest and from Coate Water Country Park, on Swindon's south-east edge. I have found larval feeding sites opposite the Richard Jefferies Museum at Coate, in Swindon. In 2019 I saw a female in the Cotswold Water Park on the Wiltshire–Gloucestershire border near Cricklade, representing recent colonisation. Sallows abound around the old gravel pits, and it must simply be a matter of time before a sizeable population develops there.

South of Swindon, the Purple Emperor is well known from Savernake Forest near Marlborough, and from the surrounding woods. This is another honeypot site, with easy access. The vast majority of people wishing to see the butterfly there visit the area around the Column (a 27-metre-tall folly erected in praise of 'mad' King George III) at the southern edge of the forest.

In fact, the butterfly occurs throughout the forest and in nearly all of its satellite woods, often in greater numbers than in the main forest block. It has been seen as far away as Ramsbury to the east, suggesting a presence in the Kennet Valley there. The population then stretches right up to the Hampshire and Berkshire borders, and in woodland south of Hungerford, in the old Shute Forest area. There is also a sizeable satellite population on Ministry of Defence land on the northern edge of Salisbury Plain, south-east of Pewsey.

Curiously, the Purple Emperor emerges somewhat later in much of Wiltshire than it does elsewhere in the south. Savernake Forest, in particular, is a distinctly 'late-flying' site (in 2018 the Emperor season there commenced a week after the first sightings had been recorded in five other southern counties). Heslop noticed this county lateness, which is less pronounced in south Wiltshire.

Gloucestershire

I have lived in Gloucestershire since 1992 but have scarcely searched for the Purple Emperor there. The county should be diffusely Purple, but systematic searches have yet to take place. There is a scatter of recent records from the wooded valleys that dissect the Cotswold dip slope and from the valley of the Windrush, a tributary of the Thames. A male was photographed by the National Trust's ticket office at Chedworth Roman Villa in 2014 and I found a hibernating larva along the old railway line there in December 2018. Also, individuals have recently been seen at Gawcombe Woods, Crickley Hill, Dumbleton and Naunton, on the National Trust's Sherborne estate and in Littleton Wood on the Trust's Snowshill estate. It could well be that the butterfly has a modest presence in the Windrush Valley (I found a larva at Sherborne Common in November 2019). There is much suitable habitat in the Frome Valley west of Cirencester. In addition, a female was seen at Lower Woods Nature Reserve, near Wickwar in south Gloucestershire, in 1989. I searched in vain there during the late 1990s, but during an era when sallows were being cleared for conservation reasons.

West of the River Severn, the Purple Emperor has an intriguing if confusing history in the Forest of Dean area (part of which is in Herefordshire). The records come in pulses, the first during the late Victorian era, when it was at times quite numerous, at least locally. There is a record of as many as 20 Purple Emperors coming to bait in a single day near Newland in 1884. The butterfly was reputed to be fairly plentiful in the Wye Valley up to around 1920. There is another pulse of records from the 1930s and a record of two being seen in 1941. Then records cease, until the butterfly was reported from the Cinderford area during the late 1980s. I struggle with the Forest of Dean (it is vast, and far too heavily coniferised for my liking), but I have located highly suitable-looking broad-leaved sallows in several of the valley bottoms. A proper search is required. One issue the Dean poses is why, if the butterfly is there, are there no records of males feeding along the numerous gravelled forest rides? However, few people look, and it may simply be that the Forest of Dean race are oak-sap feeders, rather than dung feeders, and seldom descend.

South East England

Hampshire

The Purple Emperor has long been known from Hampshire, and the county is rightly regarded as one of the butterfly's national strongholds. In all probability the insect has some form of presence in most of the wooded areas away from the central area of the New Forest. It appears to be on the increase in the county – expanding and infilling – but recording effort has also increased tremendously, inspired and led by Ashley Whitlock, Purple Emperor Champion for the Hampshire and Isle of Wight Branch of Butterfly Conservation. This means that the account of the status and distribution of the Purple Emperor in Hampshire I penned for *The Butterflies of Hampshire* (2000) has been outgrown.

The *Hampshire & Isle of Wight Butterfly Report* for 2018 shows that the Purple Emperor was recorded from 174 tetrad squares (squares of 2 x 2 kilometres) in Hampshire during the period 2005–18. This effectively makes it as widespread as the Dingy Skipper in the county.

As with most of the Purple counties, there are a small number of honeypot sites which attract a great many visitors, and detract recording effort away from elsewhere. Hampshire's main honeypot is Alice Holt Forest, an 851-hectare Forestry England holding on the border with Surrey. It has been renowned for its Purple Emperors since before the Second World War. For many years the Lodge Inclosure was regarded as the best area within the forest for the butterfly, but in recent decades the strongholds have been Straits Inclosure and Abbotts Wood Inclosure, at the forest's southern end, which are sited on Gault Clay. In a good summer it is possible to see upwards of 30 apparent individuals on one day in these southern parts, though this is partly because a number of male territories were discovered by intense survey work during the early 2000s, as documented in *In Pursuit of Butterflies* (2015). Few other Hampshire sites, if any, produce such numbers. The butterfly's fortunes in Alice Holt Forest fluctuate according to Forestry England's treatment of sallows. The truth is that 'Alice' and its wooded environs support a fully functioning metapopulation of this living jewel, with the females tracking sallow growth wherever it develops.

Elsewhere in the county, it is hard to find an area of woodland on the clays (London Clay and Gault Clay) and the Clay-with-Flints that is not utilised, at least periodically. Also, there are some sizeable populations in woods on the chalk, notably Crab Wood and West Wood, just west of Winchester. The Purple Emperor occurs in modest numbers in several of the Forest of Bere woods, in the south of the county. Some well-known sites, though, support only small populations, notably Pamber Forest, a Local Nature Reserve north of Basingstoke. The main problem for recording, though, is that access is difficult to many of Hampshire's woods on account of pheasant-shooting interests, including in the vast Harewood Forest, east of Andover.

There are also populations on many of Hampshire's wooded heaths, where sallows grow in areas of impeded drainage. There is a conflict here in that Purple Emperor colonies are easily lost when sallow scrub is cleared during heathland restoration work. The heathland populations appear to be generally weak.

The status of the Purple Emperor in the New Forest is decidedly unclear. For decades, the butterfly was known from the silvicultural inclosures (planted woods) on the more clayey soils where broad-leaved sallows grew: to the south of Lyndhurst, to the east and south of Brockenhurst, and in the south-westerly inclosures near Sway. Today, Pondhead Inclosure, immediately south of Lyndhurst, looks eminently suitable, possessing a fair number of the favoured broad-leaved sallows. It is currently managed by a small trust, and is unlike any other part of the Forest. Strangely, the butterfly has yet to be discovered there.

Elsewhere in the New Forest woods, broad-leaved sallows are incredibly rare, having been steadfastly eliminated under post-war forestry policy (an account is given by Rear Admiral Torlesse, one of the last of the New Forest collectors, quoted in *The Butterflies of Hampshire*). Today, sallow regeneration is being prevented by high populations of deer. Broad-leaved sallows, and sizeable-leaved sallows in general, are now all but restricted to the edges of major roads, such as the A337 between Cadnam and Lyndhurst, which are fenced off from grazing animals. The only recent records of Purple Emperors in the New Forest come from Costicles Inclosure, on the forest's eastern edge near Ashurst, Wotton Coppice Inclosure, near Sway, and an individual at Hale Purlieu in the north-west corner of the open forest. Although sallows occur in profusion in many of the damper areas of the New Forest they are invariably of the small-leaved, narrow-leaved varieties (Grey Willow and its close hybrids). These leaves may be too small to feed the large early summer Purple Emperor larvae, and too coarse for the first-instar larvae later in the summer. My feeling is that the Purple Emperor should occur in places just outside the New Forest's perimeter (or perambulation, as it is known). The butterfly also awaits discovery, or rediscovery, in the woods in Hampshire's extreme south-west peninsula, west of the River Avon, where the county fingers deep into Wiltshire and Dorset.

The Purple Emperor is now being discovered in some of Hampshire's major river valleys, where sallow carr and willows often abound. There are recent records from the Dever Valley at

Wonston, the upper Test Valley at Whitchurch, and the Loddon
Valley at Old Basing on the east edge of Basingstoke (where I
found a hibernating larva in early December 2018). Public access
to the Test and Itchen valleys is restricted, due to angling interests,
so the discovery of the Purple Emperor there is likely to be a
slow process.

However, the butterfly is turning up more and more in urban
Hampshire, notably in the cities of Southampton, Winchester
and Portsmouth. It has been seen on Southampton Common,
where it could well be breeding, and is regularly reported from
woods on the city's northern fringes. In Winchester, there have
been recent sightings in the cathedral grounds. There was even
an incident when an Empress stole the show at a christening
there, and another when a male parascended into a street theatre
event at the annual Winchester Hat Fair. The butterfly has also
been seen weaving its way among traffic in the high street. These
records came into focus on 19 September 2019 when I found a
larva in a sallow thicket just downstream of Winchester College –
the Purple Emperor is breeding in fen-carr habitat there (I was
there to celebrate the bicentenary of the composition of John
Keats's ode, '*To Autumn*', and found that larva among 'the river
sallows' Keats mentions). Portsmouth is even more remarkable,
as buildings are densely packed there, but there is potential
habitat at North Harbour and Hilsea Lines, and a male was
recently seen in a shopping mall in Gunwharf Quays. Hampshire
seems to be becoming increasingly Purple.

Isle of Wight
There are precious few records of Purple Emperors from the Isle
of Wight. There is a single record from Parkhurst Forest in 1890,
and others from that era from the Brading and Yarmouth areas.
Then, no more were recorded until a male was seen at Brighstone
in 1952. This was followed by another lengthy gap before one
was recorded at Stag Copse Nature Reserve, Newport, in 1977.
In 2013, singletons were reported from the southern end of
Parkhurst Forest, west of Newport, and from Firestone Copse
near Ryde. These records suggest intermittent colonisation.

Theoretically, the butterfly should be reasonably well established on the island, given the profusion of (generally narrow-leaved) sallows in and around the woods on the clays in the island's northern sector. Firestone Copse looks quite suitable, and there is also potential for the butterfly in Combley Great Wood, Parkhurst Forest, Rowlands Wood and along the old railway line near Wootton Common, between Newport and Ryde. There is also modest potential for the Purple Emperor in and around Newtown meadows in the north-west of the island. It shouldn't take much fieldwork to declare the Isle of Wight properly Purple. However, the scarcity of frosts there might hinder larval hibernation, and lead to high winter mortality rates – which again supports the theory of intermittent colonisation. Also, climate change, in the form of milder winters, may render the island unsuitable for this species.

Sussex

If Hampshire is the epicentre of the Purple Empire, West Sussex is the fulcrum. Heslop aptly describes the A272, which in his day ran from Stockbridge deep into East Sussex, as the 'backbone of the Purple Empire' (since then, the sacred road has been truncated at either end).

Much of the surface geology of Sussex is highly conducive to sallow growth, not least the Weald Clay of the Low Weald, the Gault Clay of the greensand edge and the hotchpotch of other clays that occur in the High Weald of East Sussex and beyond. Add to this the Clay-with-Flints that covers parts of the South Downs, the alluviums of the river valleys that dissect the downs, and various damp and boggy hollows and 'laggs' (wet shallow valleys), and you have a veritable kingdom of sallow – or you would, if humankind permitted it. The point here is that much of Sussex away from the coastal plain is low-grade agricultural land, which bakes hard in high summer but turns into a veritable bog in other seasons – sallow heaven.

The Butterflies of Sussex (2017) lucidly explains the Purple Emperor's occupation of Sussex, highlighting its long history of retreats and advances and its recent spread back into East Sussex. During the early 1990s the butterfly was all but restricted to woods on the Weald clay and to the wooded escarpment and crests of the West Sussex downs. Since then it has spread throughout the western reaches of East Sussex, into Ashdown Forest, and as far afield as Hurst Green and Wadhurst on the Kent border. Also, and perhaps more interestingly, it has colonised southwards down the dip slope of the downs, occupying wooded combes there, and is now threatening to conquer the coastal plain (there it will struggle, as the coastal plain is high-grade agricultural land). Its ambition is clear: total occupation. Much of East Sussex should readily fall under its spell.

However, the fast-draining sandy soils of the Lower Greensand and the dry open chalklands rein the butterfly's ambitions in considerably, though both sallows and Purple Emperors occur readily in damp valley bottoms within the greensand system. The butterfly is known from the woody heaths to the west of Midhurst, and from Chailey Common south-east of Haywards Heath.

The Purple Emperor's larval foodplants benefitted hugely from the great storms of October 1987 and January 1990, both in Sussex and in the adjoining counties of Hampshire, Surrey and Kent. Those storms opened up many closed-canopy woods, and one of the trees to benefit from the new openings was, of course, the humble sallow. The butterfly has simply followed its foodplant.

Interestingly, the Purple Emperor reaches many of the highest points in West Sussex. Males have been recorded recently on the wooded crest above Heyshott (227 metres above mean sea level), Graffham (222 metres) and Bignor (200 metres). A number of male territories have been located on wooded high points along the western downs.

Traditionally, Purple Emperor numbers have always been highest – or, rather, least low – in Southwater Forest and in the parts of Chiddingfold Forest that lie in Sussex (the bulk of this forest lies in Surrey; see p. 362). I used to be able to see 30 apparent individuals on a good day in the Southwater Forest woods during the early 1970s, especially during the excellent Purple Emperor season of 1975.

Those numbers, and the dreams associated with them, paled into utter insignificance when the new nature land of Knepp

Wildland sprung into being during the early 2000s. Sallow seed rained down on bare fields taken out of arable cultivation and sowed the most extensive Purple Emperor breeding grounds ever documented in Britain. The Purple Emperor colonised quickly, and was flourishing there by 2009. In 2018, the best Purple Emperor season of my 49-year experience, three separate recorders achieved day counts in excess of 300 apparent individuals. That set a new bar for Purple Emperor population density nationally, if not for western Europe, and illustrates the potential the Sussex clay lands hold for this butterfly.

Elsewhere in Sussex, there are modest populations on the western downs at Eartham Wood near Slindon and in Houghton Forest north of Arundel, in various Forestry England and privately owned woods in the Loxwood and Plaistow area, and in privately owned woods north of Billingshurst. The overall impression, however, is of a diffuse presence almost throughout non-coastal West Sussex and over the clay lands of the High Weald in East Sussex – ones and twos here and there, mainly in the form of ever-violent males battling for the control of territories in canopy gaps up in the oak crowns. The key to this success is the living matrix of oak and sallow habitat that dominates much of the Sussex landscape. This matrix includes green lanes, roadside manorial wastes, oak-lined hedges, wooded commons and greens, and myriad shaws and wooded laggs.

Missing from the Sussex Empire, at least for now, is the entire south-east corner, which includes significant amounts of woodland around Battle, Robertsbridge, Broad Oak and Beckley. Beckley Woods, near Rye, looked suitable when I visited one late winter day 20 years ago. Also, the butterfly has yet to be found in the few blocks of woodland that exist on the East Sussex South Downs (Friston Forest) and, most notably, in Abbot's Wood by Hailsham, which was formerly a renowned butterfly collecting site.

Kent
The British passion for the Purple Emperor began in Kent. The initial epicentres were Darenth Wood, near Dartford, and Great Chattenden Wood, close to Rochester, short train rides from

London. Butterfly collectors flocked to these woods during the mid- and late Victorian eras, and there are tales of great daring in the entomological literature, particularly in the writings of Tutt and Frohawk, as summarised in Chapter 1. Heslop named one of his Purple Emperor aberrations ab. *chattendeni*.

Today, the Purple Emperor is well established in the northwest sector of Kent, in a block running north from the East Sussex border, across the M25 and reaching into the south-east fringes of London; with an eastern boundary running roughly down the south-east corridor of the M25, from the Swanley Interchange, and down through Sevenoaks, Tonbridge and Royal Tunbridge Wells. The south-easternmost population may well be the one I discovered in Scotney Woods, Lamberhurst, in July 2014. It is interesting that the population runs quite far into south-east London, with recent records from around Downe (where Charles Darwin lived), Petts Wood at Orpington and, most significantly, on Shooters Hill near the Woolwich Ferry.

This favoured block contains much clay land, but also wooded greensand ridges and wooded chalk hill land. The woods on the downs and greensand hilltops were extensively damaged by the Great Storm of October 1987. Sallows benefitted hugely from the extensive clear-up operations that followed the storm, though that generation of sallows is now starting to be outcompeted by taller-growing trees. This enabled much colonisation by the Purple Emperor, for example on National Trust land at Toys Hill and Ightham Mote, between Westerham and Tonbridge.

There are also Purple outposts to the north and south-east of Rochester and in Orlestone Forest (also known as Ham Street Woods), south of Ashford. Heslop considered the Orlestone race to be unusually large, and theorised that it might have been breeding on Aspen. There are few records, though, from the wooded terrain in between these population centres, the most significant of which is my discovery of a small population in Sissinghurst Woods, near Cranbrook, in mid-July 2015. That suggests that the butterfly may well be present in woods around Biddenden and Tenterden, which would link the Sissinghurst and Orlestone populations.

The Purple Emperor has never been recorded from the many woods on the North Downs east of Maidstone, or in the vast Blean Woods complex to the west and north of Canterbury. That represents a huge area of *terra nova*. Sallows are, however, decidedly rare in the Blean Woods, where the soils are too fast-draining, but it would be surprising if the butterfly proved to be absent from those North Downs woods. At present, the Purple Emperor seems to be a Kentish butterfly, rather than a butterfly of Kent, being all but restricted to the land west of the Medway (a Man or Maid of Kent lives east of the Medway, a Kentish Man or Maid to the west).

The sites most frequently visited by butterfly watchers are the woods around Markbeech, south-east of Edenbridge, and Dene Park Woods at Shipbourne, on the A227 north of Tonbridge. However, all populations in Kent appear to be small. The best-looking Purple Emperor site I have seen in the county is the remnants of Great Chattenden Wood at Rochester. This includes the adjoining Ministry of Defence disposal land at Lodge Hill, the site of a development dispute. My assessment is that Chattenden, where our curious relationship with this insect effectively began, supports one of the best populations of the Purple Emperor in the UK, but the size of the population there has yet to be recognised.

Surrey
If Kent is where Emperoring began, Surrey is the county where Emperoring ecology began, with Bookham Common being the 'type locality' where Ken Willmott conducted most of his pioneering work into the ecology of the butterfly.

For decades, the Purple Emperor was thought to occur only in Chiddingfold Forest, which lies on the Weald Clay in the south of the county, and at outposts at Bookham Common and nearby Ashtead Common. This proved to be erroneous thinking, for the butterfly has been found to be far more widespread, so much so that the latest book on Surrey's butterflies (*Butterflies of Surrey Revisited*, 2013) states that the butterfly 'probably occurs in most suitable woodlands' – and leafy Surrey is the most wooded county in England.

Much of Surrey's woodland is potentially suitable for the Purple Emperor, and its sallows, given the extent of clay soils (Gault Clay and London Clay, primarily) and alluviums. Also, the damp valleys within the Lower Greensand, which occupies much of south-west Surrey, are rich in sallows, the river valleys support sallows and willows, and many of the wooded combes on the chalk also support sallow stands. Little of Surrey, then, is of low potential for the butterfly and its larval foodplants – mainly the dry heaths on the Bagshot, Windlesham and Camberley Sand Formations, and the urban sprawl (Surrey supports a human population in excess of 1.2 million).

The distribution map in *Butterflies of Surrey Revisited* indicates that the Purple Emperor is very widespread in Surrey, occurring extensively in clay woodland, a surprising number of woods on the chalk, several of the south-west Surrey heaths, and along canal and river corridors where it may be using White Willow (*S. alba*). There are a number of known male territories along the crest of the North Downs escarpment. On the (wooded) heaths, the Emperor is known from Ash and Pirbright ranges, Chobham Common, Thursley Common and Witley Common. The last of these supported a sizeable population during the 1970s, which has recently declined. On the downs, the butterfly has been seen almost annually on Box Hill since 1992. It is probable that it is currently under-recorded in the south-east corner of Surrey, down the M23 and A22 corridor and along the Kent border.

Recording suggests, I think strongly, that the Purple Emperor has spread systematically northwards in Surrey since the early 1990s, though recorder effort has also increased during that time. In 1994 it was found in woods at Coulsdon, Epsom and Oxshott, and has been seen well into suburbia almost annually since. Best of all are records from a Surbiton kitchen in 2015, Wimbledon Common in 2016, Putney Heath in 2013 and a bathroom in Worcester Park in 2019. This suggests a butterfly pushing deep into London's suburbs. There are also a number of garden records, of wanderers. It may well be that the number of male territories in gardens and paddocks in Surrey is in at least three figures.

As with other counties, Surrey has several sites that are popular with Emperorphiles, which happen to support the strongest (known) populations. These are Ashtead Common, which is just inside the M25, Bookham Common (or technically, Bookham Commons plural) at Leatherhead, the Botany Bay and Tugley Wood sector of Chiddingfold Forest, and Sheepleas Nature Reserve at West Horsley. These sites can produce tallies of 20 or more Emperors in a day, for the diligent. It is likely that Surrey also supports several other (relatively) strong populations that await discovery.

Berkshire

The Royal County of Berkshire is drained by the River Thames and its tributary, the Kennet. The western half is rural, the eastern half largely urban or suburban. West Berkshire consists of lightly wooded chalkland – the Berkshire Downs and a small section of downland south of Hungerford, separated by the River Kennet, a classic southern chalk stream. Much of the rest of the county is river valley clay land, the exception being the sandy acidic soils of the Bagshot Formation in the county's south-east, along the meandering border with Surrey.

The 1994 atlas of *The Butterflies of Berkshire, Buckinghamshire and Oxfordshire* suggests that the Purple Emperor is a rare butterfly in the county, showing just a scatter of records from (west) Berkshire during a six-year survey period. Since then, increasing recording effort has raised the butterfly's status considerably, such that the Purple Emperor can now be described as being widespread throughout the county, though seemingly weak on the Lambourn Downs and on the Bagshot Sands.

In west Berkshire the species occurs in the Kennet Valley upstream and downstream of Newbury, in woods on the Wickham Ridge just north-west of Newbury, in woods on the high chalkland up against the Hampshire and Wiltshire border to the south of Hungerford, on the Lambourn Downs, and in the undulating, well-wooded terrain of the rolling downs between Hermitage and Goring. There is also a handful of records from the Greenham Common area, to the south-east of Newbury.

There are a number of recent records from the Reading area, ranging from Pangbourne, down towards Aldermaston and into Reading itself (including a male in the Tesco supermarket car park at Earley, on the south-east edge of Reading, where there is a surprising amount of sallow-rich habitat).

Downstream of Reading, the Purple Emperor seems to be more fragmentary in occurrence, though that may be due to lower recorder coverage. It occurs in Maidenhead Thicket and is recorded in most years from various places within Windsor Great Park and Windsor Forest.

The overall impression is that the butterfly is probably quite well established in Berkshire today, including in riverine woodland in the Kennet and Thames corridors, where it may be breeding on true willows (as opposed to sallows). No sizeable populations are known, though, and it may simply be that the butterfly has a rather diffuse presence almost throughout Berkshire.

Oxfordshire

It was inevitable that at some stage in these county accounts the structure would fail because of the unobliging nature of county borders. That happens here, as the boundary between Oxfordshire and Buckinghamshire meanders randomly through the heart of Bernwood Forest, the epicentre of the Purple Empire in the two counties. This forest has been famous for its Purple Emperors since the 1930s. Its western half is in Oxfordshire.

Oxfordshire is blessed with large areas of clays rich in sallows, with belts of Oxford Clay, Kimmeridge Clay and Gault Clay running north-eastwards through the middle swathe of the county. Much of this clay land is also wooded, heavily in places, as is the county's sector of the Chiltern Hills. There are also the river vales of the Thames and its Oxfordshire tributaries, the Ray, Cherwell, Evenlode and Windrush, with riverine woodland and in places abundant willows. Conversely, much of north Oxfordshire is only lightly wooded, apart from to the north of Bicester.

The Purple Emperor occurs in just about all the woods within the Oxfordshire sector of Bernwood Forest, though it must be emphasised that many of the smaller woods are in

private ownership, offering limited or no public access. The
main centres, and best populations, are in Waterperry Wood,
parts of which were made into a nature reserve for this butterfly
in the late 1960s, and the county wildlife trust reserve of
Whitecross Green Wood. Both afford open access. The species
effectively occurs in most if not all the woods around the villages
of Beckley, Stanton St John and Horton-cum-Studley. It can also
occasionally be seen along wooded roadsides, green lanes and
treed hedges in the wider Bernwood landscape.

Ranging towards Oxford, where Bernwood Forest ends, the
Purple Emperor is known from Sydlings Copse, just north of
Headington, and is regularly seen in Brasenose Woods and
Shotover Country Park on the east edge of Oxford. Not to be
outdone, it also occurs on the west edge of Oxford, around
Cumnor Hill, in Wytham Great Wood at Botley, and around
Farmoor Reservoir. A little to the north-west, it flies in and
around the Blenheim estate woods at Woodstock. Bagley Wood,
at the southern end of Oxford, was a famous locality many
decades ago, but there are no recent records.

All of this begs the question of whether the Purple Emperor
actually occurs in Oxford itself. Port Meadow, which runs the
length of the Cherwell almost into the heart of Oxford near
Magdalen Bridge, looks suitable, with frequent broad-leaved
sallows and numerous tall willows in its thick hedges. Will
someone please discover the Purple Emperor in Port Meadow,
before some bright spark finds it in the city of Cambridge.
Never mind the annual Varsity Match or eternal academic
rivalry; this matter is of far higher importance.

The Purple Emperor is quite well established in the
Oxfordshire sector of the south Chilterns, which is heavily
wooded, though it appears to have been unknown from here
until the 1970s. Sallows occur readily in combe bottoms, and
where there are Clay-with-Flints deposits.

West Oxfordshire is an enigma, beginning with the incredibly
private, and poorly recorded, Wychwood Forest, north of Witney,
from where there are no recent records – due to the prohibition
of access. However, since 2013 the Purple Emperor has been

discovered in several places in west Oxfordshire: at Foxholes Nature Reserve north of Burford, at a private site north of Chipping Norton, in woods to the south-west of Burford, and in Badbury Forest, west of Faringdon. This means that the butterfly is now pressing against the Gloucestershire border.

Late in 2019, I discovered a highly isolated population in relict oak pasture-woodland owned by the National Trust at Ashdown, in the extreme south-west corner of Oxfordshire. The butterfly may have been there for decades, if not centuries, breeding on about 50 veteran sallow trees.

Buckinghamshire

Buckinghamshire is now a premier county for the Purple Emperor. This is remarkable as *The Butterflies of Berkshire, Buckinghamshire and Oxfordshire* (1994) strongly suggests otherwise. The butterfly is currently widespread and well established in woods on the clay lands of the Vale of Aylesbury and in the Chiltern woods. This is partly due to natural spread, with the butterfly colonising the Chiltern woods spectacularly from the mid-1970s, but also to diligent recorder effort, by Dennis Dell, who lived in Aylesbury between 2002 and 2017, and by Mick and Wendy Campbell, who have dedicated innumerable hours to surveying for Purple Emperors in Buckinghamshire and Oxfordshire. The Campbells' technique is simple, and time efficient: they prospect new habitat during the darker months, then home in on possible male territories during the flight season.

The Purple Emperor's occurrence in the Chilterns amazes me, for I lived there during the late 1960s and early 1970s and searched hard in the mid-Chilterns, without any success. Sallows were decidedly rare then, weeded out by foresters who wished only to grow Beech or conifers. Yet several of the woods I frequented subsequently became, and remain, pleasantly Purple. The butterfly seems to be particularly well established in woodland to the north of High Wycombe, reaching right up to the county border at Tring. However, it rather peters out eastwards, towards Chalfont St Giles and Chesham, as the land becomes increasingly suburbanised and habitat increasingly fragmented.

In the extreme south-east corner of Buckinghamshire, there are recent Emperor records from the National Trust's Cliveden estate on the Thames, just upstream of Slough (recorded there in 2013 and 2016), the extensive woodlands of Burnham Beeches and Farnham Common, and from Black Park and Langley Park on the east edge of Slough.

The Vale of Aylesbury is wondrously Purple. The Emperor has been seen in almost every wood in the Buckinghamshire sector, the few exceptions being closed-canopy neglected oak woods lacking open rides, glades and sallows. For a time, the Buckinghamshire part of the main block of Bernwood Forest (Hell Coppice, York's Wood, Shabbington Wood and Oakley Wood) was regarded as the epicentre, but investigations discovered denser colonies in several other woods to the north and north-east. Most of these woods are in private ownership, but Finemere Wood and Rushbeds Wood are both county wildlife trust reserves which support sizeable populations.

One local landowner in the Vale of Aylesbury manages his woods with the Purple Emperor, and other wildlife, firmly in mind. His conversion came after an epiphanic encounter with a resplendent male in his tractor cab, while mowing the grassy rides one hot summer day. His rides are now gloriously lined with sallows, coppicing is extensively practised and the woods support one of the strongest populations in the country, where 50 Purple Emperors can be counted in a day. Good counts are also obtained, in some years, from the main block of Bernwood Forest and from a small, private wood a little to the north.

The Purple Emperor becomes a little thin on the ground in the extreme north of the county, as does woodland cover, but it occurs in woods around Stowe and Silverstone and actually in, as well as around, Milton Keynes new town. The latter is important, as it shows that this butterfly can readily occur in greener suburban environments.

East of England
The counties that form the East of England region have been systematically surveyed for Purple Emperors by Liz Goodyear

and Andrew Middleton, and a small team of helpers active at county or district level. Liz and Andrew began in Hertfordshire and Middlesex, effectively finishing in those counties between 2010 and 2012, before moving into Essex and Suffolk. In 2015 they started to concentrate on Norfolk, researching old records and making contact with people who had more recent records. Much of their work has been self-funded, but they have received useful grant aid from the Butterfly Conservation Hertfordshire and Middlesex branch, the Hertfordshire Natural History Society, the Robert Kiln Trust and two private benefactors. Since 2015 their work has been entirely self-funded. They have systematically painted much of Hertfordshire, Middlesex and East Anglia Purple, making a series of major discoveries, often in districts from where the butterfly was considered to be long extinct. Their discovery of the Purple Emperor in Bradfield Woods, Suffolk, in 2016, is especially noteworthy. Between 1999 and 2014 they found at least 35 male assembly areas (territories) in the region. Since 2015 they have added about 25 more. Their sightings have rarely occurred by chance, but after hours of detailed study and preparation. They published a major report in 2015.

Hertfordshire
The Boys and the Butterflies by James Birdsall (1988) chronicles the adventures of three young evacuees after they were removed from London to the village of Walkern, just east of Stevenage, in May 1940. They spent halcyon summer days collecting butterflies in an idyllic landscape. The Purple Emperor was beyond their wildest dreams, for the butterfly was considered long gone from Hertfordshire, though it had occurred in one of their favoured haunts, St John's Wood, within living memory. There seem to be no records from the county between 1896 and 1944, when the butterfly was seen in a wood west of Stevenage. This was followed by sightings at Broxbourne in 1950 and from Northaw, near Cuffley, in the early 1960s, though these were dismissed as being unlikely by the experts of the time.

A scatter of subsequent records was treated by the contempo-rary County Butterfly Recorders as being improbable

– misidentifications, or releases of bred specimens (e.g. near St
Albans in 1950, near Radlett in 1975, near Stevenage in 1978 and
again in woodland west of Stevenage, in the mid-1980s). The butterfly was pronounced firmly extinct in Hertfordshire. Then, in
1986, the insect appeared unequivocally to the west of Stevenage,
and 10 years later it was seen in Wormley Woods, Broxbourne.

All this stimulated Liz and Andrew to launch a thorough
investigation into the status of the Purple Emperor in the county.
Their initial study period, from 1999 to 2002, discovered small
populations at six sites within three 10-kilometre squares. They
also gathered and analysed historical records, and reached the
conclusion that the butterfly may well have had a continual
presence in Hertfordshire since it was discovered there in 1833.
They produced a report in 2003.

Bitten by a mighty bug, they continued with what had
become a calling, first in Hertfordshire, then in adjoining
Middlesex, and then into all the other counties that make up
eastern England, culminating in a major report produced in
2015. Their technique was simply to conduct homework –
historical research, perusal of maps (paper and online), and
identification of wooded high points (mainly along wood edges),
which could host male territories – and then home in on likely
spots (they call them assembly points) during the flight season. It
worked, spectacularly.

The Purple Emperor is now known to be fairly widespread
in Hertfordshire, occurring in most of the woodland systems in
the county. Several male assembly areas are now monitored
annually. However, populations are almost invariably small.

In the south-west of the county, an early find was a colony at
Tring Park, on the summit of the Chiltern escarpment. The
butterfly was also discovered in extensive woodland on the
National Trust's Ashridge Estate, near Berkhamsted. Males
are occasionally seen from the observation platform at the top of
the 33-metre-tall Bridgewater Monument there, and at a better
assembly area a little to the north.

Elsewhere in south Hertfordshire, colonies have been found in
woods around Chorleywood and Bushey, in Whippendell Woods

just west of Watford, in Cassiobury Park in Watford, at Hilfield Park Reservoir between Watford and Borehamwood, at Bricket Wood by Potters Bar, in the privately owned Mimms Wood complex just north of the South Mimms Services on the M25, at Northaw Great Wood near Cuffley and, especially, within the Broxbourne Woods and Wormley Woods woodland system just west of Broxbourne. That's impressive, matching status levels in any of the core counties of the Purple Empire south of the Thames.

Around Hertford, colonies have been found at Balls Wood, just south of the town, Golding's Wood to the south-east, and Panshanger Park to the west. There was an interesting sighting of a stray male in a garden at Thundridge in 2014. Best of all, in 2016 Liz saw a female in her garden in Ware, which had perhaps wandered from the heavily sallow-lined A10 corridor nearby. Such sightings suggest that the butterfly is wandering through the landscape.

Around Welwyn Garden City, colonies exist in woodland to the west, Sherrardspark Wood which is almost in the town, Bramfield Wood to the north-east and Mardley Heath to the north. The butterfly is also known from woods around Hatfield House, Hatfield.

In the north of the county, between Luton and Stevenage, the Purple Emperor is known from Knebworth Woods, from small woods near Preston and St Paul's Walden just west of Stevenage, and from Box Wood on the east edge of Stevenage. In the north-east, it is known from Plashes Wood, well north of Ware, and has appeared in a garden in Bishop's Stortford.

We can only speculate as to the extent to which the Purple Emperor has resurged in Hertfordshire, or whether it has always occurred there in low numbers. Liz and Andrew adhere to the latter theory, and so do I. Send for the Birdsall boys! Let them know that *iris* is back in their beloved Box Wood, and needs searching for in their other childhood heartlands of St John's Wood and High Wood.

Middlesex (old county of)

Few would have thought that the Purple Emperor could occur in twenty-first-century Middlesex. There is, though, a long history of the butterfly occurring in this highly urbanised county (there is a somewhat obtuse record for Caen Wood – possibly Ken Wood at Hampstead – from the 1850s). Nonetheless, the county is Purple, and nicely too, either due to recent recolonisation or because the butterfly had never died out.

A record from 1976 at Whitewebbs Park, part of old Enfield Chase close to the intersection of the M25 and the A10, was the first for Middlesex since a male was seen wandering down Ruislip High Street in 1955 (recorded by the Ruislip Natural History Society). Then something remarkable happened: in 1999 the Purple Emperor was seen at Ruislip Common, and in 2003 one turned up at Forty Hall, close to Whitewebbs Park at Enfield.

Since then, populations have been discovered in and around Ruislip Woods National Nature Reserve, where the Purple Emperor is now seen annually at a male assembly area in Park Wood. Whitewebbs Park was also found to be hosting a population, and a male assembly area has been located there – well away from any sallows. In addition, a number of wanderers have been recorded recently; for example, at Abney Park Cemetery, in Stoke Newington.

Best of all, the Purple Emperor was discovered on Hampstead Heath in 2012. This monumental event was announced on Twitter by the Corporation of London. Since then, the butterfly has been recorded from several different parts of the Heath. Also, in 2018 a well-occupied male assembly area was discovered, after much searching, on ridge-top veteran oaks at Totteridge Green, between Finchley and Barnet.

Purple Emperor numbers are perhaps predictably low in Middlesex, with a maximum of three in a vista at well-known male assembly areas in Ruislip Woods and Whitewebbs Wood. However, there is a fair scatter of small woods, many country parks, and relict areas of old field systems with oak and willows within a landscape in which farming is in retreat. The butterfly awaits full discovery in the Grand Union Canal and Lea Valley corridors, where sallows abound locally.

Essex

The first record of the Purple Emperor in Britain comes from Essex, at Castle Hedingham, to the north of Braintree, way back in 1695.

In the south of the county, it was first recorded from Epping Forest, near Waltham Abbey, in 1833. After a lengthy period of assumed extinction (last record in 1939), the butterfly was seen again in Epping Forest during the great Purple Emperor season of 1983. A trickle of sightings took place between 2000 and 2010. Since then, butterfly recorders have seen Purple Emperors in Epping Forest annually, finding it from Lord's Bushes and Buckhurst Hill in the forest's extreme south end and Pole Hill at Chingford in the south-west corner, right up to Woodridden Hill and Bell Common at the north end. By 2018, 10 male assembly areas had been identified, six of which produced a total of 14 males that summer. Further discoveries were made during 2019. This is a considerable achievement given the dense structure of the forest. It is not an easy site to work, being a long-wooded ridge. Liz and Andrew believe that the butterfly has remained continuously present in Epping Forest throughout entomological history.

Elsewhere in south Essex, the Purple Emperor is known from Hainault Forest at Chigwell, Havering Country Park and Bedfords Park at Romford, Thorndon Country Park at Brentwood, Norsey Wood near Billericay, Langdon Hills at Basildon, Eastbrookend Country Park at Hornchurch and Hickley Woods just north of Southend. Brentwood can claim some earlier fame, as it was here in 1758 that pioneer entomologist Dru Drury 'beat' four larvae off sallows. He gave one to Moses Harris, who reared it through. These were the first Purple Emperor larvae found in the UK, and the first to be bred. Havering Country Park is also a place of interest, as it holds a great landmark territory – a clump of giant Wellingtonias, which can be seen from Epping Forest 20 kilometres away, standing out like a cathedral spire. Emperor males may travel far to gather here, and as many as four can be seen in the air at a time.

In the Harlow area, the butterfly has been rediscovered in Ongar Park Woods, close to Epping. All this means that there is a fairish chance of a wandering Emperor turning up in the The Purple Emperor pub in Harlow, perhaps to create chaos at one of the live music events for which the pub is renowned.

The Purple Emperor has been found to be well established in Hatfield Forest and its outlying woods, just east of Bishop's Stortford, and also in small woods either side of Great Dunmow. The top count at Hatfield in 2018 was an impressive 10 individuals, achieved by local naturalist Lawrence Drummond.

In north-west Essex, the butterfly is known from small woods around Duddenhoe End and up against the Cambridgeshire border near Saffron Walden.

In central Essex, the Purple Emperor seems to occur in many of the small, scattered woods that characterise the landscape, for example around Writtle. It has also been discovered at several spots along the Danbury Ridge since 2014, and also in woodland to the south-east of Colchester. In addition, in the early 2000s the butterfly was introduced to the Marks Hall estate, north of Coggeshall, though it may well have already been present there, or was poised to colonise. The Purple Emperor is doing well on this estate; sallows are encouraged, and the butterfly's presence there is greatly valued.

The Purple credentials of north-east Essex, an historically important part of the Purple Empire, are currently being investigated. In all, it appears that the butterfly is quite widespread in Essex, though populations are, as elsewhere, generally small. Much surveying has been carried out by Laurence Drummond, in liaison with Liz and Andrew, and by Brentwood naturalist Colin Jupp. Others will follow; this county is – and probably always has been – nicely Purple.

Suffolk
The county butterfly atlas produced by Mendel and Piotrowski in 1986 paints a fairly dismal picture of the Suffolk butterfly fauna, pointing out that the county had lost more species than any other, including the Purple Emperor. The subsequent *Millennium Atlas of Suffolk Butterflies*, produced by the Suffolk Naturalists' Society in 2001, lists the Purple Emperor as so long

extinct that it did not merit a species account. The last county record was from 1962, and prior to that, 1947.

Then things started happening. In 2012 it came to light that a wildlife-friendly farmer had seen a male Emperor perched on his tractor south-east of Thetford in 1985. The significance of that record was not recognised at the time.

Things kicked off in 2013, when the butterfly was discovered in the famous ancient coppices of Bradfield Woods, south-east of Bury St Edmunds. It has subsequently been found in several of the other small woods in that flatland area. Five were seen in the worked coppices of Bradfield Woods on one day in 2018, suggesting a population increase (and enhanced searching). The male assembly area there is above the visitor centre. This provides an example of how easily overlooked this butterfly can be.

Also, south of Bury St Edmunds, the butterfly was found recently near Stanstead, north of Long Melford. A singleton was seen in Lavenham in 2018. Closer to Bury St Edmonds, the Purple Emperor was discovered in woods on the National Trust's Ickworth estate in 2018, and in a wood near the village of Whepstead. It is just starting to be found north of Bury St Edmonds. Thetford Forest in the Brecks is mostly too dry and sandy for sallows, and too coniferised, but some of the woods between Thetford and Bury St Edmunds may be suitable. A Purple Emperor was seen in a garden in this area in 2013, and, north-east of Bury St Edmunds, one was seen near Ixworth village in 2018.

In 2015, the Purple Emperor was recorded in the RSPB's reserve at Wolves Wood near Hadleigh, west of Ipswich. Three were subsequently seen in a nearby wood. Further searches may reveal more sites in the Ipswich and Woodbridge area, although in 2019 it became apparent that several locally extinct butterfly species were being clandestinely reintroduced to this district by well-meaning enthusiasts.

All these discoveries were made by Liz and Andrew, working closely with the Suffolk branch of Butterfly Conservation. The rediscovery of the Purple Emperor in Suffolk represents a monumental achievement and reflects much hard work. It also shows what can be achieved when people go out in search of this butterfly.

Rightly or wrongly, the Purple Emperor was introduced to Theberton Wood, just north-east of Saxmundham, in the early 2000s. Annual releases were made between 2001 and 2004 (see account in the passage on introductions in Chapter 2, p. 61). The butterfly has taken quite well there, and has spread to other woods — at times on its own volition, and at other times with some human assistance, through further releases. In addition, translocations took place to woods around Halesworth, which generated sightings in 2014 and 2015. The initial introductions were made before the Purple Emperor was rediscovered in Suffolk and have inadvertently masked natural spread.

Norfolk

Despite the fact that Norfolk, and north Norfolk in particular, can probably boast more naturalists per square mile than any other county (with the possible exception of Dorset), the status of the Purple Emperor in the county remains something of an enigma. The situation is made stranger by the fact that much of north Norfolk lies on the Boulder Clay, on which sallows will grow prolifically. Yet there are surprisingly few old records from the county, which includes among its alumni the butterfly colossus F W Frohawk.

As with so many other counties, the Purple Emperor was considered to be long extinct in Norfolk. The last known site seems to have been Foxley Wood, halfway between Norwich and Fakenham, where the butterfly persisted at least into the 1970s. But there are also records from Holt Country Park, in north Norfolk, from 1995 and 2006, and one from Upton Broad in the Broads in 1973.

Then, things kicked off. In early August 2016 an old male Emperor was observed from the hilltop gazebo in the National Trust's Sheringham Park, east of Cromer. The following year Liz and Andrew saw a territorial male in nearby Sheringham Park Wood, a female was sighted among the sallows by Weybourne Pond there, and National Trust ranger Mark Webster subsequently saw two males close by. The butterfly was also seen in Sheringham Park Wood in 2018.

Nearby, on Beeston Common, a female was photographed in 2017, and two, possibly three, individuals were recorded there in 2018. It also came to light that a Purple Emperor had been seen in a Beeston garden in 2014, and that one had apparently been photographed at the National Trust's Felbrigg Hall in 2011. I spent time in the woods in the district in early October 2017, finding a number of the best-looking pure Goat Willows (not hybrids, for once) I had seen in years. Holt Country Park, in particular, looked eminently suitable. Sure enough, Liz and Andrew saw a female there in 2018, and several other sightings were subsequently made, including one of a fresh-looking female feeding on a garden Buddleia at Northrepps, south-east of Cromer, in 2019.

Elsewhere in Norfolk, in 2011 a Purple Emperor was seen in the Holkham Gap, close to the sea near Wells-next-the-Sea; another was seen south of Sandringham in north-west Norfolk back in 2004; in 2015 one was reported from woodland near Upgate, north-west of Norwich; and in 2017 one was recorded at Fritton, inland between Great Yarmouth and Lowestoft.

Down on the border with Suffolk, west of Diss, a Purple Emperor was seen at Redgrave and Lopham Fen National Nature Reserve in 2015, a site I considered to be suitable when I visited in 2000. Another was seen close by in Bressingham (just inside Norfolk) in 2017.

In mid-July 2019 Liz and Andrew rediscovered the Purple Emperor in its old haunt of Foxley Wood, now a wildlife trust nature reserve. Perhaps it had remained there all along, functioning below Heslop's 'observation threshold'? Additionally, in 2019 individual Purple Emperors were seen at Ashwellthorpe, south-west of Norwich, and at Swanton Novers National Nature Reserve, between Holt and Fakenham.

It is open to speculation as to whether the butterfly had survived in Norfolk all along, if it has recolonised (from Suffolk, Cambridgeshire or even perhaps from across the North Sea), or if it has been clandestinely introduced by well-meaning butterfly breeders? The case history provided by other counties would suggest that the first option provides the most likely explanation.

Meanwhile, the Purple Emperor still remains in need of discovery in the Norfolk Broads – there are two tantalising records, from 1973 and 2006. Andrew and Liz, who sails the Broads and knows and loves them well, have searched, though as yet without success – though Andrew had a brief but inconclusive distant sighting at Hickling Broad in 2019. Normal rules of engagement, though, might not apply in the Broadland sallow-carr jungles – the butterfly may be behaving rather differently there.

The message to Norfolk is simple: the Purple Emperor desires to become your premier butterfly, deposing your esteemed Swallowtail.

Cambridgeshire (including old Huntingdonshire)

Declaring the Purple Emperor extinct in a county seems to wind the butterfly up rather nicely, as is indicated by the tale of its spectacular resurgence in Cambridgeshire and old Huntingdonshire, after it had been categorised as 'extinct' in *The Butterflies of Cambridgeshire* (2006).

The Purple Emperor was well known from Monks Wood, Huntingdon, in the distant past, though it (and its sallows) suffered severely from extensive felling work there during the First World War. In 1897 no fewer than 50 were seen in a day there, one of the highest counts on record prior to the twenty-first century. The butterfly was recorded in Monks Wood in 1964, and again in the great Emperor year of 1983. By 2018, it had returned, as part of a countywide resurgence.

In 2011, the Purple Emperor appeared at Woodwalton Fen National Nature Reserve, in the Cambridgeshire Fens between Huntingdon and Peterborough, a short distance from Monks Wood. That was a 'first' for this well-recorded site, with the butterfly breeding in Grey Willow carr. By 2014 it was relatively numerous there, with males assembling on oaks around the site of Charles Rothschild's stilted bungalow. This is unusually open terrain for the Purple Emperor, and males can be seen crossing low over the Fen to assemble on these oaks. In 2018, three males

were seen in woodland a few miles to the west, indicating
significant spread. Earlier, in 2013, the Purple Emperor had
appeared at Brampton Wood Nature Reserve, just to the south-
west of Huntingdon, reappearing there in 2015.

West of Peterborough, in the extreme north-west of the
county, the Purple Emperor was seen in 2014 at Bedford Purlieus
National Nature Reserve, Southey Wood, and Castor Hanglands
National Nature Reserve. It has subsequently proved to be
comfortably established in that district.

In south Cambridgeshire, a singleton was seen at Bar Hill,
north-west of Cambridge, in 2011. Then, in 2013, a colony was
discovered near Balsham, on the border with Essex. Here, males
sometimes perch on, and defend, a concrete water tower outside
the wood edge. In 2014, another population was discovered at
Ditton Park Wood, a Forestry Commission (now Forestry
England) wood south of Newmarket. Ten males were counted
there on 2 July 2018.

In the south-west of the county, the butterfly appeared in
woodland near Gamlingay in 2012. Since then, it has been
found in at least three woods around there. In addition, in 2016
a male called in at visitor reception at the National Trust's
Wimpole Hall, a little to the east, where he was duly meeted-
and-greeted.

It is likely that the Purple Emperor invaded Cambridgeshire
(and old Huntingdonshire) from its stronghold in east
Northamptonshire, where populations have burgeoned since
the millennium, and also from Hertfordshire and Essex to the
south, in a pincer movement. There is a reasonable chance, of
course, that the butterfly had lingered on all along at a few sites
in Cambridgeshire, in which case those populations would have
been bolstered by incomers. What is significant, though, is that
the Purple Emperor moved into fen-carr habitats in the county,
breeding on Grey Willow carr, as in Holland. It will be interesting
to see when the butterfly appears at Wicken Fen National
Nature Reserve, deep in the Cambridgeshire Fens. It may
already be there, though one experienced recorder looked
without success in 2019.

Bedfordshire

Long ago, Bedfordshire was a noted county for the Purple Emperor, but it seems that the butterfly had died out before the publication of the Victoria County History account in 1904. Miraculously, it began to return in the early 1980s, when one was seen a little to the east of Milton Keynes. Two other sightings were made during the mid-1990s. The butterfly has expanded impressively during the present century, though recording effort has also increased.

In south Bedfordshire, the Purple Emperor appeared at King's Wood and Rushmere National Nature Reserve, just north of Leighton Buzzard, in the mid-1990s. It reappeared there in 2008 and sightings subsequently increased, suggesting full colonisation.

Just a little to the south, a male was seen in a nature reserve along a disused railway line near Dunstable, in 2006. The following year His Imperial Majesty was observed going about his business in the hippopotamus enclosure of Whipsnade Zoo. He has visited the zoological park on at least two occasions since. There are also records of individuals wandering over the adjacent Dunstable Downs, during 2012 and 2013. The Purple Emperor may have been breeding in National Trust woodland on top of the downs then. In addition, there are recent records from privately owned woodland in the vicinity.

North of Luton and Dunstable, in central Bedfordshire, a Purple Emperor was seen near Harlington in 2008, and a population has recently been located near Woburn. In 2000 one was seen along The Embankment, which runs along the Great Ouse River in the middle of Bedford – a riverside wanderer, but from where? There are no known sites close to Bedford. More recently, it has turned up in South Mills Pits, and in Forestry England's Potton Wood, part of Ampthill Forest, east of Sandy. North-west of Bedford, Purple Emperors have recently been seen in a series of small woods around Harrold and Souldrop.

The best-known site in Bedfordshire is Chicksands Wood, near Clophill. The butterfly has been recorded here annually since appearing there in 2006. Numbers increased well in 2009, and the following year a maximum of five was seen – the first time more than singletons had been recorded in the county for decades. Individuals have been observed in other woods in that area, notably around Old Warden and in Maulden Wood, Amphill. The latter is currently providing regular sightings. It may well be that the Purple Emperor is now fairly widespread in Bedfordshire. In 2018 it appeared at the RSPB's headquarters at The Lodge, Sandy.

East Midlands

Northamptonshire

The Purple Emperor has a long and fascinating history in Northamptonshire, the Rose of the Shires, a county blessed with oak forests on heavy clay soils. It is a tale of riches to rags, and from rags back to riches.

The Victoria County History states that the butterfly occurred commonly in most of the county's larger woods. Rockingham Forest, which stretched from Kettering to Peterborough, was the main stronghold. The insect was widespread and locally numerous there. Perhaps the most renowned locality was Ashton Wold, in the extreme north-east corner of the Forest. This was the domain of the Reverend William Bree (1822–1917), Rector of Polebrook and second-generation butterfly collector (see Chapter 1).

During the twentieth century the Purple Emperor became increasingly rare, until it was considered to be extinct in the county during the 1960s. It died out from Ashton Wold during the Second World War. As happened in other counties, many of Northamptonshire's oak woods were converted to dense conifer plantations, from where sallows were assiduously weeded out. Other woods were simply abandoned, and degenerated into dense mature English Oak or Ash woods, lacking open rides – sallows were choked out, and there was no possibility of regeneration. Also, and incredibly, it appears that the Purple Emperor was lost from its stronghold in Salcey Forest after the Forestry Commission aerial sprayed the forest with insecticide during the 1960s, in an attempt to control an outbreak of Green Oak Tortrix moth. The details rightly lie buried within the sanctums of the Forestry Commission – we have all moved

on, and forests are most adept at moving on. Salcey was the
setting for BB's boyhood masterpiece *Brendon Chase* (1944), in
which the Purple Emperor appears almost as a mystical being.

BB, or to reiterate his proper name, Denys Watkins-Pitchford
(1905–1990), was Northamptonshire through and through. He
was born in Lamport in the centre of the county, and after
studying in London and teaching art at Rugby he moved to east
Northamptonshire, which became his heartland. In 1973 he
began releasing garden-reared Purple Emperors into the nearby
woods – the main block of the Fermyn Woods complex
consisting of Oxen, Titchmarsh, Green Side, Souther and Lady
woods. It is a matter of conjecture as to whether the butterfly
was previously extinct there or not. My feeling is that the scatter
of veteran sallows along the wood edges there suggests that the
insect may have survived in and around Fermyn Woods all along,
but at a low population density. However, BB was convinced
that these were 'his' Emperors, and I love and admire his writing,
artwork, nature-first values and dedication to the Purple
Emperor too much to dispute his claim. They are forever his, at
least in spirit.

The main block of Fermyn Woods had been replanted with
Norway Spruce before and after the Second World War. For a
while the spruce trees grew well, apparently favouring the
Boulder Clay, on which they had never been grown before.
Then they stopped growing, and started to die back – as
happened in Norway Spruce plantations on clay land elsewhere.
Over a period of about 20 years the Forestry Commission
cleared them away (there are relict areas of the diseased Norway
Spruce slums in Lilford Wood and Wadenhoe Great Wood, small
outliers to the east of this main block). They then did something
wonderful: they left the woods to natural regeneration. Broad-
leaved trees appeared in profusion – Ash, Field Maple and
English Oak, plus a profusion of pioneer colonising hybrid
sallows. Sallows adore the Boulder Clay, which covers about 50
per cent of Northamptonshire.

By the mid-1990s the Purple Emperor was resurging
throughout the Fermyn Woods complex. In 1998 it was recorded

in Harry's Park Wood, to the north of Brigstock. By the good summer (and great Emperor season) of 2003 it was clear that a large Purple Emperor population was developing in Fermyn Woods, something which had not happened anywhere in the UK for decades, perhaps not since the advent of mass coniferisation and sallow weeding following the establishment of the Forestry Commission in 1919. Sallows, and their associated butterfly, were proliferating. The next two good summers, 2006 and 2009, saw further increases. The butterfly also expanded further in range during the great summer of 2013, by which time most of the vast generation of new sallows had become suitably tall. The Fermyn Woods complex was now supporting what was probably the largest and the most extensive population of the Purple Emperor anywhere in Britain since the heyday of Kent's Great Chattenden Wood back in the mid-Victorian era. The butterfly had also spread to other woods in the vicinity, including the privately owned Geddington Chase, Southwick Wood and Grafton Park Wood.

Currently, the Purple Emperor is established in most of the Rockingham Forest woods, from Kettering through to Peterborough, and down to Thrapston in the south-east. This includes woods to the west of Corby, and just to the north of Kettering. In 2017, I found it in King's Wood, an ancient woodland relict trapped in Corby new town, and it colonised the renowned Black Hairstreak site of Glapthorn Cow Pastures, north of Oundle, where I had searched for it in vain in 2010 and 2013. In 2015 it appeared in Fineshade Wood, in the north of Rockingham Forest, off the road to Stamford. The butterfly's future now depends on the extent to which Forestry England can balance the needs of this butterfly with other forest aims.

Away from Rockingham Forest and east Northamptonshire, the Purple Emperor began to colonise Forestry Commission woodland between Kettering and Northampton in 2014. The following year it was recorded in a wood to the west of Northampton.

South of Northampton, the Purple Emperor reappeared in Yardley Chase in 2009 and in nearby Salcey Forest in 2011. It is increasing and expanding nicely in this former stronghold area, notably in Yardley Chase. Likewise, it reappeared in Hazelborough Woods, in the old Whittlebury Forest around Silverstone, back in 1999, having presumably spread back over the border from Buckinghamshire. Since then, it has been found in nearby Bucknell Wood, Whistley Wood and Wicken Wood, and now appears to be well established in this woodland complex.

Finally, in 2015 the Purple Emperor was recorded near Everdon, to the south-east of Daventry, in the lightly wooded countryside of south-west Northamptonshire. This means that virtually all of Northamptonshire is now strongly Purple, the exception being the western and north-western fringes, and the central area around Lamport.

Rutland

Rutland may be small, but it has a great heart, which is Purple. The county won its colours at 10 am on 3 July 2014, when a pristine male Purple Emperor was photographed in the RSPB's visitor centre car park at Egleton on the west side of Rutland Water. Since then, Purple Emperors have been seen in some of the small woods to the north of the reservoir. The butterfly is also known from woodland just over the border into Lincolnshire.

Lincolnshire

Lincolnshire is the one English county I do not know well. Most people don't even travel through it. I know only the extreme south.

Much of Lincolnshire is on clay, and parts are well wooded. This means that there is a long history of the Purple Emperor occurring there. In fact, historically Lincolnshire was regarded as a stronghold county. The only areas the butterfly has not been recorded from are the coastal strip land, which includes the resorts of Mablethorpe and Skegness, the open flatland around Sleaford, and the Lincolnshire Fens around Boston and Spalding. During the late Victorian and Edwardian eras the Purple Emperor was recorded from many of the woodland systems, particularly between Oakham (in Rutland) and Bourne in the south of the county, around Lincoln itself, around Louth on the eastern edge of the Lincolnshire Wolds, and near Market Rasen.

Incredibly, there seem to be no records between 1904, when the insect was recorded from Laughton Forest, which was then a heathy expanse north of Gainsborough, and the late 1980s, when it was discovered in woodland just south of Louth, on the eastern edge of the Wolds. Much oak woodland was, though, cleared during that time, to make way for agriculture. The fact that Louth is well away from the borders of any other county suggests that either the butterfly had lingered on in that district all along, or that it had been clandestinely introduced. The former seems the most likely scenario.

During the present century, the Purple Emperor has resurged strongly in south Lincolnshire. In 2015 it appeared in woodlands just north of Bourne and a few miles to the west near Colsterworth. Since then it has been found in other woods close to Bourne. These may have been recolonisations spawned by the burgeoning population in Northamptonshire to the south.

In addition, a sizeable population has been established in and around Chambers Farm Wood, to the east of Lincoln, following releases there in 2014 and 2015 (see the passage on introductions in Chapter 2, p. 63). It may be that those woods would have been colonised naturally in the near future, given the rate at which the butterfly seems to be moving north (but that is not to pass judgement). In 2018 the Purple Emperor was discovered in two new woods close to Lincoln, suggesting further northward spread.

Nottinghamshire
Historically, the Purple Emperor was known from the area around Mansfield and Sherwood Forest, and from smaller woods to the east, towards Newark-on-Trent. The first record comes from Sherwood Forest in 1859. The butterfly seems to have been reasonably well known from the Sherwood area around the turn of the nineteenth century, and in the woods to the east. The last batch of records comes from 1939, when the species was recorded from Thieves Wood on the southern edge of Mansfield, three sites in and around Sherwood Forest, and a small wood at

Winkburn, towards Newark-on-Trent. The butterfly then appears to have died out from the county, or sunk to a level at which detection was all but impossible.

During the mid-1960s the Purple Emperor was released into Cotgrave Forest, to the south-east of Nottingham (see the passage on introductions in Chapter 2, p. 61). George Hyde, one of the three co-authors of *Notes & Views of the Purple Emperor*, was involved. It is likely that some topping up subsequently occurred. What is interesting is that the butterfly's presence there remained a secret until 2015, by which time much of the site had become a country park. Much of Cotgrave is new woodland over colliery waste deposits, with older, rather damaged woodland (in private ownership) to the west and east. There is now a thriving Purple Emperor population there, in atypically open habitat, where the butterfly is unusually visible. On 26 June 2017 one observer recorded 15 sightings in 90 minutes, including two vistas of pairs of patrolling males. Also in 2017, a magnificent male ab. *lugenda* was photographed down on a path. This is now a well-known site for the butterfly, and is sympathetically managed.

Leicestershire

Leicestershire came out and declared itself Purple in 2018, after decades of assumed or actual extinction, when the Purple Emperor was seen in woodland straddling the M1 on the north-west fringe of Leicester. The species was seen again there in 2019. Better still, on 16 July 2019 a male Purple Emperor was photographed at Charnwood Lodge National Nature Reserve, near Coalville, a few miles to the north-west. These records suggest that the species is re-establishing itself in the Charnwood Forest area.

The Coalville record is particularly important, as the town lies close to the new National Forest, which runs in a broad swathe from Leicester north-west to and beyond Burton upon Trent in Staffordshire, and overspills nicely across the border into south Derbyshire. Sallows abound in many of the newly created woods, most of which are sited where coal spoil has been spread, or on clay. Many of these young woods, notably around Ashby-de-la-Zouch in Leicestershire and Ticknall in neighbouring Derbyshire, constitute some of the best-looking Purple Emperor habitat I have seen, on a par with the dense sallow jungles of Fermyn Woods and Knepp Wildland. Unfortunately, I have only been able to search for larvae in mid-April – a difficult time of year to locate them. It is, I believe, only a matter of time before south Derbyshire declares itself Purple.

West Midlands

Warwickshire

The reintroductions of the Purple Emperor in 2004 to Ryton Wood, to the south-east of Coventry, and to Oversley Wood, near Alcester, are covered in the piece on introductions in Chapter 2 (p. 63). It is worth emphasising here that by the end of 2018 the butterfly had spread so well that it been recorded from 22 tetrad squares (squares of 2 x 2 kilometres) in the county, and was present in at least 17 woods (probably more like 20). By 2018 the butterfly had spread from Ryton as far south as woodland near Southam, and from Oversley as far east as Wellesbourne, the other side of Stratford-upon-Avon.

It would appear that the majority of recent records result from natural colonisation from these two release sites. Some, however, may result from natural spread from Northamptonshire, particularly those from copses in lightly wooded farmland on the border. In 2018 and 2019 the butterfly was recorded in woodland further north, towards Daventry. These records are important as they indicate that the Purple Emperor may be able to persist in lightly wooded farmed countryside.

Of particular interest is the Purple Emperor's colonisation of parts of the new Heart of England Forest, which aims to establish 12,500 hectares of new woodland in the south-west of the county, between Redditch and Evesham, close to the Oversley Wood release site. By early 2019, over 2,500 hectares of new woodland had been created in four woodland centres. Many sallows have been planted, and others have planted themselves. This new forest may shortly become the premier locality for the Purple Emperor in Britain.

In addition, there are interesting modern records from the RSPB's Middleton Lakes reserve outside Sutton Coldfield, on the Staffordshire border, from 2014, and also from Hollywood on the southern edge of Birmingham in 2015. These two sightings could, though, result from butterflies released at social events such as weddings, as a company started including Purple Emperors in 'butterfly confetti' packages around then. Having said that, there are numerous suitable-looking sallows along the railway line running into Birmingham New Street station from the south-west, notably around Longbridge and King's Norton. Moreover, much of the Tame Valley is rich in sallows. The latter runs east through the wildlife-rich Sandwell Valley at West Bromwich, before turning north and heading past Tamworth.

Historically, most of the scatter of Warwickshire records for the Purple Emperor come from woods to the east of Coventry. Many of those woods have now been recolonised by natural spread from Ryton Wood.

Worcestershire
There are only four records from Worcestershire in the Biological Records Centre/Butterflies for the New Millennium database, all old: one from Tenbury Wells, on the border with north Herefordshire, from the unlikely early date of 5 June 1918; one from Bredon Hill, near Pershore, in the great summer of 1976, when Purple Emperors turned up in many new places; and two from Park Wood at Upper Colwall in the Malvern Hills, in 1864 and 1899. There is also a 'near Malvern' record from 1950 which could relate to Park Wood, which is just in Worcestershire, or to other woods on the west flank of the Malverns, which are in Herefordshire (the summit of the Malverns straddles the two counties).

There should be more Worcestershire records, for the county is quite well wooded. Parts of the Forest of Feckenham, between Worcester and Redditch, look modestly suitable today. There is also suitable habitat in the woods due west of Pershore. Sure enough, late in the 2019 Purple Emperor season a ragged female was photographed in Tiddesley Wood, on the west edge of

Pershore. This may have been a wanderer from the burgeoning population in nearby south-west Warwickshire, and could herald the colonisation of much of Worcestershire.

Herefordshire

In addition to the Malvern Hills records mentioned above, the Purple Emperor was also known from Eastnor Park, near Ledbury, on the south-western edge of the Malvern Ridge. There is also a scatter of largely old records from far-flung places in the county: Little Cowarne, south-west of Bromyard in east Herefordshire; Great Doward on the River Wye in the north-west corner of the Forest of Dean; and Pontrilas, up against the Welsh border below the Brecon Beacons. Most of these records are dated 1908, though the butterfly was known from Great Doward over many years, and was seen there as recently as 1976. The final record is even more disparate, coming from just south of Hay-on-Wye in 1984.

I have looked in vain for the Purple Emperor in Herefordshire, at Haugh Wood to the south-east of Hereford and in Dymock Woods near Newent. Both areas of woodland look eminently suitable. I may have visited just a trifle late in the (2016) flight season.

Strangely, the butterfly has never been recorded in the vast Wyre Forest, on the Worcestershire–Shropshire border.

Staffordshire

There seems to be little in the way of deep history of the Purple Emperor occurring in this county – just the odd record from the Cannock Chase area during the Victorian era. Then, on 18 July 2019 a male was photographed while fluttering at a window near Rugely in Cannock Chase. This stimulated other reports from that district, which await verification. At the time of going to print, though, it looks as though the Purple Emperor may well have returned to south Staffordshire – in which case, sallow-rich land on the northern and north-eastern fringes of Birmingham, to the immediate south of Cannock, could be in the process of being colonised.

Wales and beyond

There are five old records of Purple Emperors occurring in wooded valleys in North Wales, none more recent than the 1930s. Two are from the Snowdonia area, one from near Machynlleth, one from near Llanidloes, Powys, and the fifth from near Montgomery. These records are beyond my understanding, but involve valley-bottom woodland, where sallows grow along wooded river corridors. Oddly, there are no substantiated records from South Wales, even from Monmouthshire (Sir Fynwy), which is well wooded. This is odd, as Frohawk (1924) says that 'it is not uncommon in Monmouthshire'.

In the nineteenth century, the Purple Emperor was recorded from three areas of Shropshire: the Ellesmere district, Haughmond Hill to the east of Shrewsbury, and Ragleth Wood on the edge of Church Stretton. These suggest that the butterfly may have been more widespread in the county.

Further north, there is a record from Thurstaston Common, a largely wooded heath on the Wirral Peninsula, Merseyside. I went there in the late 1990s, and it looked suitable. It represents the most north-westerly recorded site for the Purple Emperor in Britain.

Yorkshire would like to have the last word, and so it shall. *The Butterflies of Yorkshire* (2005) suggests that the Purple Emperor may well have occurred around Doncaster during early Victorian times, perhaps in Edlington Wood, which is not too far from Sherwood Forest, Nottinghamshire, from where the butterfly was then known. The book also mentions a male from Ewden Head, north-west of Sheffield, in 1941, though on the absurdly late date of 22 September – which is surely an error – and also of a male which appeared in a York garden in early August 1997, perhaps an escapee or release. The book concludes, rightly, that Yorkshire should be keeping close watch for the arrival of the Purple Emperor in its broad acres – before Lancashire gets colonised. Yorkshire may have already won this battle, as the Purple Emperor is now rumoured to occur in woods around Maltby, just east of Rotherham – in which case the white rose can be recoloured Purple.

Glossary

The Purple Emperor is a mindset, and like all mindsets it has generated its own language over time. This language will continue to evolve. With all the terms below, the originator's name is in brackets. Some standard nature conservation terms are also included here.

Assembly area (Oates): Favoured treetop territory location used by more than one male, where airspace and canopy perching points are disputed. Can consist of a single tree or a clump. See also master oak/tree and territory – these terms are synonyms.

Baiting (Hulme): The practice of spreading bait, such as shrimp paste, along open rides in order to encourage Purple Emperors to descend to feed. This began in early Victorian times and has resurged in recent years. Hulme calls 'laying the filth'.

Basking (biology): A butterfly's habit of sitting in the sun with its wings spread open. To raise its body temperature it holds its wings in a 'V' shape, to funnel sunshine on to its body, which, unlike the wings, absorbs heat (though there are also heat sensor patches on the wings).

Breeding ground (biology): In this context, a distinct area of land where a butterfly's foodplant grows in environmental conditions suitable for breeding.

Canopy gap (biology): A prominent gap in the foliage between tall trees, effectively acting as a mountain pass.

Clash and chase (Goodyear and Middleton): The key part of territorial dispute behaviour, in which rival males will circle around each other before one chases the other away, at speed, above the treetops, often reaching heights of 50 metres above the canopy. The victor, and sometimes the vanquished, will return. This behaviour usually involves pairs of males, but may involve small groups.

De-titting (Hulme): Pursuit and eviction of one or more birds of the tit family from the tree canopy. Both sexes of the Purple Emperor do this: males from territories, females from sallow stands. In winter, tits are major predators of hibernating Purple Emperor larvae. There seems to be some form of stored resentment.

Egging (Hulme): Diagnostic behaviour of a female butterfly clearly intent on laying eggs.

Emperoring (Oates): The peaceful, pleasurable and utterly innocent
pastime of searching for Purple Emperors.

Feeder tree (Heslop): A stressed or diseased tree, usually oak, possessing
an obvious sap run or minor sap bleeds from fissures, on which adult
Purple Emperors (of both sexes) feed. These trees are usually
seasonal, and often function intermittently, even ephemerally.

Flight season (biology): The time of year when the adult stage of a
butterfly is flying.

Foliage bowl (biology): A large indentation in the foliage cover of a
mature tree or a group of trees along a wood edge, where the air
temperature is warmer and conditions are stiller. Purple Emperors
gather in these foliage bowls late in the day, and in cool weather.

Foodplant (biology): Technically, the larval pabulum; that is, what the
larva or caterpillar eats.

Grounding (Hulme): An instance of a Purple Emperor, usually a
male, descending to feed on substances on the ground.

Herself (Oates): The Empress, or female Purple Emperor.

Himself (Oates): The Emperor, or male Purple Emperor.

His Imperial Majesty (Victorian): One of the Purple Emperor's
many epithets, in use since at least early Victorian times.

Instar (biology): A distinct growth phase of a caterpillar or larva,
separated by skin changes (ecdysis). The larva of the Purple
Emperor has five instars, separated by four skin changes. These
instars are abbreviated to L1, L2 etc.

Master oak or master tree (Heslop): A tree, or distinct group of
trees, invariably occupied by one or more territorial males in
suitable weather on afternoons during the flight period.

Metapopulation (biology): A network of populations, large, small
and transient, within an area of landscape, between which some
exchange of adults will occur. Within a metapopulation structure,
individual colonisations and extinctions will occur naturally.

Microclimate (biology): A highly localised pocket where climatic
conditions are different from those in the surrounding area.

Monitoring (biology): Assessing how a population or a group of
populations is faring, by means of standardised methodology. This
is usually distinct from surveying.

Oak edging (Oates): The habit Purple Emperor males have of flying
along tree edges in search of females. Males so engaged ignore the
normally favoured treetops, instead flying in a searching manner
along the mid-tree zone, where females are most likely to perch,
along rides and wood edges.

Observation threshold (Heslop): The population density above which a Purple Emperor population is likely to be observed; the assumption being that at many localities the butterfly exists below the level at which it can readily be noticed, even by skilled observers. It is likely that this threshold has been lowered in recent years, as naturalists have become more skilled at finding Purple Emperor populations. Much depends on how open or dense a site is.

People of Purple Persuasion (Oates): The Purple Emperor fan club, who all share a blissful state of mind and exist to help others experience and value this miraculous butterfly. It is a very broad church: no one is excluded, so long as they're Purple.

Pupation (biology): The process of changing from larva (caterpillar) to pupa (chrysalis).

Purple Empire (Heslop): The known range of the Purple Emperor in Britain. Also, the name of the Purple Emperor blog.

Rejection drop (Willmott): Distinctive flight behaviour where a mated female rejects male advances by fluttering down to the ground, with her ardent suitor(s) swooping around her, before pulling out at the last second and scuttling off at speed, often causing the male to crash-land. Some other butterflies behave similarly, notably the Swallowtail. Also called a Tumbledown.

Sallow searching (Oates): The Emperor's habit of searching sallow thickets and scrub containing sallow bushes for freshly emerged virgin females, and perhaps also for about-to-hatch pupae containing females. Sallow-searching is commonplace during the first half or two-thirds of the Purple Emperor season, ceasing once all the females have emerged and have been mated, and when the males are ageing. Males may indulge in sallow searching at all times of day, but mainly do so during the late morning period – which is why they seldom appear at known territories before midday.

Silking (Oates): The larva's habit of spinning silk, from its mouthparts, to create a silk pad on which it can cling firmly, a safe highway along the leaf midrib, and to affix the seat leaf stem on to its twig at the petiole join, and to create a pupation pad and secure a leaf for pupation.

Single occupancy (Oates): Assembly areas, master trees or territories which on a specific afternoon are occupied only by solitary males, and consequently tend to be quiescent (especially in hot weather when few birds and other insects are flying).

Surveying (biology): Searching, systematically, for new populations. This is (usually) distinct from monitoring, though the two overlap in the area called 'repeat survey'.

Taxa (biology): Plural of taxon; a taxonomic grouping within the
classification of organisms. In this context, a generalised group of
species, subspecies and hybrids. Taxonomy (the system for naming
and organising things, especially plants and animals, into groups
that share certain characteristics) is rather a dark art. No name or
system seems to stay put for long. Changes are forever being made;
at times, one fears, to keep taxonomists in work. Taxonomists fall
into two camps: lumpers and splitters. The former wish to see as
few separations and as much generality as possible; the latter are
fascinated by species being split down into minutiae, even micro-
species. The splitters are in vogue now. Both entomology and
botany are bedevilled by all this, to the eternal confusion of the
humble beginner and at the expense of those who seek simplicity
in life. Naturalists, who are primary and often unwitting users,
suffer in silence. This is part of the context for reaching some
semblance of understanding of the Purple Emperor, an anarchic
animal which relishes chaos at the best of times; only, for once,
don't blame the butterfly.

Territory (Willmott): Airspace around canopy gaps, and nearby
boughs used for perching, occupied and defended by territorial
males during the afternoon and evening periods. Territories can be
divided into primary (used annually, from start to finish of the
flight season, in virtually all weathers) and secondary (occupied
usually by solitary males in times of high population, or when
primary territories are too windswept).

Tumbledown (Hulme): Synonym for rejection drop, above.

References and further reading

Asher, J, Warren, M S, Fox, R, Harding, P, Jeffcoate, G and Jeffcoate, S. 2001. *The Millennium Atlas of Butterflies in Britain and Ireland*. Oxford University Press, Oxford.

Bucknell, W R. 1892. New Forest – collecting notes. *Entomologist's Record* 3: 264.

Coleman, W S. 1860. *British Butterflies*. Routledge, Warne & Routledge, London.

Dell, D. 2004. Experiences from breeding *Apatura iris* (L.) Nymphalidae in Switzerland from 1982 to 2002. *Entomologist's Record* 116: 179–187.

Dell, D, Sparks, T H and Dennis, R L H. 2005. Climate change and the effect of increasing spring temperatures on emergence dates of the flagship butterfly *Apatura iris* (Lepidoptera: Nymphalidae). *European Journal of Entomology* 102: 161–167.

Dunk, H C. 1954. Observations of the early stage of *Apatura iris* L. *Entomologist's Record* 66: 135–137.

Eeles, P. 2019. *Life Cycles of British & Irish Butterflies*. Pisces Publications, Newbury.

Eernisse, E. 2017. *Knepp Castle Estate Scrub and Hedgerow Changes 2001–2015 Southern Block*. Contract report, published on Knepp Castle Estate website.

Emmet, A M. 1991. *The Scientific Names of the British Lepidoptera: their history and meaning*. Harley Books, Colchester.

Ford, E B. 1945. *Butterflies*. Collins New Naturalist, London.

Fox, B W. 2005. The larva of the White Admiral butterfly, *Limenitis camilla* – a master builder. *Entomologist's Gazette* 56: 225–236.

Fox, R, Asher, J, Brereton, T, Roy, D and Warren, M S. 2006. *The State of Butterflies in Britain and Ireland*. Pisces Publications, Newbury.

Fox, R, Brereton, T M, Asher, J, August, T A, Botham, M S, Bourn, N A D, Cruickshanks, K L, Bulman, C R, Ellis, S, Harrower, C A, Middlebrook, I, Noble, D G, Powney, G D, Randle, Z, Warren, M S and Roy, D B. 2015. *The State of the UK's Butterflies 2015*. Butterfly Conservation and the Centre for Ecology & Hydrology, Wareham.

Friedrich, E. 1977. *Die Schillerfalter.* Die Neue-Büchere. 505: 112 S., Ziemsen Verlag, Wittenberg (in German, passages translated for me by Dr Dennis Dell).

Frohawk, F W. 1924. *Natural History of British Butterflies.* Hutchinson & Co., London

Goodyear, E and Middleton, A. 2003. *The Hertfordshire Purple Emperor* Apatura iris. Hertfordshire Natural History Society.

Goodyear, E and Middleton, A. 2015. *Eastern Region Purple Emperor* Apatura iris *Report for 2014.* Dispar website.

Harmer, A S. 2000. *Variation in British Butterflies.* Paphia Publishing Ltd, Lyndhurst.

Hermann, G. 2007. *Tagfalter suchen im Winter* (Searching for Butterflies in Winter). Books on Demand, Norderstedt.

Heslop, I R P, Hyde, G E and Stockley, R E. 1964. *Notes & Views of the Purple Emperor.* Southern Publishing, Brighton. (Most chapters previously published as papers in entomological journals.)

Hesseltine, G. 1888. *Apatura iris* in Hants. *Entomologist* 21: 209–201.

Hewett, G M A. 1895. Iris. *Entomologist's Record* 6: 145–147.

Holden, B. (ed.) 2013. *BB's Butterflies: a celebration of one man's passion for the Purple Emperor.* Roseworld Productions, Solihull.

Hudson, W H. 1902. *Hampshire Days.* J. M. Dent & Sons, London.

Jarvis, F V L. 1954. Larval Diapause in *Apatura iris* L. *Entomologist's Record* 66: 212–217 and 234–240.

Leatherdale, S. 1999. In defence of sallow. *Quarterly Journal of Forestry* 93 (3): 177–180.

Leraut, P. 2016. *Butterflies of Europe and Neighbouring Regions.* NAP Editions, France.

Lipscomb, C G. 1970. The habits of *Apatura iris* L. the Purple Emperor. *Entomologist's Record* 82: 159–160.

Luckens, C J. 1976. Successful hibernation of second instar larva of *Apatura iris* L. *Entomologist's Record* 88: 26.

Marren, P. 2015. *Rainbow Dust.* Penguin Random House, London.

Marren, P. 2019. *Emperors, Admirals and Chimney Sweepers: The naming of butterflies and moths.* Little Toller Books, Dorset.

Meikle, R D. 1984. *Willows and Poplars of Great Britain and Ireland.* Botanical Society of the British Isles Handbook No. 4, London.

Oates, M R. 2005. Extreme butterfly-collecting: a biography of I R P Heslop. *British Wildlife* 16: 164–171.

Oates, M R. 2008. The myth of the master tree. *British Wildlife* 19: 330–337.

Oates, M R. 2012. Adventures with caterpillars: the larval stage of the Purple Emperor butterfly. *British Wildlife* 23: 335–342.

Oates, M R. 2015. *In Pursuit of Butterflies*. Bloomsbury, London.

Oates, M R. 2017. *Beyond Spring*. Fair Acre Press, Oswestry.

Pantelić, D, Ćurčić, S, Savić-Šević, S, Korać, A, Kovačević, A, Ćurčić, B and Bokić B. 2011. High angular and spectral selectivity of Purple Emperor (Lepidoptera: *Apatura iris* and *A. ilia*) butterfly wings. *Optics Express* 19 (7): 5817–5826.

Page, R J C. 2010. Perching and patrolling continuum at favoured hilltop sites on a ridge: a mate location strategy by the Purple Emperor butterfly *Apatura iris*. *Entomologist's Record* 122: 61–70.

Pitman, C M R. 1954. A note on *Apatura iris* Linn. *Entomologist's Record* 66: 118–119.

Robinson, P T, Flacke, G L and Hentschel, K M. 2017. *The Pygmy Hippo Story: West Africa's enigma of the rainforest*. Oxford University Press, Oxford.

Russworm, A D. 1978. *Aberrations of British Butterflies*. E W Classey, Faringdon.

Salway, R E. 1881. A month in the New Forest. *Entomologist* 14: 199–200.

Sandars, E. 1939. *A Butterfly Book for the Pocket*. Oxford University Press, London.

Settele, J. *et al.* 2008. *Climatic Risk Atlas of European Butterflies*. BioRisk 1 (special issue). Pensoft, Sofia.

Sheehy, E and Lawton, C. 2014. Population crash in an invasive species following recovery of a native predator: the case of the American grey squirrel and the European pine marten in Ireland. *Biodiversity Conservation* 23: 753–774.

Sheehy, E, Sutherland, C, O'Reilly, C and Lambin, X. 2018. The enemy of my enemy is my friend: native pine marten recovery reverses the decline of the red squirrel by suppressing grey squirrel populations. *Proceedings of the Royal Society B* 285: 20172603.

South, R. 1906. *The Butterflies of the British Isles*. Frederick Warne & Co., London.

Stace, C. 2019. *New Flora of the British Isles* (4th edition). Cambridge University Press, Cambridge.

Symes, H. 1954. Notes on the larva of *Apatura iris* L. *Entomologist's Record* 66: 40–43.

Thomas, J A and Lewington, R. 2014. *The Butterflies of Britain & Ireland*. British Wildlife Publishing, Oxford.

Tree, I. 2018. *Wilding*. Picador, London.

Tubbs, C R. 2001. *The New Forest: History, Ecology & Conservation*. New Forest Centenary Trust, Lyndhurst.

Tutt, J W. 1896. *British Butterflies*. George Gill & Sons, London.

Wilkinson, G W. 1857. *Apatura iris*. *The Entomologist's Weekly Intelligencer* 2: 148–149.

Willmott, K J. 1987. *The Ecology and Conservation of the Purple Emperor Butterfly (*Apatura iris*)*. Report for World Wildlife Fund 1984–1986.

Willmott, K J. 1990. *The Purple Emperor Butterfly (Apatura iris)*. British Butterfly Conservation Society (Butterfly Conservation), Colchester.

Wykes, N., in Matthews, P. (ed.) 1957. *The Pursuit of Moths and Butterflies: an Anthology*. Chatto & Windus, London.

References: County butterfly books and reports

Asher, J. 1994. *The Butterflies of Berkshire, Buckinghamshire and Oxfordshire*. Pisces Publications, Newbury.

Barker, A. (ed.) 2019. *Hampshire & Isle of Wight Butterfly & Moth Report for 2018*. Butterfly Conservation Hampshire and Isle of Wight Branch.

Blencowe, M and Hulme, N. 2017. *The Butterflies of Sussex*. Pisces Publications, Newbury.

Bristow, C R, Mitchell, S H and Bolton, D E. 1993. *Devon Butterflies*. Devon Books, Tiverton.

Dexter, A. 2010. *Butterflies in Somerset and Bristol*. Butterfly Conservation Somerset and Bristol Branch.

Duddington, J and Johnson, R. 1983. *The Butterflies and Larger Moths of Lincolnshire and South Humberside*. Lincolnshire Naturalists' Union, Lincoln.

Duncan, I, Seal, P, Tilt, J, Wasley, R and Williams, M. 2016. *Butterflies of the West Midlands*. Pisces Publications, Newbury.

Ffennell, D W H. 1977. The status of the Purple Emperor (*Apatura iris* Linn.) in the Isle of Wight. *Entomologist's Record* 89: 341–342.

Field, R, Perrin, V, Bacon, L and Greatorex-Davies, N B. 2006. *The Butterflies of Cambridgeshire*. Butterfly Conservation Cambridgeshire and Essex Branch.

Frost, H M. (ed.) 2005. *The Butterflies of Yorkshire*. Butterfly Conservation, Wareham.

Fuller, M. 1995. *The Butterflies of Wiltshire: their history, status and distribution 1982–1994*. Pisces Publications, Newbury.

Fuller, M. 2018. *Wiltshire Butterfly Report for 2017*. Butterfly Conservation Wiltshire Branch.

Goater, B. 1974. *The Butterflies & Moths of Hampshire and the Isle of Wight*. EW Classey, Faringdon.

Goddard, D and Wyldes, A. 2012. *The Butterflies of Northamptonshire*. Butterfly Conservation Bedfordshire and Northamptonshire Branch.

Goodyear, E and Middleton, A. 2003. *The Hertfordshire Purple Emperor Apatura iris*. Hertfordshire Natural History Society.

Goodyear, E and Middleton, A. 2006. *Purple Emperor Project Progress Report 2004 & 2005*. Butterfly Conservation Hertfordshire and Middlesex Branch.

Goodyear, E and Middleton, A. 2015. *Eastern Region Purple Emperor Apatura iris Report for 2014*. Dispar website.

Mendel, H and Piotrowski, S H. 1986. *The Butterflies of Suffolk: an atlas and history*. Suffolk Naturalists' Society, Ipswich.

Newton, J and Meredith, D G. 1984. Macrolepidoptera of Gloucestershire. *Proceedings of the Cotteswold Naturalists' Field Club* 39: 21–134.

Oates, M R, Taverner, J and Green, D. 2000. *The Butterflies of Hampshire*. Pisces Publications, Newbury.

Penhallurick, R D. 1996. *The Butterflies of Cornwall and the Scilly Isles*. Dyllansow Pengwella, Truro.

Plant, C. 1988. *The Butterflies of the London Area*. London Natural History Society.

Pratt, C R. 2011. *A Complete History of the Butterflies and Moths of Sussex*. Self-published.

Sawford, B. 1987. *Butterflies of Hertfordshire*. Castlemead Publications, Hertford.

Slater, M. *in press*. *The Conservation of Warwickshire's Butterflies*. Pisces Publications, Newbury.

Stewart, R. 2001. *Millennium Atlas of Suffolk Butterflies*. Suffolk Naturalists' Society, Ipswich.

Thomas, J A and Webb, N. 1984. *The Butterflies of Dorset*. Dorset Natural History and Archaeological Society, Dorchester.

Wacher, J, Worth, J and Spalding, A. 2003. *A Cornwall Butterfly Atlas*. Pisces Publications, Newbury.

Willmott, K J, Bridge, M, Clarke, H E and Kelly, F. 2013. *Butterflies of Surrey Revisited*. Surrey Wildlife Trust, Woking.

Acknowledgements

A multitude of people have helped towards this book in diverse ways. Their numbers are too legion for them all to be named here. The roll of honour dates back to 1964, when the Purple Emperor first entered my life, and must be headed by my late mother, Helen Oates (née Martin). The sufferings of my wife, Sally, and family must be dutifully recorded here – my four children have long referred to this butterfly as *The Preciousss*, rightly.

I am particularly grateful to Charlie and Issy Burrell of Knepp Castle Estate, and their staff and volunteers – most notably Penny Green and Rachel Knott – for making my wildest dream come true, through the Purple paradise that is Knepp Wildland. Equally foremost are my dear friends Neil Hulme, who has been my kindred spirit in all things Purple for many years; Ken Willmott, whom I have known closely since the long hot summer of 1976 and who pioneered ecological work on the Purple Emperor; Dr Dennis Dell, an octogenarian who serves as a role model for my later years and who read through and commented helpfully on many of the chapters in this book, as did my longstanding friend Gail Jeffcoate; and Liz Goodyear and Andrew Middleton, who have systematically and brilliantly surveyed for Purple Emperors in Hertfordshire, Middlesex and East Anglia, and commented constructively on several draft chapters here.

Katy Roper, of Bloomsbury Publishing, managed to knock the first draft of this book into shape before going on maternity leave. Jenny Campbell took over from her, and saw the project through to fruition, aided and abetted by Jim Martin. I am deeply grateful to them, and to Tim Bernhard for providing line drawings, and to Darren Woodhead for a deeply memorable day at Knepp Wildland in July 2019 when he, in the company of his delightful family, captured ideas for the book's front cover; and to copy-editor Liz Drewitt for spotting and correcting various mistakes.

It is a pleasure also to acknowledge the People of Purple Persuasion (the official Purple Emperor fan club): notably Derek Longhurst, who has accompanied me on this journey since our schooldays together and established the Purple Emperor website and blog; Mike Fuller and Bill Shreeves, longstanding butterfly recorders for the counties of Wiltshire and Dorset, respectively; Doug Goddard and Andy Wyldes, who fly the Purple flag in Northamptonshire; Mike Slater, who has assiduously recorded the Purple Emperor's spread in Warwickshire, and provided much practical conservation advice and cutting-edge thinking; Ashley Whitlock, who has been the Purple standard bearer in Hampshire for many years; Chris Winnick, for use of his extensive library, and Lynn and Paul Fomison for use of their caravan; butterfly breeders Derek Smith, Martin White and Colin Wiskin, whose expertise has been invaluable to this book; and Paul Fosterjohn, for the production of umpteen Purple Emperor badges, flags and paraphernalia, and for his 69-page risk assessment form for the dangerous pursuit of Emperoring; Dr Richard

Harrington for advice on aphid ecology; Andy Foster for advice on beetles and weevils; the Catalan contingent of Jimmy Evarts, Mike Lockwood and Dr Constanti Stefanescu; and the Dutch contingent headed by Dr Michiel Wallis de Vries. My dearest schoolfriend, Dr Nigel Fleming, also needs thanking – for encouraging me to live the most discordant of lives.

Finally, several people who are with us only in spirit are reverently acknowledged here: notably BB (Denys Watkins-Pitchford), in whose wonderful children's book *Brendon Chase* I first discovered the Purple Emperor; M H Jones and N T Fryer, naturalist-masters of Christ's Hospital school, just north of Knepp Castle Estate, who both failed to teach me an iota of maths but were otherwise strongly instrumental in my development; Dr Roger Clarke of Bernwood Forest; and the man whose writings captured my imagination forever, I R P Heslop. I am especially grateful to the Heslop family for their support during my researches, notably I R P Heslop's youngest daugher, Jane Murray.

It is also a pleasure to acknowledge the positive work conducted by today's Forestry England (formerly the Forestry Commission), most notably for its careful stewardship of Savernake Forest, in liaison with Savernake Estate. The National Trust's ranger teams, too, have done sterling work for both the conservation of this butterfly and for people's experience of it. Here I must highlight the work carried out for decades by ranger Ian Swinney of Bookham Commons.

Data were provided from the Butterflies for the New Millennium recording scheme, courtesy of Butterfly Conservation. Above all, this book would not have been

possible without the fellowship provided by Butterfly
Conservation, its staff, retired Chairman Dr Jim Asher,
members and branches, and the expert assistance of the
County Butterfly Recorders. It is as much their book as
it is mine.

Matthew Oates
June 2020

Index of species and scientific names

General index